OTTOMAN AND
TURKISH LAW

OTTOMAN AND TURKISH LAW

Eskisehir 2013, the Capital City of
Culture for the Turkic World

Fatih Öztürk
Faculty of Law, Istanbul University

iUniverse LLC
Bloomington

OTTOMAN AND TURKISH LAW

iUniverse books may be ordered through booksellers or by contacting:

iUniverse LLC
1663 Liberty Drive
Bloomington, IN 47403
www.iuniverse.com
1-800-Authors (1-800-288-4677)

ISBN: 978-1-4917-2991-5 (sc)
ISBN: 978-1-4917-2990-8 (e)

Library of Congress Control Number: 2014905878

Printed in the United States of America.

iUniverse rev. date: 04/09/2014

This work is dedicated to my longtime friend, Fatih ONCU, whose impressive career skills inspired me to believe that I was capable of authoring a book.

Contents

Foreword..ix

Chapter 1. The Ottoman Millet System 1

Chapter 2. The Ottoman Millet System and the Protection
of Religious Minority Groups and Women.............23

Chapter 3. The Ottoman Muslim Turkish Women
and Divorce 71

Chapter 4. The Republic of Turkey and Women in
Divorce Cases 109

Chapter 5. A Theory of Liberal Minority Rights
of Will Kymlicka 149

Chapter 6. Critics of Will Kymlicka's Liberal Minority
Rights Theory: Failure to Protect Religious
Minorities...189

Chapter 7. Introduction to Minority Issues in Turkey—
The Constitution—Making Process and
Eu Integration..205

References...221

FOREWORD

I would like to thank and recognize for their efforts in guiding me in the process of bringing myself to provide this work for the Turkic World, as a piece for Eskişehir 2013—the Capital City of Culture—my friends Fatih Öncü, and Güngür Azim Tuna—Governor of Eskişehir. Broadening the accessibility of the works of Turkish authors through this endeavor would not have been possible without their insight.

In order to further the goal of achieving greater protection of human rights in modern democracies, the work is approached from the international human rights perspective. The fundamental goal is to make an argument for a better defense of the establishment and protection of the modern rule of law. The primary motivation for this is to draw attention to the inability of the Turkish legal system to rid itself of arcane and outdated legal interpretations, practices, and traditions altogether, with the hope that it will move towards a more thorough, modern, socially as well as historically relevant approach in its method and execution.

Fatih Öztürk, PhD
Istanbul, 2014

Foreword

With Eskişehir 2013, the Capital City of Culture for the Turkic World, Turkish authors embark on the journey to introduce themselves to the world and meet the international audience, thus setting us on the path to carrying out our project. In line with the vision and mission of our Republic for 2023, we believe that Turkish authors have significant contributions to make to the legacy of the literary world in international arena. It is a modern reality that the path to success lay in having the works translated into English and more accessible through online mediums—so as to escape the hindrance of delivery and postage concerns that arise with the dissemination of books.

It is with this in mind that we offer our sincere gratitude to our young academic, Fatih Ozturk, for his work in the field of Ottoman-Turkish Law; for us, an inspiring step towards introducing our authors to the world.

Güngör Azim Tuna
Governor of Eskişehir

The following four articles concerning Ottoman Law include the same or slight variations of the same information from a single source which concerns the social structure, historical background, and legal system of the Ottoman period.

The following essay was first published as: The Ottoman Millet System, 15 Journal of South-East European Researches, Issue 16, pg. 71-86 (2010).

1

THE OTTOMAN MILLET SYSTEM

This essay explores the main tenets of the millet system. The Qur'an orders that freedom of religion is one of the main principles of Islam.[1] According to the Islamic Law, Jews and Christians were accepted as people of the book. Islam provides protection for non-Muslims via agreement between the State and the group.[2] In an Islamic State, non-Muslims are protected groups thus it is a duty of the government to protect their legitimate interests.[3] Millet is an Arabic word[4] that translated into English as nation.[5] This term was

---

[1] See general Mohammad Hashim Kamali, "Freedom of Religion in Islam" 21 Cap. U. L. Rev. (1992) at 80.

[2] See Mehmet Akif Aydin, *Islam ve Osmanli Hukuku Arastirmalari* [Researches on the Islam and Ottoman Law] (Istanbul, Iz, 1996) at 230.

Professor Hamidullah notes that after the Prophet, the Second Caliphate Omer, there was a Jew whose land was taken away from him without his consent, and administrators established a Mosque. Omer made the administrators destroy the mosque and returned the land to its owner. Still, today there is "Beyt-ul Yahudi" [Jew House]. See Muhammed Hamidullah, *Islam Anayasa Hukuku* [Constitutional Law of Islam], ed., Vecdi Akyuz, (Istanbul, Beyan, 1995) at 200.

[3] See Muhammad Hamidullah, Muslim Conduct of State, Chapter 12, "The Status of Non-Muslims in Islam" available at http://www.muslim-canada.org/ch12hamid.html (accessed on August 5, 2008).

[4] See Ilber Ortayli, *Uc Kitada Osmanlilar* [Ottomans on Three Continents] (Istanbul, Timas, 2007) at 59. Professor Ortayli claims that the Ottoman was one of the three greatest empires in the region of the Mediterranean and the latest universal one.

[5] See Kemal H. Karpat, "Millets and Nationality: the Roots of the Incongruity of Nation and State in the Post-Ottoman Era" in *Christians and Jews in the Ottoman Empire: the Functioning of a Pluralist Society*, Volume I, Benjamin Braude & Bernard Lewis, eds. (NY, London, Holmes & Meier, 1982), at 141-170. Professor Karpat is well known the Ottoman historian who taught for many years in Wisconsin University in the USA.

not used only for non-Muslims, but also for any nation.[6] However, in the terminology of the Ottoman historians, it is mostly used to define non-Muslim communities.[7] The Ottoman administration system was divided into two as territorial/local (provinces) and religious divisions. People were seen in the eyes of State not on the basis of ethnicity or language, but religion.[8] "Religion, language, community, ethnicity, and family made up the socio-cultural fabric of the millet."[9] For the period of the Ottoman, the most important thing was religion and supremacy of family; in other words, the millet system was in favour of "fusion of family and the community."[10] "Religion supplied to each millet a universal belief system while ethnic and linguistic differences provided for divisions and subdivisions within each one of the two Christian millets."[11]

The "Milletbasi" either a patriarch or rabbi was the representative of his community before the State[12] like a political head. The Religious community was the form of political structure and "the source of identity" for non-Muslim communities.[13] One can assume that it was a segregation or isolation of communities from each other. Berkes notes that the millet system worked without

---

[6] See Benjamin Braude, "Foundation Myths of the Millet System" in Benjamin Braude & Bernard Lewis, id, at 69.

[7] Id.

[8] See Serif Mardin, "Religion and Secularism in Turkey" in *Ataturk: Founder of a Modern State*, Ali Kazancigil & Ergun Ozbudun (eds), 2nd ed, (London, Hurst & Company, 1997) at 199

[9] See Karpat, *supra note* 5, at 142.

[10] *Id.*

[11] See Kemal Karpat, *Studies on Ottoman Social and Political History: Selected Articles and Essays* (Leiden, Brill, 2002) at 612.

[12] See Benjamin Braude, "Foundation Myths of the Millet System" in Benjamin Braude & Bernard Lewis, *supra note* 5, at 69.

[13] See Karpat, *supra note* 11, at 17.

segregating millets (nations) into ghettos or extermination[14], they lived next to each other. However, "each group had traditions as to titles, grades, recruitment, ceremonies, discipline, but absolute loyalty to the supreme ruler."[15]The Millet system based on the Zimmi [Dhimmah] tradition that regulates public and personal rules for minorities [religious] who lives under the rule of Islamic lands.[16] In doctrines, many authors continue to perpetuate this mistaken belief; Islam or Ottoman practices provided non-Muslim communities communitarian identity and did not recognize individual autonomy and just followed and dictated orthodox socio-religious orders of the communities.[17]

---

[14] See Niyazi Berkes, *The Development of Secularism in Turkey*, (NY, Rout ledge, 1998), at 11-2. This book was originally published in Canada in 1963 by McGill University. Niyazi Berkes (1908-1988) was a leftist Turkish intellectual who escaped from Turkey after the 1960 Military Coup d'état and began to reside in Canada. He never came back to live in Turkey. See, Berkes, New Introduction by Feroz Ahmad, at XV-XXXIII.

[15] Id, at 12.

[16] See Kamran Hashemi, "The Right of Minorities to Identity and the Challenge of Non-Discrimination: A Study on the Effects of Traditional Muslims Dhimmah on Current State Practices" 13 Int. J. Min. & Gr. R. (2006) at 2.

[17] Such as one of the authors see Abdulaziz Sachedina, Guidance or Governance? A Muslim Conception of "Two-Cities", 68 Geo. Wash. L. Rev. (1999-2000) at 1093. Or see Marc Baer, "The Double Bind of Race and Religion: The Conversion of the Donme to Turkish Secular Nationalism" Soc. of Comp. Stud. of Soc. and His. (2004) at 685.

Leo Zaibert rightly critics Will Kymlicka and make balance about the Ottoman Millet system. According to Zaibert, Kymlicka pointed out that the system was not liberal even many groups lived peacefully next to each other, but none of the individual has right to exit from the group thus individual autonomy was not respected. The system did not recognize any individual freedom of conscience. Therefore, he calls it as a federation of theocracies [See Will Kymlicka, *Multicultural Citizenship: A Liberal Theory of Minority Rights* (NY, Oxford, 1995) at 152 and 157].

Zaibert claims that "I do not mean to suggest that the Ottoman Millet system was liberal in content; but it is closer to being that than to being liberal-in-form. See Leo Zaibert, Punishment and Retribution, (Aldershot, AshgateP, 2006)

The *Millet System* also;[18]

"allowed the subject Christian peoples [and the other nations] to retain their separate identities and cultures, rooted in their respective churches. Indeed the monophysite churches with Syrian, Armenian and Coptic adherents, as well as the Nestorians, survived mainly in the Muslim lands, while vanishing in the more intolerant Christian West. Along with the Jews expelled from England [actually Jews were coming into the Ottoman land since around 1390], France, Spain, and Portugal, a variety of heterodox Christians including Protestants, Unitarians, and Russian Molokans received refuge in the Ottoman Empire."

Non-Muslim minorities enjoyed nearly unfettered self-government within their religious communities, also operating their own schools.[19] During the Ottoman era, many Vezirs (State ministers) or Grand Vezirs (Prime Ministers) were appointed non-Muslims

---

[18] See Hugh Poultan, *Top Hat, Grey Wolf and Crescent: Turkish Nationalism ad the Turkish Republic* (London, Hurst & Company, 1997) at 49. See more about the Ottoman Millet System, Youssef Courbage & Philippe Fargues, Christians and Jews under Islam ((London, New York, I. B. Tauris Publishers, 1997) especially look at the chapter Five: From Multinational Empire to Secular Republic: the Lost of Christianity of Turkey, Ali Guler, Osmanli Devletinde Azinliklar [Minorities in the Ottoman] (Istanbul, Turan Publishing, 1997), Onder Kaya, Tanzimat'tan Lozan'a Azinliklar [Minorities from Tanzimat to Lausanne] (Istanbul, Yeditepe Publishing, 2004), Yavuz Ercan, *Osmanli Yonetiminde Gayrimuslimler* [Non-Muslims Under the Ottoman Administration] (Ankara, Turhan Publishing House, 2001). Professor Ercan notes that according to Islamic law or the Ottoman law; Zimmi (non-Muslims) cannot ring their bells, they cannot carry guns, they cannot ride horses, they have to bury their deaths secretly, and they cannot build their houses higher than Muslim houses. At 9. It is a very classic example of Turkish academia about the Ottoman history, even without showing any reference. However, once again, there is a lot of proof against for those kinds of arguments from the Ottoman archives that mainly located in Istanbul.

[19] See Edward Mead Earle, "The New Constitution of Turkey", 40 Pol. Sc. Q., (1925) at 77.

or other Muslim races who were not Turks.[20] In the *Millet System*, nations "were treated like corporate bodies and allowed their own internal structures and hierarchies; indeed the Ottoman State encouraged this by dealing exclusively [most of the time, but not all the time] with their head figures rather than the individual members."[21] In other words, it is a system that establishes the coexistence of religions[22] and allows different communities to live side by side in harmony. However, Abdullahi A. An-Naim notes that:

"Non-Muslim minorities within an Islamic State do not enjoy rights equal to those of Muslim majority. Some apologist Muslim writers have tended to misrepresent Sharia, the historical religious law of the Muslims, in order to minimize the seriousness of discrimination against non-Muslims. Such an approach is futile not only because current public opinion is unwilling to tolerate any degree or form of discrimination on grounds of religion or belief. On a practical level, although most of the constitutions of modern Muslim states guarantee against religious discrimination, most of these constitutions also authorize the application of Sharia. As

---

[20] See Poultan, *supra note* 18, at 44. See more L. Carl Brown (ed.) Imperial Legacy: the Ottoman Imprint on the Balkans and the Middle East (New York, CUP, 1996). See Also Justin McCarthy, *Muslims and Minorities: the Population of Ottoman Anatolia and the End of the Ottoman Empire* (NY, NYUP, 1983). See also Justin McCarthy, *Death and Exile: the Ethnic Cleansing of Ottoman Muslims, 1821-1922* (Princeton, NJ Darwin P, 1995), and *The Ottoman Peoples and of Empire (Historical Endings)* (London: Arnold; NY: Oxford, 2001).

[21] See Poultan, *supra note* 18, at 48.

[22] *Id*, at 16.

such, these constitutions sanction discrimination against religious minorities."[23]

It is argued here that the Ottoman State already made this reconciliation many centuries ago.[24] Actually, Ottoman Turks began to capture universal human rights standards at their classical age (14th Century-19th Century). In sum, in the Ottoman Era, personal rights and freedoms were very important; their legal basis was provided by the Qur'an. Even in the early 16th century before medical surgery was popular, patients had to sign a paper waiving their rights to the courts before any medical operations were performed and jobs in the Public service sector, under the Ottomans, were equal for Muslims and non-Muslims.[25] Many Christians and Jews had the position of Sadrazam, or Prime Minister of the Ottoman State.[26] It is believed that the norms like "your brothers in religion" or "your equals in creation" served as a main principle for civil society.[27] Sharing highest political positions with non-Muslim citizens was a great discovery at that time. This was another remarkable experience that shows that Ottoman practices were not involved in discriminative policies.

---

[23] See Abdullahi A. An-Naim, "Religious Minorities under Islamic Law and the Limits of Cultural Relativism" 9 Hum. R. Q. (1987) at 1. Moreover, An-Naim argues that Muslims should not discriminate non-Muslims because of Islamic cultural norms and Muslims should reconcile Shariah with fundamental human rights. At 18.

See more Javaid Rehman, "Accommodating Religious Identities in an Islamic State: International Law, Freedom of Religion, and the Rights of Religious Minorities" 7 Int. J. Min. & Gr. Rts. (2000) 139-166.

[24] In doctrine there is an essay collection of a book that consists 58 articles, however, none of them talks about the Ottoman experience. Most of the authors claim that there is no tolerance for non-Muslims in Islam. What I believe this book is heavily written under 9/11 influences. See *The Myth of Islamic Tolerance: How Islamic Law Treats Non-Muslims*, Robert Spencer, ed. (Prometheus Books, Amherst & NY, 2005)

[25] See general Ahmet Akgunduz, *Belgeler Gercekleri Konusuyor I [Documents Tell the Truths I]* (Istanbul, Nil, 1989

[26] See Ortayli, *supra note* 4, at 59-68.

[27] See Sachedina, *supra note* 17, at 1097.

However, many nationalistic authors claim that the collapse of the Ottoman Empire was due to Christian and Jews involvement in politics within the Ottoman states. Objectively, Prince Said Halim Pasa disagreed with this criticism, he believed that the Ottoman Justice and Administrative System broke down because of the lack of progression with the times and that this was the reason the State lost its power.[28] In practice Ottoman States protected non-Muslim personal rights, but in the Sultan Mehmet II, Fatih (1432-1481) era, the Sultan began declaring laws to provide more safeguards for non-Muslims.[29] However, "the Ottoman Sultans did not introduce the millet system into their empire only on the capture of Constantinople, but were already applying its principles to the non-Muslim communities under their rule."[30] After the conquest of Istanbul in 1454, Sultan Mehmed II (Fatih) declared a ferman [Sultan's Decree] to the Patriarchate Gennadios containing many rights and privileges. With this decree, the Patriarchate became the highest authority over the Orthodox Churches and Fatih's aim was to encourage the Patriarchate to stay away from political affairs and also the prevention of any possible alliance of eastern and western

---

[28] See general Said Halim Pasa, *Buhranlarimiz ve Son Eserleri* [Our Crisis and His Last Written Works], ed., M. Ertugrul Duzdag (Istanbul, Iz, 1991). Said Halim Pasa one of the latest Ottoman Sadr-i Azams [Prime Minister].

[29] See Ahmet Akgunduz & Said Ozturk, *700. Yilinda Bilinmeyen Osmanli [Unknown Ottoman on the 700th Anniversary]* (Istanbul, Osmanli, 1999) at 434.

[30] From H. A. R. Gibb & Harold Bowen, *Islamic Society and the West*, (Oxford, OUP, 1957), Volume I, Part II, at 214. See Kevork B. Bardakjian, "The Rise of Armenian Patriarchate of Constantinople" in Benjamin Braude & Bernard Lewis, *supra note 5*, at 91. Moreover, the State was enforcing the Patriarchate punishments with his orders. See Erol Ozbilgen, *Butun Yonleriyle Osmanli: Adab-i Osmaniyye* [All Aspects of Ottomans: Rules of Ottoman] (Istanbul, Iz, 2007) at 419. Ozbilgen notes that religious communities' courts verdicts enforced by State officers.

See more Richard Glogg, "The Greek Millet in the Ottoman Empire" in Benjamin Braude & Bernard Lewis, *supra note 5*, at 185-207.

churches.[31] It should be noted that in 1452 with the force of the Byzantine Emperor Constantine Paleologos, the Greek Orthodox church came under the rule of Vatican, thus Sultan Fatih was a hero who saved and gave them their freedom back. Moreover, Fatih granted the patriarch the title of Ottoman Pasha [General]. The Janissary corps [Devsirme Military Personals] and an attachment of guards are also granted to him. As well as this he had founded a jail inside the Patriarchate building within which Ottoman State law was not practiced, the Patriarchate was law.[32] Fatih also provided this kind of privileges and rights to Armenian and Jewish communities. They became all representative of Armenian and Jewish communities around the world not just religious also politics.[33] It is evident that politics controlled religion during the Ottoman era.

During Ottoman times, diversity was far from being the chaos that lay dormant in society as it too often appears to be the case in modern societies. Rather, it was a quite fundamentally absorbed normality throughout the Empire. Tolerance appeared paramount, for instance as in while Sultan Beyazid II (1481-1512) ruled; Ottoman States sent ships to Spain to save Jews from

---

[31] See Elcin Macar, *Cumhuriyet Doneminde Istanbul Rum Patrikhanesi* [Istanbul Greek Patriarchate during the Republic Era] (Istanbul, Iletisim, 2003) at 29.

[32] See Adnan Sofuoglu, *Fener Rum Patrikhanesi ve Siyasi Faaliyetleri* [Fener Greek Patriarchate and Its Political Activities] (Istanbul, Turan, 1996) at 11-15.

[33] *Id*, at 16-7.

religious persecution.[34] Their descendents remain in modern day Istanbul, evidently at peace while even continuing to carry out their lives without having to change their native tongue from Spanish. Another notable influx of Jewish refugees are those that arrived in Istanbul during World War II as Turkey took in Jews from Germany, giving them immediate citizenship status, as was especially the case with university professors.[35]

Until relatively recently, Islamic societies and Muslim states showed respect for the Bible and Torah-Talmud and never limited the production or teaching of them.[36] After the conquest of Istanbul, minorities such as Greeks, Armenians and Jews were allowed to establish a community whose master was called "patriarch."[37] With this community they were absolutely allowed to live

---

[34] See "Yahudilerin Şükran Yılları" [Jews Thanksgiving Years], 6-12 January Tempo Magazine (1991) at 26-34. See more Bernard Lewis, *Cultures in Conflict: Christians, Muslims, and Jews in the Age of Discovery* (NY & Oxford, OUP, 1995) at 50-1. See general Bernard Lewis, *The Jews of Islam* (London, Melbourne & Henley, Routledge & Keagan Paul, 1984). However, Joseph R. Hacker claims, wrongly, that under the Sultan Beyazid II, "Jews suffered severe restrictions in their religious life."

See Joseph R. Hacker, "Ottoman Policy toward the Jews and Jewish Attitudes toward the Ottomans during the Fifteenth Century" in Benjamin Braude & Bernard Lewis, *supra note* 5, at 124.

See counter arguments Mark A. Epstein, "The Leadership of the Ottoman Jews in the Fifteenth and Sixteenth Centuries" in Benjamin Braude & Bernard Lewis, *supra note* 5, at 101-15.

[35] See general Ernst E. Hirsch, *Anilarim* [My Memories] (Ankara, Tubitak, 1997). He was one of those law professors who emigrated Turkey because of Nazi persecution. His brother also was one of them who taught in the medical faculty.

[36] See Osman Sekerci, *Islam Ulkelerinde Gayri Muslimlerin Temel Haklari* [Basic Rights of Non-Muslims in Islamic Countries] (Istanbul, Nun, 1996) at 63. Professor Sekerci notes that because of these privileges and rights some non-Muslims in the past abused their rights. Because there are some bad example of fetvas produced by Islamic scholars. Today, we should not follow these steps; we have to work with non-Muslim scientists. There is no any limit in Islamic law. At 65.

[37] See Ercan, *supra note* 18, at 228.

freely their own religion, language, tradition and customs. The government completely gave the management of the authority and responsibilities for all education and cultural institutes, churches and hospitals of minorities' community to this patriarch. After the capture of Istanbul, Sultan Fatih declared that none of the State officials were going to involve the affairs of non-Muslim schools in their programs.[38]

Principally, these institutes and schools were opened and supported by rich and charitable people, not by government. In the early days of the Ottomans, non-Muslims provided religious education to their own children in the churches or synagogues.[39] However, according to Islamic law, non-Muslims cannot establish new churches or synagogues only restore the old ones, but the State of Islam can allow them to establish new ones as a State policy.[40]

During the Ottoman era, non-Muslims could be exempt from military service, while others had the option of paying an exemption tax [jizyah].[41] Women, children, and poor were exempted from paying an exemption tax.[42] However, at the same time, Muslims were paying Zekat (each year paying the earning

---

[38] See Sekerci, *supra note* 36, at 65. In another book, Sekerci strongly argues that there should not be any discrimination against non-Muslims because of their beliefs in an Islamic State.

See Osman Sekerci, *Insan Haklari Alaninda Temel Belgeler ve Islam* [Basic Human Rights Documents and Islam] (Istanbul, Nun, 1996).

[39] See Ercan, *supra note* 18, at 228. Ercan rightly claims that there are currently insufficient researches about the classical era of the Ottomans and religious education for non-Muslims.

[40] See Ahmed Akgunduz, Gayr-i Muslimlere Nasil Davrandik [How we behaved to Non-Muslims] at http://.osmanli.org.tr/yazdirilabilirosmanli.php?id=32 (accessed on July 23, 2008).

[41] Interestingly, non-Muslims of the Ottomans became highest military and State administrative officers with the Devsirme System rather than living under the Dhimmah tradition. As previously stated that State officials were exempted paying taxes. See more I. Metin Kunt, "Transformation of Zimmi into Askeri" in Benjamin Braude & Bernard Lewis, *supra note* 5, at 55.

[42] See Hamidullah, *supra note* 12.

of the capital of 1 out of 40). In order to avoid military services, many non-Muslims became more educated and specialized in medicine, literature, translation, or any social and science subjects, thus reaching the highest political administrative jobs in Islamic states.[43] It was decreed [after the 1856 Reforms] to accept one third of students from non-Muslim communities into administrative officers' schools.[44] Non-Muslims are also citizens of the Islamic country therefore they have the right to work in public jobs with the exception of those of head of the State, the commander of the

---

[43] See Yusuf Fidan, *Islam'da Yabancilar ve Azinliklar Hukuku* [Minorities and Foreigners in Islamic Law] (Istanbul, Ensar, 2005) at 333.

[44] See Ortayli, *supra note* 4, at 65-6. Because the Ottoman State population consisted one third of non-Muslim communities. It may argue that the Ottoman State policy was to eliminate discrimination from politics. According to the Tahrir Defteris' [Tax Registres] documents, around in the middle of the XVIth Century, 40 % of the population was non-Muslim. See Ozbilgen, *supra note* 30, at 414.

The Ottoman State rated five times general population counting in modern sense; in 1831, 1881/82, 1893, 1906/7 and 1914. According to 1831 census, non-Muslim population was 29.67 % in the Ottoman lands. In 1881/82 this rate was 26.61 %. In 1906/7 was 25.74 %. Lastly, in 1914 it was 18.88 %.

See Ali Guler, *Osmanli Devletinde Azinliklar* [Minorities in the Ottoman State] (Istanbul, Turan, 1997) at 128.

army, the governor or the judge because those jobs represents the
sovereignty of the Islam.[45]

Professor Ortayli correctly claims that this is one of the biggest
misinformation about non-Muslims and their military services. As
earlier stated non-Muslims had a privilege not to join the military
with paying the jizye tax [poll tax]; however, some of non-Muslims
did not use this privilege and joined the army. Many of them
became commanding officers in the military. During Christmas
time and Eastern Time, the Ottoman Naval Forces castled anchor

---

[45] See Ahmet Akgunduz & Halil Cin, *Turk Hukuk Tarihi (Ozel Hukuk), Cilt
II* [*Turkish Legal History* (*Private Law*), *Volume II* (Istanbul, Osmanli, 1996) at
332.

Professor Akgunduz proves that from the Ottoman archives which
were mainly collected in Istanbul in 1502 the era of Sultan II. Bayezid, the
legislation (Kanunname) of Istanbul Municipality orders that every one should
respect the rights of animal such as providing proper food and not make horses
or donkeys carry heavy staff. He argues that the modern world did same thing
with the U. N. Declaration of Animal Rights in 1948, thus how a civilization
protect rights of animal, but not human beings. See Ahmet Akgunduz,
Osmanli Devleti nde Insana ve Hukuka Saygi [Respecting Human Beings
and Law in the Ottoman State] at http://.osmanli.org.tr/yazdirilabilirosmanli.
php?id:97 (accessed on July 23, 2008). Professor Akgunduz currently is
the rector of Islamic University of Rotterdam, The Netherlands. He is the
recognized expert academic (Professor of history of law) uniquely fluent
in Arabic and Ottoman and spends most of his own time in the Ottoman
archives in Istanbul. Most of Turkish academia knows little Ottoman and also
lacks any knowledge of Arabic. Also until recently, due to a secularist belief
and Kemalist ideology in Turkey, the academia of Turkey attacked Ottoman
history and practices even without researching the archives and interestingly
having little knowledge about Islamic law. Akgunduz, for the last twenty
years has tried to destroy these stereotypes from Turkish academia. He writes
extensively about the legal history of the Ottoman State. For example, Ahmet
Akgunduz, *Osmanli Kanunnameleri ve Hukuki Tahlilleri* [Statute Books of the
Ottomans and Legal Analysis], total XII Volumes. Professor Akgunduz began
to write this series in the early 1990s.

See more about his biography, "Professor Ahmet Akgunduz" available
at http://www.islamicuniversity.nl/en/showpeople.asp?id=20 (accessed on
November 15, 2007).

because of non-Muslim soldiers.[46] Having this privilege not to join the army with the payment of poll tax, gave extensive power to non-Muslims to control commerce over the Ottoman lands.[47] It was the successful path to protect non-Muslim communities. In the same period, across Europe Jews or opposition Christians were crying loudly about the freedom of conscience and religion. Clearly, the Ottoman Turks had not discriminated against its non-Muslim citizens. It is arguable that that this was one of the main reasons that kept the empire strong for a long time.

Jews and Christians were also exempted from the jurisdiction of the Imperial courts when the issue at hand came down to religion and personal issues, such as family law, legitimacy, and inheritance . . . etc.[48] Non-Muslim courts' verdicts were enforced by the State authorities in the same way as Sharia court decisions.[49] We should note that non-Muslims had an optional right to either apply their own religious community court or Sharia court and when they went to Sharia court, the Muslim judge's verdicts were based on Islamic law.[50] Of course, non-Muslim religious leaders were trying to block those people who applied to Sharia court and used sanctions against those who did; still non-Muslim individuals were looking for justice before Sharia courts.[51] Non-Muslims religious leaders' authority in personal law was dependent on the individual's

---

[46] See Ortayli, *supra note* 4, at 65.

[47] See general Ali Ihsan Bagis, *Osmanli Ticaretinde Gayr-i Muslimler* [Non-Muslims in the Ottoman Commercial Life] (Ankara, Turhan, 1983).

[48] See Aydin, *supra note* 2, at 233.

[49] See Ahmet Bostanci, Urdun'de Muslumanlara ve Gayri Muslimlere Yonelik Dini Yargi Sistemi [Religious Judiciary System for Muslim and Non-Muslims in Jordan] 3 Usul Dergisi (2005) at 113. Professor Kenanoglu claims that inheritance was divided under the rules of Islamic law. See M. Macit Kenanoglu, *Osmanli Millet Sistemi: Mit ve Gercek* [*The Ottoman Millet System: Mythology and Reality*] (Istanbul, Klasik, 2004) at 251.

[50] See Kenanoglu, *id*, at 209.

[51] See general Rossitsa Gradeva, "Orthodox Christians in the Kadi Courts: The Practice of the Sofia Sheriat Court, Seventeenth Century" 4 Islamic L. & Soc'y (1997) 37-69.

choice; therefore Kenanoglu does not accept this authority/right as a full judicial privilege.[52] In other words, family law for non-Muslim individuals was based upon their own choice; either Islamic law or their own religious rule.[53] However, if one of the parties was Muslim or if it involved a criminal case, non-Muslims had to go to Sharia court.[54]

Available literature agreed without any dispute that the Ottoman State provided authority/privilege to non-Muslim religious leaders to deal with their community marriage/divorce cases.[55] The Ottoman State issued many decrees declaring that Muslim religious clerks cannot validate non-Muslim marriages.[56] On that issue, many times, non-Muslim religious leaders applied to the State authorities having validate power of marriage contracts, the reason was to prevent their own community marriages from the outside interference.[57] In the Ottoman archives there are records of Greek religious leaders applying to the Ottoman Sultan to give warning to Armenian religious leaders not to validate inter Greek-Armenian marriages.[58]

In the case of divorce, non-Muslim women went to the Sharia courts, in order to get financial benefits according to Islamic

---

[52] See Kenanoglu, *supra note* 49, at 211.

[53] See Ahmed Akgunduz, "The First Model for the EU: Ottoman State—1" From Conference: Islam in Europe or Islam of Europe?, European Parliament, 11 December 2002 at http://www.osmanli.org.tr/en/yazi.php?id=134&bolum=30 (accessed on July 25, 2008).

[54] See Kenanoglu, *supra note* 49, at 210.

[55] At 245.

[56] At 246.

[57] At 247. In the Ottoman Turkish State practices, over and over the Sultans issued and declared decrees in order to protect and enlarged non-Muslim citizen's rights in the country. See examples Murat Bebiroglu, *Osmanli Devleti'nde Gayrrimuslim Nizamnameleri* [*Non-Muslim Decrees in the Ottoman State*] (Istanbul, Akademi, 2008).

[58] At 247.

law that their own religious rules did not provide.[59]Also, where according to their own religion they cannot get divorced from their partners, they went to the Sharia court. Many Catholics took advantage of this possibility.[60] It is evident that as non-Muslims if both sides agree they can take the case before the Patriarchal or Rabbinical court, otherwise, the case went before the Sharia court. Moreover, if one of the sides preferred to take the case before its own religious court as a non-Muslim, the State Authorities may allow it.[61]

However, in the aftermath of the 1718 Treaty of Passarovitz,

"The Ottoman Turks began to look outside, more particularly to the West, for new inspiration . . . the apparent mutuality of French and Turkish interests determined where the Turkish statesmen would look for inspiration. It is worth noting that France continued to represent the West in Turkish eyes until the present century in spite of her disappointing performance in later eras and the practical ascendancy of Britain in the nineteenth century."[62]

With the 1839 *Tanzimat Declaration* and *1856 Islahat Declaration*,[63] the *Millet System* took another turn. The 1839 *Declaration* (Administrative Reforms) provided that aims of laws would be to protect lives, security of property, and decency. Before the law Muslims and non-Muslims are equal. Every citizen is equal concerning taxation and military service. This document also brought new criminal law conceptions to the Turkish legal

---

[59] See Gradeva, *supra note* 51, at 55-57.

[60] See Abdurrahman Kurt, *Bursa Sicillerine Gore Osmanli Ailesi (1839-1876)* [*According to Bursa Court Archives: The Ottoman Family (1839-1876)*] (Bursa, UUY, 1988) at 135.

[61] See Kenanoglu, *supra note* 49, at 216.

[62] See Berkes, *supra note* 14, at 25-6.

[63] See Burhan Kuzu, *Ulkemizde Kisi Ozgurlugu ve Guvenligi [Freedom and Security of Individuals in Turkey]* (Istanbul, Filiz, 1997) at 60.

See Bulent Tanor, *Osmanli-Turk Anayasal Gelismeleri [The Ottoman Turk Constitutional Developments]* (Istanbul, Alfa, 1992) at 67.

system.[64] In addition, the Sultan would also follow these rules. It appears that the French Human Rights Declaration affected this declaration so that Turkish law then began to follow European steps. The 1856 Islahat Declaration (Development Reforms) provided more rights to non-Muslims than it did to Muslims. Non-Muslims did not have to do military service but they had to pay the same tax equivalent as did the Muslims.[65] Muslims had to go to the military and it was for more than five years of service. The document declared increased rights for non-Muslims, due to European State pressure.[66] Akgunduz claims that the Ottoman State provided these rights to non-Muslims before the preparation of these documents (1839 and 1856); these documents provided hard copy of the declared rights.[67] Moreover, he claims that rather than following the European practices without question, the Ottoman should have regulated the practices of non-Muslims of that era in ways that were necessary to protect their interests. Therefore following the European footsteps did not help the reformation of the system, it caused its collapse.[68] The Reforming Decree of 1856 tried to reform the millet system and secularize [officially] the empire.[69] With the 1876 Kanun-i Esasi (Constitution), the nation of Islam was erased and the nation of the Ottoman established.[70] Article 7 of the 1876 Constitution (Kanun-Esasi) stated:

---

[64] See Kuzu, *id.*

[65] *Id.*

[66] See general Tanor, *supra note 63.*

[67] See Ahmet Akgunduz, Tarihi Acidan Azinliklara Taninan Haklar ve Biz II [From the Historical Perspective: Rights Provided to non-Muslims and We, no: 2] at http://.osmanli.org.tr/yazdirilabilirosmanli.php?id=31 (accessed on July 23, 2008).

[68] Id.

[69] See Malcolm D. Evans, *Religious Liberty and International Law in Europe* (Cambridge, CUP, 1997) at 67.

[70] See Akgunduz, *supra note 67.*

"all subjects of the Empire called Ottomans without distinction, whatever faith they profess; the status of an Ottoman is acquired and lost according to conditions specified by law."[71]

Those reforms prepared the ground for the foundation of a secular republic.[72] Interestingly, in 1879, the Ottoman State enacted a law to extend State jurisdiction to non-Muslim ecclesiastical courts to fix a uniform procedure without considering religious traditions. Two Greek patriarchs resigned from this duty and in 1890 the Patriarchate Synod closed all churches and suspended all offices for three months thus the State abolish the law.[73]

There were significant changes in the political atmosphere in the 19th Century due to the French revolution and rising nationalism and the involvement of Western powers in the Ottoman internal affairs due to the loss of Ottoman State power.[74] With the establishment of Republic of Turkey, the Millet System was abolished and a unified nationalist State was constructed in 1923. In 1918 just before the fall of the Ottoman [1922] 75 percent of the territories had been lost; in 1878, 85 percent of the population were

---

[71] See Nawaf A. Salam, "The Emergence of Citizenship in Islam" 12 Arab L. Q. (1997) at 140.

[72] See Rosella Bottoni, "The Origins of Secularism in Turkey" 9 Ecc LU (2007) at 175.

[73] *Id*, at 180.

[74] See Evans, *supra note 69*, at 60-1.

gone.[75] After winning the Independence War against the Allied power, the Republic of Turkey in 1923 signed the Lausanne Treaty. The treaty included articles for the protection of religious minorities that served in the allied powers armies (the U.K., France, Italy, and [Greece]) against Turks.[76] Since its establishment in 1923 the Republic of Turkey has faced minority rights issues. However, until today the parties to the treaty have accused Turkey of violating the Lausanne Treaty. Turkey has never accepted these allegations. Turkey argues that all people residing in the country are citizens, and the republic recognizes only non-Muslims as the minority via the Lausanne treaty. However, the republic does not discriminate against anyone based on religion, ethnicity, and language differences. Furthermore, Turkey claims it is a unified State. In addition, the constructors of the republic and their followers believe that discussing this issue in public will mean enemies are going to attack the unification of Turkey and will try to divide Turkey's

---

[75] See Virginia H. Aksan, "Ottoman to Turk" 61 Int'l J. (2005-2006) at 30. According to the 1844 General Census, the Ottoman State population was 35 million and consisting of 58 % Muslim(20,5 million), 39 % Greek Orthodox[Armenian, Bulgarian and the rest of the Balkans Orthodox included in that number] (13,7 million), 2,5 % Catholic (1 million) and 0,5 % Jews(nearly 200,000).

See Bebiroglu, *supra note* 57, at 20-1.

Greek Orthodox Church was provided more privileges than it had in the Byzantine era. The Greek Ecumenical Patriarch collectively represented of the Greek, Slavic, Albanian, Romanian, and Arab Orthodox that lived in the Ottoman land. Therefore, the Greek millet was in the prominent position in the eyes of the State and affected the Ottoman ruling class policies. Until 1910s the Greek Orthodox hold highest ranking administrative position in the Ottoman capital city and around.

See Irini Sarioglou, Turkish Policy Towards Greek Education in Istanbul 1923-1974: Secondary Education and Identity (Athens, ELIA, 2004) at 21-23.

[76] See Beirne Stedman, "The Republic of Turkey" 13 Va. L. Reg. n. s. (1927-8) at 737. Stedman notes that "Greek and Armenian partisans and paid propagandists have told terrible tales of the Turks-tales of which we only heard one side, and it is always well to take one-sided tales with a large grain of salt. It has for a long time been the writer's opinion that many of these cruelties were more or less occasioned by the aggravations furnished by non-Muslims." At 735.

land. Still "Turkey is stuck with the 1923 tradition and moreover interprets the Treaty of Lausanne incorrectly/deficiently"[77] to prove its own untenable arguments. In truth, Turkey has adhered to dogmatic taboos that have precluded discussions on the *Turkish Armed Forces, Minority Rights*, and *Secularism*. In other words, the Republic established its own taboos such as secular State, phobia of Islam and Islamic culture, Turkish military guardianship of the country.[78] One commentator, who resided in Turkey for three years as a political professor at Koc University in Istanbul, observes that:

"Turkish nationalism has weighed heaviest on Kurds, Islamist, religious minorities, and the left. A State run Turkish Reformation of Islam fallen in the 1930s; more recent attempts to nationalize Islam have turned the State into a mouthpiece for mainstream Sunni doctrine. The Turkish case suggests that in states with deep

---

[77] See Baskin Oran, "The Minority Report Affair of Turkey" 5 Regent J. Int'l L. (2007) at 74. See more Baskin Oran, Turkiye'de *Azinliklar: Kavramlar, Teori, Lozan, Ic Mevzuat, Ictihat, Uygulama* [*Minorities in Turkey: Concepts, Theory, Lausanne, Domestic Law, Jurisprudence, and Practice*] (Istanbul: Iletisim, 2005). Edip Yuksel who is a Kurdish Human Rights Activist and fled from Turkey to USA claims that that the Republic secular ideology, controls, manipulates and exploits religious believes and attack them who are not converted to official version. See Edip Yuksel "Cannibal Democracy, Theocratic Secularism: The Turkish Version" 7 Cardozo J. Int'l & Comp. L. (1999) at 467

[78] See Aksan, *supra note* 75, at 30. According to the Lausanne Treaty, non Muslim groups [Greek, Armenian and Jews recognized as non Muslims] cannot own properties for religious aims outside what they had before the establishment of the Republic of Turkey. See Niyazi Oktem, "Religion in Turkey" B.Y.U.L Rev. (2002) at 375-6.

See more M. Altug Imamoglu, Azinlik Vakiflari ve Yabancilarin Tasinmaz Edinimleri [Non-Muslims' Charities and Obtaining Property of Aliens] (Ankara, YY, 2006).

societal divisions, the dream of civic nationalism may be a coerced one . . . Religion has been nationalized."[79]

During the Republican time, 600 years Ottoman history has been denied and ignored, however, young historians began to question

---

[79] See Thomas W. Smith, "Civic Nationalism and Ethno-Cultural Justice in Turkey" 27 Hum. Rts. Q. (2005) at 436-7. In his article, Smith evidently shows that during the Republic era non-Muslims of Turkey were destroyed by the State policy and practices.

"the myopia of a self-imposed amnesia" of the Republic[80] and looking at the Ottoman archives, especially court verdicts [seriye sicilleri] to explore the facts and truths about their own past. Despite the obvious prejudices that may underscore reluctance by modern academics to make a positive example of an Islamic State, it is difficult to avoid the fact that the State guaranteed

---

[80] See Aksan, *supra note* 75, at 19. Not all young historians do these kind of challenging searches. Some of them still go on without looking into the Ottoman archives but just look at the Orieantalist studies or ultra secularist studies who believed that that past is our most hateful enemy. Such include Fatma Muge Gocek, *Rise of the Bourgeoisie, Demise of Empire: Ottoman Westernization and Social Change* (NY, OUP, 1996). Or older ones such as Deniz Kandiyoti Studies, such as "Introduction," "End of Empire: Islam, Nationalism and Women in Turkey" in *Women, Islam and the State* (London, Macmillan, 1991), Deniz Kandiyoti (ed.) without looking at the Ottoman archives or archive studies and mainly using the Western resources presented the idea of Turkish seculars rather than the Turkish nation's views. That is one of the main reasons that the West could not realize what is going on inside of Turkey. See especially in the book, chapter II, by Deniz Kandiyoti, "End of Empire: Islam, Nationalism, and Women in Turkey". These authors try to show the innocence of Turkish secular reforms in statements such as "although was not legally banned, a vigorous propaganda campaign led by Ataturk himself exhorted women to adopt modern styles of dress, and dissenters were dealt with severely." Kandiyoti shows her source at dipnote 1; "Caporal mentions trials and short prison sentences for those spreading counterpropaganda." B. Caporal, *Kemalizm ve Kemalizm Sonrasinda Turk* Kadini [*Kemalism and after Kemalism Turkish Woman*] (Ankara, TIBY, 1982) p. 649. At 23 and 44.

Kandiyoti dismisses two truths; one is that there was a law Kilik ve Kiyafet Kanunu (The Law of Clothing Style) enacted in 1925 that ordered individuals to wear clothing in the Western style and moreover, many dissenters of the reforms were hanged by the Istiklal Mahkemeleri [Freedom Courts] that were established and lived in the early years of the Republic to deal with the cases of the dissenters of the Republic.

See Sadik Albayrak, *Devrimler ve Gerici Tepkiler [Revolutions and Reactionary Movements]* (Istanbul, Arastirma Y, 1989,) Tahir-ul Mevlevi, *Matbuat Alemindeki Hayatim ve Istiklal Mahkemeleri [My Life in the Press Sector and Freedom Courts]*, Atilla Senturk (ed.), (Istanbul, Nehir, 1991), and Ahmet Nedim, *Ankara Istiklal Mahkemesi Zabitlari (1926) [Records of the Ankara Freedom Court (1926)]*, (Istanbul, Isaret, 1993).

the protection of all faiths and continued to uphold all religious privileges perhaps better than any modern political system. The prominent Ottoman scholar Kemal Karpat notes that:

"the categorical rejection of everything Ottoman became a behavioural characteristic of the Turkish modernist intelligentsia. Any good aspects of that era had to be appropriated and praised as Turkish or else the student expressing such a favourable view of the past would be branded reactionary and anti-Kemalist. The six hundred years of Ottoman history obviously received low priority, but some dedicated scholars still pursued their work."[81]

In sum, it is submitted that the "Ottoman society was a mosaic of cultures and religions and provided a peace and harmony among members of society without distinction between Muslim and non-Muslim, race, and colour."[82] Therefore, this experience should be taken into consideration in order to accommodate religious minorities in the modern world. Finally we should not see our own culture as superior to others and not humiliate them, we should try to understand and not to globalize the others, and otherwise we may not be able to eliminate cultural clashes.[83]

The following essay was published as a chapter in the following text:: The Ottoman Millet System and The Protection of Religious Minority Groups and Women in Balkan Studies III: Living Together & Culture & Education, syf. 316-357, (Skopje-Macedonia, Cyril and Methodius University, 2011).

---

[81] See Karpat, *supra note* 11, at 5.

[82] See Akgunduz, *supra note* 53.

[83] See Ahmed Akgunduz, "The First Model for the EU: Ottoman State—2 at http://www.osmanli.org.tr/en/yazi.php?id=135&bolum=30 (accessed on July 25, 2008).

2

The Ottoman Millet System
and the Protection of Religious
Minority Groups and Women

> "The West for its part has stubbornly
> refused to call the Ottoman Empire by its
> name instead labelling this multi-
> religious, multi-lingual, multi-ethnic
> polity as "Turkey" and its rulers as
> "Turks." . . . Even the republic of Turkey
> approaches its Ottoman past with
> ambivalence. The Turkey of Mustafa
> Kemal Ataturk and his successors were to
> be a nation-State in the European
> mould . . . It is, however, unacceptable to
> pass judgment on the Ottoman past and
> its possible influence on the present
> without a fair historical trial."*

The Ottoman rulers were religious people and they strictly adhered
to Islamic law. The Ottoman State "was a classic example of the
plural society."[84] This article will briefly explore its legal system and
will explore the main parameters of the 'Millet System'. The millet
system or minorities and their rights (i.e., how they exercised their
rights) will be examined as practised during the Ottoman era. In

---

* See L. Carl Brown, "The Setting: An Introduction" in *Imperial Legacy: The
Ottoman Imprint on the Balkans and the Middle East*, ed. L. Carl Brown, (NY,
CUP, 1996) at 5-6

[84] See Benjamin Braude & Bernard Lewis, "Introduction" in *Christians and
Jews in the Ottoman Empire: the Functioning of a Pluralist Society*, Volume I,
Benjamin Braude & Bernard Lewis, eds. (NY, London, Holmes & Meier,
1982) at 1.

this era, the term "minority" was exclusive to religious groups. The Ottoman Turks granted autonomy to religious minorities, a system which is believed by many scholars to work only in the poly-ethnic and multi-religious societies of that time. In the Ottoman system, Muslims, Christians, and Jews worshipped and worked side by side, enriching their distinct cultures. The legal traditions and practices of each community, particularly in matters of personal status were respected and enforced within the empire.[85] Today, it still appears that the only way to preserve the identity of religious groups, their own ideas and ways is to recognise their particular differences and in particular to allow them the privilege of operating a separate family law suitable to their particular beliefs.

During this period, minorities within a minority, particularly women of a minority group, were also protected against abusive practices of their own group by the imperial courts. However, Ottoman jurists, when dealing with a specific case were not intrusive, and thus did not touch the core values of the religious groups when they were protecting vulnerable women. In order to illustrate the pros and cons of the system, I will refer to the case-law of the era with a view to showing how the Ottoman practice provided justice for minority women with a specific focus on divorce cases. The main question here is whether or not autonomy to religious or other minority groups, particularly in the matters of separate (separate or parallel?) family law, has properly been protected in present liberal democracies. In other words, whether liberal democracies sufficiently provide room for such a model of autonomy to religious and other minority groups in the matters of separate family law, especially if the group practices seem to be conservative.

The article will contend that classical era Ottoman practices had provided a solid answer to eliminating the injustices and failures of today's minority models especially when it comes to the protection

---

[85] *Id.*

of religious minorities. In this respect, issues relating to divorce and the protection of women will be assessed to provide a closer scrutiny of the Ottoman Millet system. It will further question whether or not such elements can be harmoniously infused into modern liberal systems. The analysis will focus on the question of whether it is possible to provide a separate religious legal system for religious minorities that could also address the concerns of women in liberal State models. It will be argued that the best interests of religious minorities, regarding family law matters, should be determined by the religious group involved under minimal State control. A State's main duty should be limited to controlling people's voluntary choices, i.e., whether they join the group voluntarily and can freely exit at any time if they so wish. Other than this, the State should not be involved with the internal affairs of the groups. If the State interferes with the internal affairs of religious groups, this might be an authoritarian/intrusive practice, attempting to impose "liberalism" upon the individual members of a particular group. State

Ottoman Legal System*

The main question concerning this legal system was whether it was a multi layered judicial system or unified legal system. Basic rights and thoughts in Islam did not have the same phases that occurred in the Western world. They have been in existence since the beginning of Islam and the concept of freedom in Islam is

---

* During the Ottoman era, the most important thing was the Sharia courts in terms of legal system. Each court recorded their decision on Ser'iye Sicili which was the registration book of the courts. The oldest date goes back to 1455 from Bursa Court Ser'i Sicili. See more about Ser'iye Sicilleri-Osmanli Hukukunda Adliye Teskilatinin Yapisi ve Fonksiyonlari [Seri Sicil-Structures and Functions of the Ottoman Judiciary System] at http://.istanbulmuftulugu.gov.tr/index. php?option=com_content&task=view&id=21 . . . (accessed on August 5, 2008).

different from the notion in Western understanding.[86]The majority of people link Sharia law with obligations and Western law with rights.[87]Previously, Islamic law was known as "Fikih" [88]Fikih is mainly divided into two sections: Furu-i Fikih that deals the branches of fikih and Usulu-i Fikih that is the theoretical aspect of Sharia that looks at the primary sources of Islamic law.[89]Furu-i Fikih also had been divided into ibadat [acts of worship] and muamelat [interpersonal relations] such as family law, contract law, criminal law . . . etc.[90]

Freedom in Islam means: without harming anyone and yourself you may do anything within the borders of the legal system.[91] According to Islam, people are free, and just subjects of Allah (Abdullah).[92] Islamic law orders that no one should obey atrocious people and that they should refuse absolute freedom and call it animal freedom and describe it as being coercion of the Daemon

---

[86] See Ahmet Akgunduz, Islam ve Bati Hukukunda Insan Haklarinin Tarihi Gelisimi [Historical Phases of Human Rights in Islam and West] at http://. osmanli.org.tr/yazdirilabilirosmanli.php?id:145 (accessed on July 23, 2008).

[87] See Murteza Bedir, "Fikih to Law: Secularization through Curriculum" 11 Islamic L. & Soc'y (2004) at 379. The author provides this information from Joseph Schacht *An Introduction to Islamic Law* (Oxford, OUP, 1964) at 4. In his article, Bedir argues that the Western notion of law influenced the form of fikih into Islamic law.

[88] At 380.

[89] See general Murteza Bedir, Fikih, Mezhep ve Sunnet [Fikih, Sects, and Sunnah] (Istanbul, Ensar, 2004).

[90] See Bedir, *supra note* 87, at 380.

[91] See Akgunduz, *supra note* 86.

[92] *Id.*

and being the slave of the inner-man.[93] Moreover, Islam does not accept church [mosque] and/or priesthood.[94]

The Sunni jurisdiction of Islamic law does not make any distinction regarding public and private law. It is mainly concerned with rights of Allah [God] and Human Rights.[95] However, some current Islamic legal scholars claim that God's rights could be accepted as public law and human rights could be acknowledged as private law.[96] In Islamic law, private acts cannot be taken before the court unless there is violation of right[s] of someone and a claim made to the judiciary.[97] With this position, criminal law is the private law branch in Islam.[98] The victim and plaintiff must be present both at trial and the execution.[99]

Theoretically, it is possible to divide Islamic law into public and private.[100] One eminent Islamic scholar in Turkey, Professor Hayrettin Karaman claims that there is always a private/public law distinction in Fikih [Islamic Law].[101] He also advises that private law in Islam should be considered from the perspective of

---

[93] See Servet Armagan, *Islam Hukukunda Temel Hak ve Hurriyetler* [*Basic Rights and Freedoms in Islamic Law*] (Ankara, TDB, 1987) at 71.

[94] See Nawaf A. Salam, "The Emergence of Citizenship in Islam" 12 Arab L. Q. (1997) at 131.

See for a discussion of how Islam and secularism are incompatible, Mehrzad Boroujerdi, "Can Be Islam Secularized?" in *In Transition: Essays on Culture and Identity in Middle Eastern Societies*, M. R. Ghanoonparvar & Faridoun Farrokh (eds.), (Texas, A & M IUP, 1994).

[95] See Armagan, *supra note 93*, at 118.

[96] *Id*.

[97] See Abdulaziz Sachedina, Guidance or Governance? A Muslim Conception of "Two-Cities", 68 Geo. Wash. L. Rev. (1999-2000) at 1079. The author gathers this information from Joseph Schacht, *An Introduction to Islamic Law* (Oxford, OUP, 1964) at 189-90.

[98] At 1094.

[99] *Id*.

[100] See Hayrettin Karaman, Mukayeseli Islam Hukuku, 1. Cilt [Comparative Islamic Law, Volume 1] (Istanbul, Iz, 1999) at 20 hereafter.

[101] At 39.

continental legal system.[102] Others claim that "the Qur'anic vision of an ideal order is not based on the separation of the private and public"; rather, it is the finding of your own true way.[103]In other words, public and private life is integrated and with the Qur'an's reference, individual freedom of conscience is the cornerstone of this communal life.[104] The Qur'an intertwines religion and civil responsibility, Christianity divides the world "between the sacred and secular."[105]In Islam, religion is not taken away from the public arena. Bedir claims that traditionally, public law is less developed in Islamic law compared to the Western legal tradition.[106]

As stated earlier, private law in Islamic law developed the notion of relationship between "the individual and the social good."[107] Professor Emon, using Western sources, mistakenly argues that Hanafi jurists sacrifice the individual for the public interest or the community.[108] Islam treats all rights equally, whether or not they could be considered major or minor rights. Without the consent of an individual person his/her right cannot be sacrificed in the

---

[102] See general Hayrettin Karaman, Mukayeseli Islam Hukuku, 3. Cilt [Comparative Islamic Law, Volume III] (Istanbul, Iz, 1999)

[103] See Sachedina, *supra note* 97, at 1089.

[104] *Id.*

[105] At 1090.

[106] See Bedir, *supra note* 87, at 400. The same argument was made by many Ottoman legal historians such as Ebul'ula Mardin who was one of the prominent Turkish legal scholars and thought the Islamic law subject in the law faculty of Istanbul University in the early years of the Republic.

See about Ebul'ula Mardin's biography, Turgut Akpinar, *Istanbul Universitesinde 50 Yil Oncesi Bazi Buyuk Hocalarimiz* [*50 Years Ago Some of Our Eminent Professors in Istanbul University*] (Istanbul, Kitabevi, 2004).

[107] See Anver M. Emon, Huquq Allah and Huquq Al-Ibad: A Legal Heuristic for A Natural Rights Regime, 13Islamic L.&Soc'y (2004) at 327.

[108] At 331-33. See parallel idea from Turkish academia "individualistic interpretations of the Sacred law were not allowed." See Heper, *supra note* 285, at 45.

name of society. Bediuzzaman Said Nursi[109] from Turkey repeats this notion of Islamic justice in a modern sense;

"Pure justice and relative justice may be explained like this: according to the allusive meaning of the verse,—"if anyone slew a person—unless it be for murder or for spreading mischief in the land—it would be as if he slew the whole people, [Holy Qur'an 5:32]"—the rights of an innocent man cannot be cancelled for the sake of all the people. A single individual may not be sacrificed for the good of all. In the view of Almighty God's compassion, right is right, there is no difference between great and small. The small may not be annulled for the great. Without his consent, the life and rights of an individual may not be sacrificed for the good of the community. If he consents to sacrifice them in the name of patriotism, that is a different matter. A particular is sacrificed for the good of the universal; the rights of an individual are not considered in the face of the community. A sort of relative justice is attempted to be applied as the lesser of two evils. But if it is\possible to apply pure justice, relative justice may not be attempted, if it is, it is wrong."[110]

---

[109] Bediuzzaman Said Nursi (1877-1960)who is of Kurdish origin but was born and died in Turkey and influenced the Islamic thought in modern world—justifies that true enemies are in the century of "science-reason-and civilization-" materialism and atheism and their source is materialist philosophy. To fight against this problem he chose the jihad of the word in other words non-physical jihad and positive action means that maintenance of public order and security that harmed by the acts of unbelief could be repaired by the healing of the truths of the Qur'an. At, http://.www.nursistudies.com

[110] See Bediuzzaman Said Nursi, Letters, The Fifteenth Letter, at 79, at http://www.nur.gen.tr/en.html#leftmenu=Risale&maincontent=Risale&islem=read&KitapAd=Letters&KitapId=21&BolumId=732&Page=79.

In the Ottoman court, the judge sat on the bench alone; however, there were officials who helped him.[111] Judges also served as a mayor and chief of police of their local area.[112] A Kadi [judge] acted as a mediator and brought the sides to an acceptable solution; in other words, bargaining and negotiation was part of Ottoman law.[113] Until 1864 and the establishment of the Nizamiye Courts, Sharia courts were the only courts.[114] When we compare the Islamic legal system with other systems of today we see a similarity to common law, for example the role of a judge and the jury system. A Kadi (judge) describes and develops rules and cases and also took care of cases with a jury that consisted of five or six trustworthy individuals from the local community.[115] Every court recorded its decisions in special record books, a practise ordered by the Ottoman State.[116]

In the Ottoman era, the main principle between the State and its people was justice [adalet].[117] "Justice was the protection of the rural and urban producers against abuses of the military elite."[118] Many post-classical Ottoman political studies mention that justice was the main cornerstone during the Ottoman era for legitimate

---

[111] See Ahmet Bostanci, Urdun'de Muslumanlara ve Gayri Muslimlere Yonelik Dini Yargi Sistemi [Religious Judiciary System for Muslim and Non-Muslims in Jordan] 3 Usul Dergisi (2005) at 107. The author claims that the Jordanian Judiciary system is the continuation of the Ottoman Judiciary system that offers a choice for Muslim and non-Muslim in private family law.

[112] See Ahmet Akgunduz, "Application of Islamic Legislation in the Ottoman State: Sharia Courts and Sharia Records" at http://www.osmanli.org.tr/en/the_articles.php?bolum=30&id=338 (accessed on July 28, 2008).

[113] See Haim Gerber, *State, Society, and Law in Islam: Ottoman Law in Comparative Perspective* (NY, NYSUP, 1994) at 177 and 179.

[114] See Bostanci, *supra note* 111, at 109.

[115] See Necdet Sevinc, *Osmanli'nin Yukselisi ve Cokusu* [The Rise and fall of the Ottoman] (Istanbul, Birharf, 2005), at 93.

[116] See Akgunduz, *supra note* 112.

[117] See Erol Ozbilgen, *Butun Yonleriyle Osmanli: Adab-i Osmaniyye* [All Aspects of Ottomans: Rules of Ottoman] (Istanbul, Iz, 2007), at 117.

[118] See A. Ergene Bogac, "On Ottoman Justice: Interpretations in Conflict (1600-1800)" 8 Islamic L. & Soc'y (2001) at 52.

governance.[119] The Ottoman believed that justice is the protection of legitimate order and recognized mutual rights and obligations in order to continue in a healthy society.[120] Moreover, around the XVIII Century some rebellions occurred against the Sultanate Orders in the name of justice.[121] The Ottoman legal system was defined by hierarchies of codes, justice according to Ser'i Law [Sharia]. [122] Everyone in the country, including the Sultans, was amenable before the law; they were not seen as being above the law.[123] Here, the Ottoman legal system "in practice . . . clearly, distinguished [between] the State and religion, dealing with issues that concerned political power and administration independently from religion."[124] It could be said that before French secular practices, there were Ottoman ones in terms of separation of religion and politics. However, the Ottoman version should be distinguished from the French counterpart. During the Ottoman era, with few exceptions of State suppression caused by Shia movements, there were no sect uprisings[125] anywhere in Europe. Even in its beginnings, the Ottoman State believed one should "give back to Caesar what is Caesar's and to God what is God's".

This separation of State and religion gave rise to the order of law followed by the Ottomans. However, this hierarchy was not always adhered to in practice. Hierarchical order in the Ottoman legal system were—first, the Qur'an [God's Orders]-Hadis [Prophet

---

[119] At 54.

[120] At 86.

[121] See general Mustafa Akdag, Turk Halkinin Dirlik ve Duzenlik Kavgasi: Celali Isyanlari [Fight of Turkish People for Social and Political Order: Celali Rebellions] (Ankara, BKBY, 1999).

[122] Halil Cin & Ahmed Akgunduz, *Turk Hukuk Tarihi1. Cilt, Kamu Hukuku* [*History of Turkish Law, Volume I, Public Law*] (Istanbul, OAV, 1995) at 225.

[123] *Id*, at 226.

[124] See Halil Inalcik, "The Meaning of Legacy" in *Imperial Legacy: The Ottoman Imprint on the Balkans and the Middle East*, ed. L. Carl Brown, (NY, CUP, 1996) at 21.

[125] See general Taha Akyol, *Osmanli'da ve Iran'da Mezhep ve Devlet* [Mezhep and State in the Ottoman and Iran] (Istanbul, Milliyet, 1999).

Mohammad's Orders and Practices]-Icma[Collective Decisions of Islamic Jurists and Scholars]-Kiyas[Analogy]-Orders of the Sultan that complied with Islamic law-Regulations of Islamic States— Legal Codes of Newly Captured Lands that complied with Islamic law-Legal Customs that complied with Islamic law-Agreements with Foreign Governments-Principle of Reciprocity in International law-Istihsan[leaving general rule and establishing an exceptional rule because of necessity] and Istishab[if there is no absolute rule, then it is permissible]-and Previous Prophets' Sharia.[126] Even if this order defined societal laws, the Ottomans also considered the new introductions into its society and altered laws according to changing values and sometimes adopted other legal customs, or established a secular-universal thought, while still maintaining its Sunni philosophy.

Among the main four Sunni mezhebs (sects) the Hanefi school of thought was followed by the Ottoman Turks as being the most rational and liberal.[127] This selection also helped to rationalise the legal system. Especially, in the field of criminal law, where the State chose not to use capital punishment and authorities preferred to give amends or blood money (compensation to the victim's family) thus, the Ottomans tried to be a role model for a universality [of human rights] and promote harmony.[128]

To further pursue their hopes for universality and harmony, the Ottomans adopted Tacit (customary) law that influenced and shaped its legal system, this law was never practiced as it

---

[126] See Ozbilgen, *supra note* 34, at 117. See more Cin & Akgunduz, *supra note* 35, at 159-64. See more additional info about those terminological words and their explanations, Mehmet Erdogan, Fikih ve Hukuk Terimleri Sozlugu [Dictionary of Terminology of Islamic Law and Law] (Istanbul, Ragbet, 1998).

[127] See Ozbilgen, *supra note* 117, at 122.

[128] See Ilber Ortayli, *Uc Kitada Osmanlilar* [Ottomans on Three Continents] (Istanbul, Timas, 2007) at 113. Professor Ortayli claims that the Ottoman was one of the three greatest empires in the region of the Mediterranean and the latest universal one. See general, Ilber Ortayli, *Son Imparatorluk Osmanli* [Last Empire Ottoman] (Istanbul, Timas, 2006).

had been by the Ottomans in other Islamic societies or states.[129] Thus, the Ottoman State became more multi-ethnic, multi-lingual-and multi-religious. It made the Ottoman more of a State than an imperial kingdom. If newly attained countries or land had no legal tradition contrary to Islamic law, the Ottoman rulers made and permitted their practices as new codes of the State,[130] for example, adoption of taxation laws came from many countries that later joined the empire, a reason why new citizens of the State acknowledged the power of their new rulers. It also helped people keep custody and interpretation of their traditions. In practice, Ottoman Sultan orders were limited by Sharia law or the Customs of people[131] and some customary laws were in opposition to Islamic law, but the State still accepted them as their own legal rule.[132] Law of the Ottoman was secular and politic not religious.[133] Famous Ottoman historians Stanford Shaw, Ira Lapidus, and Professor Halil Inalcik claimed in numerous writings that with the acceptance of customary practices the Ottoman State became a secular State.[134] However, Professor Akgunduz counter claims that Sharia law permitted the Sultan (Ulul-Emr, head of the State) to make laws, but that this law should have complied

---

[129] During the Ottoman era, judges went through a three step procedure to pass as candidate judge. After finishing medrese, their first duty was to be a consultant and answer people's questions, second, he had to teach at a medrese and finally if he was successful on these two duties he might be able to become a judge. See Ilber Ortayli, *Osmanliýi Yeniden Kesfetmek* [Re-exploration of the Ottomans] (Istanbul, Timas, 2006) at 128. A judge also controlled all officials within his own area. Moreover, judges were routinely supervised by higher judges. *Id*, 128-9.

[130] See Cin & Akgunduz, *supra note* 122, at 166-70.

[131] *Id*, at 197-8. See also Ozbilgen, *supra note* 117, at 123.

[132] See Akyol, *supra note* 125, at 151.

[133] *Id*.

[134] See Stanford Shaw, *History of the Ottoman Empire and Modern Turkey,* Volume I, (Cambridge, CUP, 1987) at 134. Ira Lapidus, *a History of Islamic Societies,* (Cambridge, CUP, 1988) 319. Halil Inalcik, the Middle East and the Balkans under the Ottoman Empire, (Bloomington, 1987) at 86.

with the Sharia.[135] However, it could be said that Professor Akgunduz observations on the Devsirme system are misplaced. This was a system that permitted many non-Muslims to access high bureaucratic and administrative positions, all but the position of Sultan itself. This action is a clear violation of Classical Islamic law, where high State positions were only granted to Muslim citizens. This demonstrates the Ottoman separation of religion and politics or what one might call secularism.

Since the establishment of the Ottoman State all orders and customs accepted as legal rules were registered by a State official (Nisanci).[136] This person was the State's highest legal advisor, even Seyhul-Islam, or the executive State clergy came to the Nisanci for interpretation of rules.[137] Registrars wrote legal documents after discussions held between legal and religious scholars with the approval of the Sultan. The commands of previous Sultans were followed by their successors except if, and when, there were new situations that needed amendment to retain societal trust of the legal system.[138]

Even during the 14th century there was advancement in the legal system far beyond the norm of the time. Until the 18th Century, the Ottoman State was seen in the eyes of European excursionists and philosophers as a source of inspiration and the "most modern government" in the world.[139] The Ottomans developed a universality of this system through understanding and a desire for the well-being of its citizens. Worth noting was how judges' verdicts were not changed by Sultan orders.[140] Moreover, governors had no

---

[135] See Ahmet Akgunduz, *Osmanli Kanunnameleri ve Hukuk Tahlilleri* [Legal Rules of the Ottomans and Legal Analysis], Volume I (Istanbul, Fey, 1990) at 60.

[136] See Ozbilgen, *supra note* 117, at 108.

[137] See Akyol, *supra note* 125, at 150.

[138] See Ozbilgen, *supra note* 117, at 127-8.

[139] See Asli Cirakman, "From Tyranny to Despotism: The Enlightenments of Unenlightent Image of Turks" 33 Int. J. MES (2001) at 49.

[140] See Halil Inalcik, *Turkey and Europe in History* (Istanbul, Eren, 2006) at 64.

jurisdiction over judges appointed by the Sultan's ministry.[141] This made the Ottoman justicial system independent from legislators and executive powers. The Ottoman political system resembled that of the modern United States of America, the legislative and executive are mixed, but the justice branch was completely separate. In other words, the separation of powers seemed to work. Like today, judges, defendants and offenders were able to call expert witnesses into courts.[142] One of the most important features of the Ottoman system was that nobody was sentenced to punishment without a judge's order.[143] No other State at the time possessed this type of law, again a step in the direction of universality. If, during the trial one of the parties provided new evidence, the judge needed to review the case again, and any one party could apply to the Divan-i Human, State's main council, located in the capital city, where experienced higher court judges could examine the case,[144] in effect, a right of appeal. This was a significant development in the way of State law. According to the Ottoman legal system, each party to the case was able to confer with a legal scholar before going to court, which usually helped parties to reach a settlement,[145] similar to a Mediation-Arbitration system in common law. In sum, with the assimilation of customary law practices, the Ottoman created a more global, secular legal system one that was devout in the separation of mosque and State.

---

[141] *Id.*

[142] See Sevince, *supra note* 115, at 93-4.

[143] See Cin & Akgunduz, *supra note* 122, at 270-1. See Ozbilgen, *supra note* 117, at 219.

[144] See Ozbilgen, *supra note* 117, at 32. See also Cin & Akgunduz, *supra note* 122, at 239-40.

[145] See Cin & Akgunduz, *supra note* 39, at 223.

Foundations of the Millet System

The Qur'an orders that freedom of religion is one of the main principles of Islam.[146] According to the Islamic Law, Jews and Christians were accepted as people of the book. Islam provides protection for non-Muslims via agreement between the State and the group.[147] In an Islamic State, non-Muslims are protected groups thus it is a duty of the government to protect their legitimate interests.[148] Millet is an Arabic word[149] that translated into English as nation.[150] This term was not used only for non-Muslims, but also for any nation.[151] However, in the terminology of the Ottoman historians, it is mostly used to define non-Muslim communities.[152] The Ottoman administration system was divided into two as territorial/local (provinces) and religious divisions. People were seen in the eyes of State not on the basis of ethnicity or language, but

---

[146] See general Mohammad Hashim Kamali, "Freedom of Religion in Islam" 21 Cap. U. L. Rev. (1992) at 80.

[147] See Mehmet Akif Aydin, *Islam ve Osmanli Hukuku Arastirmalari* [Researches on the Islam and Ottoman Law] (Istanbul, Iz, 1996) at 230.

Professor Hamidullah notes that after the Prophet, the Second Calphate Omer, there was a Jew whose land was taken away from him without his consent, and administrators established a Mosque. Omer made the administrators destroy the mosque and returned the land to its owner. Still, today there is "Beyt-ul Yahudi" [Jew House]. See Muhammed Hamidullah, *Islam Anayasa Hukuku* [Constitutional Law of Islam], ed., Vecdi Akyuz, (Istanbul, Beyan, 1995) at 200.

[148] See Muhammad Hamidullah, Muslim Conduct of State, Article 12, "The Status of Non-Muslims in Islam" available at http://www.muslim-canada.org/ch12hamid.html (accessed on August 5, 2008).

[149] See Ortayli, *supra note 45*, at 59.

[150] See Kemal H. Karpat, "Millets and Nationality: the Roots of the Incongruity of Nation and State in the Post-Ottoman Era" in Benjamin Braude & Bernard Lewis, *supra note 1*, at 141-170. Professor Karpat is well known the Ottoman historian who taught for many years in Wisconsin University in the USA.

[151] See Benjamin Braude, "Foundation Myths of the Millet System" in Benjamin Braude & Bernard Lewis, *supra note 84*, at 69.

[152] *Id.*

religion.[153] "Religion, language, community, ethnicity, and family made up the socio-cultural fabric of the millet."[154] For the Ottoman period, the most important thing was religion and supremacy of family; in other words, the millet system favoured "fusion of family and the community."[155] "Religion supplied each millet with a universal belief system while ethnic and linguistic differences provided for divisions and subdivisions within each one of the two Christian millets."[156]

The "Milletbasi" either a patriarch or rabbi was the representative of his community before the State[157] like a political head. The Religious community was the form of political structure and "the source of identity" for non-Muslim communities.[158] One can assume that it was a segregation or isolation of communities from each other. Berkes notes that the millet system worked without segregating millets (nations) into ghettos or extermination[159], they lived next to each other. However, "each group had traditions as to titles, grades, recruitment, ceremonies, discipline, but absolute loyalty to the supreme ruler."[160]The Millet system based on the Zimmi [Dhimmah] tradition that regulates public and personal rules for minorities [religious] who lives under the rule of Islamic

---

[153] See Serif Mardin, "Religion and Secularism in Turkey" in *Ataturk: Founder of a Modern State*, Ali Kazancigil & Ergun Ozbudun (eds), 2nd ed, (London, Hurst & Company, 1997) at 199

[154] See Karpat, *supra note* 150, at 142.

[155] *Id.*

[156] See Kemal Karpat, *Studies on Ottoman Social and Political History: Selected Articles and Essays* (Leiden, Brill, 2002) at 612.

[157] See Benjamin Braude, "Foundation Myths of the Millet System" in Benjamin Braude & Bernard Lewis, *supra note* 84, at 69.

[158] See Karpat, *supra note* 150, at 17.

[159] Niyazi Berkes, *The Development of Secularism in Turkey*, (NY, Rout ledge, 1998) at 11-2. This book was originally published in Canada in 1963 by McGill University. Niyazi Berkes (1908-1988) was a leftist Turkish intellectual who escaped from Turkey after the 1960 Military Coup d'état and began to reside in Canada. He never came back to live in Turkey. See, Berkes, New Introduction by Feroz Ahmad, at XV-XXXIII.

[160] *Id*, at 12.

lands.[161] In doctrines, many authors continue to perpetuate this mistaken belief; Islam or Ottoman practices provided non-Muslim communities communitarian identity and did not recognize individual autonomy and just followed and dictated orthodox socio-religious orders of the communities.[162]

---

[161] See Kamran Hashemi, "The Right of Minorities to Identity and the Challenge of Non-Discrimination: A Study on the Effects of Traditional Muslims Dhimmah on Current State Practices" 13 Int. J. Min. & Gr. R. (2006) at 2.

[162] Such as one of the authors see Sachedina, *supra note* 14, at 1093. Or see Marc Baer, "The Double Bind of Race and Religion: The Conversion of the Donme to Turkish Secular Nationalism" Soc. of Comp. Stud. of Soc. and His. (2004) at 685.

Leo Zaibert rightly critics Will Kymlicka and make balance about the Ottoman Millet system. According to Zaibert, Kymlicka pointed out that the system was not liberal even many groups lived peacefully next to each other, but none of the individual has right to exit from the group thus individual autonomy was not respected. The system did not recognize any individual freedom of conscience. Therefore, he calls it as a federation of theocracies [See Will Kymlicka, *Multicultural Citizenship: A Liberal Theory of Minority Rights* (NY, Oxford, 1995) at 152 and 157].

Zaibert claims that "I do not mean to suggest that the Ottoman Millet system was liberal in content; but it is closer to being that than to being liberal-in-form. See Leo Zaibert, Punishment and Retribution, (Aldershot, AshgateP, 2006)

The millet system also;[163]

"allowed the subject Christian peoples [and the other nations] to retain their separate identities and cultures, rooted in their respective churches. Indeed the monophysite churches with Syrian, Armenian and Coptic adherents, as well as the Nestorians, survived mainly in the Muslim lands, while vanishing in the more intolerant Christian West. Along with the Jews expelled from England [actually Jews were coming into the Ottoman land since around 1390], France, Spain, and Portugal, a variety of heterodox Christians including Protestants, Unitarians, and Russian Molokans received refuge in the Ottoman Empire."

Non-Muslim minorities enjoyed nearly unfettered self-government within their religious communities, also operating their own schools.[164] During the Ottoman era, many Vezirs (State ministers) or Grand Vezirs (Prime Ministers) were appointed non-Muslims or

---

[163] See Hugh Poultan, *Top Hat, Grey Wolf and Crescent: Turkish Nationalism ad the Turkish Republic* (London, Hurst & Company, 1997) at 49. See more about the Ottoman Millet System, Youssef Courbage & Philippe Fargues, Christians and Jews under Islam ((London, New York, I. B. Tauris Publishers, 1997) especially look at the article Five: From Multinational Empire to Secular Republic: the Lost of Christianity of Turkey, Ali Guler, Osmanli Devletinde Azinliklar [Minorities in the Ottoman] (Istanbul, Turan Publishing, 1997), Onder Kaya, Tanzimat'tan Lozan'a Azinliklar [Minorities from Tanzimat to Lausanne] (Istanbul, Yeditepe Publishing, 2004), Yavuz Ercan, *Osmanli Yonetiminde Gayrimuslimler* [Non-Muslims Under the Ottoman Administration] (Ankara, Turhan Publishing House, 2001). Professor Ercan notes that according to Islamic law or the Ottoman law; Zimmi (non-Muslims) cannot ring their bells, they cannot carry guns, they cannot ride horses, they have to bury their deaths secretly, and they cannot build their houses higher than Muslim houses. At 9. It is a very classic example of Turkish academia about the Ottoman history, even without showing any reference. However, once again, there is a lot of proof against for those kinds of arguments from the Ottoman archives that mainly located in Istanbul.
[164] See Edward Mead Earle, "The New Constitution of Turkey", 40 Pol. Sc. Q., (1925) at 77.

other Muslim races who were not Turks.[165] In the millet system, nations "were treated like corporate bodies and allowed their own internal structures and hierarchies; indeed the Ottoman State encouraged this by dealing exclusively [most of the time, but not all the time] with their head figures rather than the individual members."[166] In other words, it is a system that establishes the coexistence of religions[167] and allows different communities to live side by side in harmony. However, Abdullahi A. An-Naim notes that:

"Non-Muslim minorities within an Islamic State do not enjoy rights equal to those of Muslim majority. Some apologist Muslim writers have tended to misrepresent Sharia, the historical religious law of the Muslims, in order to minimize the seriousness of discrimination against non-Muslims. Such an approach is futile not only because current public opinion is unwilling to tolerate any degree or form of discrimination on grounds of religion or belief. On a practical level, although most of the constitutions of modern Muslim states guarantee against religious discrimination, most of these constitutions also authorize the application of Sharia. As

---

[165] See Poultan, *supra note* 163, at 44. See more L. Carl Brown (ed.) Imperial Legacy: the Ottoman Imprint on the Balkans and the Middle East (New York, CUP, 1996). See Also Justin McCarthy, *Muslims and Minorities: the Population of Ottoman Anatolia and the End of the Ottoman Empire* (NY, NYUP, 1983). See also Justin McCarthy, *Death and Exile: the Ethnic Cleansing of Ottoman Muslims, 1821-1922* (Princeton, NJ Darwin P, 1995), and *The Ottoman Peoples and of Empire (Historical Endings)*

(London: Arnold; NY: Oxford, 2001).

[166] See Poultan, *supra note* 163, at 48.

[167] *Id*, at 16.

such, these constitutions sanction discrimination against religious minorities."[168]

It is held that the Ottoman State already made this reconciliation many centuries ago, if fact, Ottoman Turks began to capture universal human rights standards at their classical age (14th Century-19th Century). [169] In sum, in the Ottoman Era, personal rights and freedoms were very important; their legal basis was provided by the Qur'an. Even in the early 16th century, before medical surgery was popular, patients had to sign a paper waiving their rights to the courts before any medical operations were performed. Jobs in the Ottoman Public service sector, were filled by Muslims and non-Muslims alike.[170] Many Christians and Jews had the position of Sadrazam, or Prime Minister of the State.[171] It is believed that norms like "your brothers in religion" or "your equals in creation" served as a main principle for civil society.[172] Sharing highest political positions with non-Muslim citizens was a great discovery at that time. This was another remarkable experience that illustrates non-discriminative policies. However, many nationalistic authors claim that the collapse of the Ottoman

---

[168] See Abdullahi A. An-Naim, "Religious Minorities under Islamic Law and the Limits of Cultural Relativism" 9 Hum. R. Q. (1987) at 1. Moreover, An-Naim argues that Muslims should not discriminate non-Muslims because of Islamic cultural norms and Muslims should reconcile Shariah with fundamental human rights. At 18.

See more Javaid Rehman, "Accommodating Religious Identities in an Islamic State: International Law, Freedom of Religion, and the Rights of Religious Minorities" 7 Int. J. Min. & Gr. Rts. (2000) 139-166.

[169] In doctrine there is an essay collection of a book that consists 58 articles, however, none of them talks about the Ottoman experience. Most of the authors claim that there is no tolerance for non-Muslims in Islam. What I believe this book is heavily written under 9/11 influences. See *The Myth of Islamic Tolerance: How Islamic Law Treats Non-Muslims*, Robert Spencer, ed. (Prometheus Books, Amherst & NY, 2005)

[170] See general Ahmet Akgunduz, *Belgeler Gercekleri Konusuyor I [Documents Tell the Truths I]* (Istanbul, Nil, 1989

[171] See Ortayli, *supra note* 128, at 59-68.

[172] See Sachedina, *supra note* 97, at 1097.

Empire was due to Christian and Jews involvement in politics within the State. Objectively, Prince Said Halim Pasa disagreed with this criticism, he believed that the Justice and Administrative System broke down because of the lack of progression with the times and that this was the main reason the State lost its power.[173] In practice Ottoman States protected non-Muslim personal rights, but Sultan Mehmet II, Fatih (1432-1481) began declaring laws to provide stronger safeguards.[174] However, "the Ottoman Sultans did not introduce the millet system into their empire only on the capture of Constantinople, but were already applying its principles to the non-Muslim communities under their rule."[175] After the conquest of Istanbul in 1454, the Sultan declared a ferman [Sultan's Decree] to the Patriarchate Gennadios containing many rights and privileges. With this decree, the Patriarchate became the highest authority over the Orthodox Churches and Fatih's aim was to discourage his involvement in political affairs and the prevention of any possible alliance of eastern and western churches.[176] It should be noted that in 1452 with the force of the Byzantine Emperor Constantine Paleologos, the Greek Orthodox church came under

---

[173] See general Said Halim Pasa, *Buhranlarimiz ve Son Eserleri* [Our Crisis and His Last Written Works], ed., M. Ertugrul Duzdag (Istanbul, Iz, 1991). Said Halim Pasa one of the latest Ottoman Sadr-i Azams [Prime Minister].

[174] See Ahmet Akgunduz & Said Ozturk, *700. Yilinda Bilinmeyen Osmanli [Unknown Ottoman on the 700th Anniversary]* (Istanbul, Osmanli, 1999) at 434.

[175] From H. A. R. Gibb & Harold Bowen, *Islamic Society and the West*, (Oxford, OUP, 1957), Volume I, Part II, at 214. See Kevork B. Bardakjian, "The Rise of Armenian Patriarchate of Constantinople" in Benjamin Braude & Bernard Lewis, *supra note* 84, at 91.

Moreover, the State was enforcing the Patriarchate punishments with his orders.

See Ozbilgen, *supra note* 117, at 419. Ozbilgen notes that religious communities' courts verdicts enforced by State officers.

See more Richard Glogg, "The Greek Millet in the Ottoman Empire" in Benjamin Braude & Bernard Lewis, *supra note* 84, at 185-207.

[176] See Elcin Macar, *Cumhuriyet Doneminde Istanbul Rum Patrikhanesi* [Istanbul Greek Patriarchate during the Republic Era] (Istanbul, Iletisim, 2003) at 29.

the rule of Vatican, thus Sultan Fatih was returned their freedom. Moreover, Fatih granted the patriarch the title of Ottoman Pasha [General]. The Janissary corps [Devsirme Military Personals] and an attachment of guards were also granted. He also founded a jail inside the Patriarchate building within which Ottoman State law was not practiced, the Patriarchate was law.[177] Fatih also provided this kind of privileges and rights to Armenian and Jewish communities. They became all representative, in religion and politics, of Armenian and Jewish communities around the world.[178] It is evident that politics controlled religion during the Ottoman era.

During Ottoman times, diversity was far from being the chaos that lay dormant in society as often appears to be the case in modern societies. Rather, it was a quite fundamentally absorbed normality throughout the Empire. Tolerance appeared paramount, for instance as in while Sultan Beyazid II (1481-1512) ruled; Ottoman States sent ships to Spain to save Jews from religious persecution.[179] Their descendents remain in modern day Istanbul, evidently at peace while even continuing to carry out their lives without having to change their native tongue from Spanish. Another notable

---

[177] See Adnan Sofuoglu, *Fener Rum Patrikhanesi ve Siyasi Faaliyetleri* [Fener Greek Patriarchate and Its Political Activities] (Istanbul, Turan, 1996) at 11-15.

[178] *Id*, at 16-7.

[179] "Yahudilerin Şükran Yılları" [Jews Thanksgiving Years], 6-12 January Tempo Magazine (1991) at 26-34. See more Bernard Lewis, *Cultures in Conflict: Christians, Muslims, and Jews in the Age of Discovery* (NY & Oxford, OUP, 1995) at 50-1. See general Bernard Lewis, *The Jews of Islam* (London, Melbourne & Henley, Routledge & Keagan Paul, 1984). However, Joseph R. Hacker claims, wrongly, that under the Sultan Beyazid II, "Jews suffered severe restrictions in their religious life."

See Joseph R. Hacker, "Ottoman Policy toward the Jews and Jewish Attitudes toward the Ottomans during the Fifteenth Century" in Benjamin Braude & Bernard Lewis, *supra note* 84, at 124.

See counter arguments Mark A. Epstein, "The Leadership of the Ottoman Jews in the Fifteenth and Sixteenth Centuries" in Benjamin Braude & Bernard Lewis, *supra note* 84, at 101-15.

influx of Jewish refugees are those that arrived in Istanbul during World War II as Turkey took in Jews from Germany, giving them immediate citizenship status, especially in the case of university professors.[180]

Until relatively recently, Islamic societies and Muslim states showed respect for the Bible and Torah-Talmud and never limited the production or teaching of them.[181] After the conquest of Istanbul, minorities such as Greeks, Armenians and Jews were allowed to establish a community whose master was called "patriarch."[182] With this community they were absolutely allowed to live freely their own religion, language, tradition and customs. The government completely gave the management of the authority and responsibilities for all education and cultural institutes, churches and hospitals of minorities' community to this patriarch. After the capture of Istanbul, Sultan Fatih declared that none of the State officials were going to involve the affairs of non-Muslim schools in their programs.[183]

Principally, these institutes and schools were opened and supported by rich and charitable people, not by government. In the early

---

[180] See general Ernst E. Hirsch, *Anilarim* [My Memories] (Ankara, Tubitak, 1997). He was one of those law professors who emigrated Turkey because of Nazi persecution. His brother also was one of them who taught in the medical faculty.

[181] See Osman Sekerci, *Islam Ulkelerinde Gayri Muslimlerin Temel Haklari* [Basic Rights of Non-Muslims in Islamic Countries] (Istanbul, Nun, 1996) at 63. Professor Sekerci notes that because of these privileges and rights some non-Muslims in the past abused their rights. Because there are some bad example of fetvas produced by Islamic scholars. Today, we should not follow these steps; we have to work with non-Muslim scientists. There is no any limit in Islamic law. At 65.

[182] See Ercan, *supra note* 163, at 228.

[183] See Sekerci, *supra note* 98, at 65. In another book, Sekerci strongly argues that there should not be any discrimination against non-Muslims because of their beliefs in an Islamic State.

See Osman Sekerci, *Insan Haklari Alaninda Temel Belgeler ve Islam* [Basic Human Rights Documents and Islam] (Istanbul, Nun, 1996).

days of the Ottomans, non-Muslims provided religious education to their own children in the churches or synagogues.[184] However, according to Islamic law, non-Muslims cannot establish new churches or synagogues only restore the old ones, but the State of Islam can allow them to establish new ones as a State policy.[185]

During the Ottoman era, non-Muslims could be exempt from military service, while others had the option of paying an exemption tax [jizyah].[186] Women, children, and poor were exempted from paying an exemption tax.[187] However, at the same time, Muslims were paying Zekat (each year paying the earning of the capital of 1 out of 40). In order to avoid military services, many non-Muslims became more educated and specialised in medicine, literature, translation, or any social and science subjects, thus reaching the highest political administrative jobs in Islamic states.[188] It was decreed [after the 1856 Reforms] to accept one third of students from non-Muslim communities into administrative

---

[184] See Ercan, *supra note* 163, at 228. Ercan rightly claims that there are currently insufficient researches about the classical era of the Ottomans and religious education for non-Muslims.

[185] See Ahmed Akgunduz, Gayr-i Muslimlere Nasil Davrandik [How we behaved to Non-Muslims] at http://.osmanli.org.tr/yazdirilabilirosmanli.php?id=32 (accessed on July 23, 2008).

[186] Interestingly, non-Muslims of the Ottomans became highest military and State administrative officers with the Devsirme System rather than living under the Dhimmah tradition. As previously stated that State officials were exempted paying taxes. See more I. Metin Kunt, "Transformation of Zimmi into Askeri" in Benjamin Braude & Bernard Lewis, *supra note* 1, at 55.

[187] See Hamidullah, *supra note* 147.

[188] See Yusuf Fidan, *Islam'da Yabancilar ve Azinliklar Hukuku* [Minorities and Foreigners in Islamic Law] (Istanbul, Ensar, 2005) at 333.

officers' schools.[189] Non-Muslims are also citizens of the Islamic country therefore they have the right to work in public jobs with the exception of those of head of the State, the commander of the army, the governor or the judge because those jobs represents the sovereignty of the Islam.[190]

Professor Ortayli claims this as a major misconception about non-Muslims and their military services. As earlier stated non-Muslims had a privilege not to join the military with paying the jizye tax [poll tax]; however, some of non-Muslims did not use this privilege and joined the army. Many of them became commanding officers in the military. During Christmas time and Eastern Time, the Ottoman Naval Forces castled anchor because of non-Muslim soldiers.[191] Having this privilege not to join the army with the payment of poll tax, gave extensive power to non-Muslims to control commerce over the Ottoman lands.[192] It was the successful path to protect non-Muslim communities. In the same period, across Europe Jews or opposition Christians were crying loudly about the freedom of conscience and religion. Clearly, the Ottoman Turks had not discriminated against its non-Muslim citizens. It is

---

[189] See Ortayli, *supra note* 128, at 65-6. Because the Ottoman State population consisted one third of non-Muslim communities. It may argue that the Ottoman State policy was to eliminate discrimination from politics. According to the Tahrir Defteris' [Tax Registres] documents, around in the middle of the XVIth Century, 40 % of the population was non-Muslim. See Ozbilgen, *supra note* 117, at 414.

The Ottoman State rated five times general population counting in modern sense; in 1831, 1881/82, 1893, 1906/7 and 1914. According to 1831 census, non-Muslim population was 29.67 % in the Ottoman lands. In 1881/82 this rate was 26.61 %. In 1906/7 was 25.74 %. Lastly, in 1914 it was 18.88 %.

See Ali Guler, *Osmanli Devletinde Azinliklar* [Minorities in the Ottoman State] (Istanbul, Turan, 1997) at 128.

[190] See Ahmet Akgunduz & Halil Cin, *Turk Hukuk Tarihi (Ozel Hukuk), Cilt II* [*Turkish Legal History (Private Law), Volume II* (Istanbul, Osmanli, 1996).

[191] See Ortayli, *supra note* 128, at 65.

[192] See general Ali Ihsan Bagis, *Osmanli Ticaretinde Gayr-i Muslimler* [Non-Muslims in the Ottoman Commercial Life] (Ankara, Turhan, 1983).

arguable that that this was one of the main reasons that kept the empire strong for a long time.

Jews and Christians were also exempted from the jurisdiction of the Imperial courts when the issue at hand came down to religion and personal issues, such as family law, legitimacy, and inheritance . . . etc.[193] Non-Muslim courts' verdicts were enforced by the State authorities in the same way as Sharia court decisions.[194] We should note that non-Muslims had an optional right to either apply their own religious community court or Sharia court and when they went to Sharia court, the Muslim judge's verdicts were based on Islamic law.[195]Of course, non-Muslim religious leaders were trying to block those people who applied to Sharia court and used sanctions against those who did; still non-Muslim individuals were looking for justice before Sharia courts.[196] Non-Muslims religious leaders' authority in personal law was dependent on the individual's choice; therefore Kenanoglu does not accept this authority/right as a full judicial privilege.[197]In other words, family law for non-Muslim individuals was based upon their own choice; either Islamic law or their own religious rule.[198] However, if one of the parties was Muslim or if it involved a criminal case, non-Muslims had to go to Sharia court.[199]

---

[193] See Aydin, *supra note* 147, at 233.

[194] See Bostanci, *supra note* 111, at 113. Professor Kenanoglu claims that inheritance was divided under the rules of Islamic law. See M. Macit Kenanoglu, *Osmanli Millet Sistemi: Mit ve Gercek* [*The Ottoman Millet System: Mythology and Reality*] (Istanbul, Klasik, 2004) at 251.

[195] See Kenanoglu, *id*, at 209.

[196] See general Rossitsa Gradeva, "Orthodox Christians in the Kadi Courts: The Practice of the Sofia Sheriat Court, Seventeenth Century" 4 Islamic L. & Soc'y (1997) 37-69.

[197] See Kenanoglu, *supra note* 194, at 211.

[198] See Ahmed Akgunduz, "The First Model for the EU: Ottoman State—1" From Conference: Islam in Europe or Islam of Europe?, European Parliament, 11 December 2002 at http://www.osmanli.org.tr/en/yazi. php?id=134&bolum=30 (accessed on July 25, 2008).

[199] See Kenanoglu, *supra note* 194, at 210.

Available literature agreed without any dispute that the Ottoman State provided authority/privilege to non-Muslim religious leaders to deal with their community marriage/divorce cases.[200]The Ottoman State issued many decrees declaring that Muslim religious clerks cannot validate non-Muslim marriages.[201]On that issue, many times, non-Muslim religious leaders applied to the State authorities having validate power of marriage contracts, the reason was to prevent their own community marriages from the outside interference.[202]In the Ottoman archives there are records of Greek religious leaders applying to the Ottoman Sultan to give warning to Armenian religious leaders not to validate inter Greek-Armenian marriages.[203]

In the case of divorce, non-Muslim women went to the Sharia courts, in order to get financial benefits according to Islamic law that their own religious rules did not provide.[204]Also, where according to their own religion they cannot get divorced from their partners, they went to the Sharia court. Many Catholics took advantage of this possibility.[205] It is evident that as non-Muslims if both sides agree they can take the case before the Patriarchal or Rabbinical court, otherwise, the case went before the Sharia court. Moreover, if one of the sides preferred to take the case before its own religious court as a non-Muslim, the State Authorities may allow it.[206]

---

[200] At 245.

[201] At 246.

[202] At 247. In the Ottoman Turkish State practices, over and over the Sultans issued and declared decrees in order to protect and enlarged non-Muslim citizen's rights in the country. See examples Murat Bebiroglu, *Osmanli Devleti'nde Gayrrimuslim Nizamnameleri* [*Non-Muslim Decrees in the Ottoman State*] (Istanbul, Akademi, 2008).

[203] At 247.

[204] See Gradeva, *supra note* 196, at 55-7.

[205] See Abdurrahman Kurt, *Bursa Sicillerine Gore Osmanli Ailesi (1839-1876)* [*According to Bursa Court Archives: The Ottoman Family (1839-1876)*] (Bursa, UUY, 1988) at 135.

[206] See Kenanoglu, *supra note* 194, at 216.

However, in the aftermath of the 1718 Treaty of Passarovitz,

"The Ottoman Turks began to look outside, more particularly to the West, for new inspiration . . . the apparent mutuality of French and Turkish interests determined where the Turkish statesmen would look for inspiration. It is worth noting that France continued to represent the West in Turkish eyes until the present century in spite of her disappointing performance in later eras and the practical ascendancy of Britain in the nineteenth century."[207]

With the 1839 *Tanzimat Declaration* and *1856 Islahat Declaration*,[208] the *Millet System* took another turn. The 1839 *Declaration* (Administrative Reforms) provided that aims of laws would be to protect lives, security of property, and decency. Before the law Muslims and non-Muslims are equal. Every citizen is equal concerning taxation and military service. This document also brought new criminal law conceptions to the Turkish legal system.[209] In addition, the Sultan would also follow these rules. It appears that the French Human Rights Declaration affected this declaration so that Turkish law then began to follow European steps. The 1856 Islahat Declaration (Development Reforms) provided more rights to non-Muslims than it did to Muslims. Non-Muslims did not have to do military service but they had to pay the same tax equivalent as did the Muslims.[210] Muslims had to go to the military and it was for more than five years of service. The document declared increased rights for non-Muslims, due to European State pressure.[211] Akgunduz claims that the Ottoman State provided these rights to non-Muslims before the

---

[207] See Berkes, *supra note* 159, at 25-6.
[208] See Burhan Kuzu, *Ulkemizde Kisi Ozgurlugu ve Guvenligi [Freedom and Security of Individuals in Turkey]* (Istanbul, Filiz, 1997) at 60.

　　See Bulent Tanor, *Osmanli-Turk Anayasal Gelismeleri [The Ottoman Turk Constitutional Developments]* (Istanbul, Alfa, 1992) at 67.
[209] See Kuzu, *id*.
[210] *Id*.
[211] See general Tanor, *supra note* 208.

preparation of these documents (1839 and 1856); these documents provided hard copy of the declared rights.[212] Moreover, he claims that rather than following the European practices without question, the Ottoman should have regulated the practices of non-Muslims of that era in ways that were necessary to protect their interests. Therefore following the European footsteps did not help the reformation of the system, it caused its collapse.[213] The Reforming Decree of 1856 tried to reform the millet system and secularize [officially] the empire.[214] With the 1876 Kanun-i Esasi (Constitution), the nation of Islam was erased and the nation of the Ottoman established.[215] Article 7 of the 1876 Constitution (Kanun-Esasi) stated:

"all subjects of the Empire called Ottomans without distinction, whatever faith they profess; the status of an Ottoman is acquired and lost according to conditions specified by law."[216]

Those reforms prepared the ground for the foundation of a secular republic.[217] Interestingly, in 1879, the Ottoman State enacted a law to extend State jurisdiction to non-Muslim ecclesiastical courts to fix a uniform procedure without considering religious traditions. Two Greek patriarchs resigned from this duty and in 1890 the Patriarchate Synod closed all churches and suspended all offices for three months thus the State abolish the law.[218]

---

[212] See Ahmet Akgunduz, Tarihi Acidan Azinliklara Taninan Haklar ve Biz II [From the Historical Perspective: Rights Provided to non-Muslims and We, no: 2] at http://.osmanli.org.tr/yazdirilabilirosmanli.php?id=31 (accessed on July 23, 2008).

[213] *Id*.

[214] See Malcolm D. Evans, *Religious Liberty and International Law in Europe* (Cambridge, CUP, 1997) at 67.

[215] See Akgunduz, *supra note* 212.

[216] See Salam, *supra note* 94, at 140.

[217] See Rosella Bottoni, "The Origins of Secularism in Turkey" 9 Ecc LU (2007) at 175.

[218] *Id*, at 180.

There were significant changes in the political atmosphere in the 19th Century due to the French revolution and rising nationalism and the involvement of Western powers in the Ottoman internal affairs due to the loss of Ottoman State power.[219] With the establishment of Republic of Turkey, the Millet System was abolished and a unified nationalist State was constructed in 1923. In 1918 just before the fall of the Ottoman [1922] 75 percent of the territories had been lost; in 1878, 85 percent of the population were gone.[220] After winning the Independence War against the Allied power, the Republic of Turkey in 1923 signed the Lausanne Treaty. The treaty included articles for the protection of religious minorities that served in the allied powers armies (the U.K., France, Italy, and [Greece]) against Turks.[221] Since its establishment in 1923 the Republic of Turkey has faced minority rights issues. However, until today the parties to the treaty have accused Turkey of violating

---

[219] See Evans, *supra note* 214, at 60-1.

[220] See Virginia H. Aksan, "Ottoman to Turk" 61 Int'l J. (2005-2006) at 30. According to the 1844 General Census, the Ottoman State population was 35 million and consisting of 58 % Muslim(20,5 million), 39 % Greek Orthodox[Armenian, Bulgarian and the rest of the Balkans Orthodox included in that number] (13,7 million), 2,5 % Catholic (1 million) and 0,5 % Jews(nearly 200,000).

See Bebiroglu, *supra note* 202, at 20-1.

Greek Orthodox Church was provided more privileges than it had in the Byzantine era. The Greek Ecumenical Patriarch collectively represented of the Greek, Slavic, Albanian, Romanian, and Arab Orthodox that lived in the Ottoman land. Therefore, the Greek millet was in the prominent position in the eyes of the State and affected the Ottoman ruling class policies. Until 1910s the Greek Orthodox hold highest ranking administrative position in the Ottoman capital city and around.

See Irini Sarioglou, Turkish Policy Towards Greek Education in Istanbul 1923-1974: Secondary Education and Identity (Athens, ELIA, 2004) at 21-23.

[221] See Beirne Stedman, "The Republic of Turkey" 13 Va. L. Reg. n. s. (1927-8) at 737. Stedman notes that "Greek and Armenian partisans and paid propagandists have told terrible tales of the Turks-tales of which we only heard one side, and it is always well to take one-sided tales with a large grain of salt. It has for a long time been the writer's opinion that many of these cruelties were more or less occasioned by the aggravations furnished by non-Muslims." At 735.

the Lausanne Treaty. Turkey has never accepted these allegations. Turkey argues that all people residing in the country are citizens, and the republic recognizes only non-Muslims as the minority via the Lausanne treaty. However, the republic does not discriminate against anyone based on religion, ethnicity, and language differences. Furthermore, Turkey claims it is a unified State. In addition, the constructors of the republic and their followers believe that discussing this issue in public will mean enemies are going to attack the unification of Turkey and will try to divide Turkey's land. Still "Turkey is stuck with the 1923 tradition and moreover interprets the Treaty of Lausanne incorrectly/deficiently"[222] to prove its own untenable arguments. In truth, Turkey has adhered to dogmatic taboos that have precluded discussions on the *Turkish Armed Forces, Minority Rights*, and *Secularism*. In other words, the Republic established its own taboos such as secular State, phobia of Islam and Islamic culture, Turkish military guardianship of the country.[223] One commentator, who resided in Turkey for three years as a political professor at Koc University in Istanbul, observes that:

---

[222] See Baskin Oran, "The Minority Report Affair of Turkey" 5 Regent J. Int'l L. (2007) at 74.

See more Baskin Oran, Turkiye'de *Azinliklar: Kavramlar, Teori, Lozan, Ic Mevzuat, Ictihat, Uygulama* [*Minorities in Turkey: Concepts, Theory, Lausanne, Domestic Law, Jurisprudence, and Practice*] (Istanbul: Iletisim, 2005). Edip Yuksel who is a Kurdish Human Rights Activist and fled from Turkey to USA claims that that the Republic secular ideology, controls, manipulates and exploits religious believes and attack them who are not converted to official version. See Edip Yuksel "Cannibal Democracy, Theocratic Secularism: The Turkish Version" 7 Cardozo J. Int'l & Comp. L. (1999) at 467

[223] See Aksan, *supra note* 137, at 30. According to the Lausanne Treaty, non Muslim groups [Greek, Armenian and Jews recognized as non Muslims] cannot own properties for religious aims outside what they had before the establishment of the Republic of Turkey. See Niyazi Oktem, "Religion in Turkey" B.Y.U.L Rev. (2002) at 375-6.

See more M. Altug Imamoglu, Azinlik Vakiflari ve Yabancilarin Tasinmaz Edinimleri [Non-Muslims' Charities and Obtaining Property of Aliens] (Ankara, YY, 2006).

"Turkish nationalism has weighed heaviest on Kurds, Islamist, religious minorities, and the left. A State run Turkish Reformation of Islam fallen in the 1930s; more recent attempts to nationalize Islam have turned the State into a mouthpiece for mainstream Sunni doctrine. The Turkish case suggests that in states with deep societal divisions, the dream of civic nationalism may be a coerced one . . . Religion has been nationalized."[224]

During the Republican time, 600 years Ottoman history has been denied and ignored, however, young historians began to question

---

[224] See Thomas W. Smith, "Civic Nationalism and Ethno-Cultural Justice in Turkey" 27 Hum. Rts. Q. (2005) at 436-7. In his article, Smith evidently shows that during the Republic era non-Muslims of Turkey were destroyed by the State policy and practices.

"the myopia of a self-imposed amnesia" of the Republic[225] and looking at the Ottoman archives, especially court verdicts [seriye sicilleri] to explore the facts and truths about their own past. Despite the obvious prejudices that may underscore reluctance by modern academics to make a positive example of an Islamic State, it is difficult to avoid the fact that the State guaranteed

---

[225] See Aksan, *supra note 223*, at 19. Not all young historians do these kind of challenging searches. Some of them still go on without looking into the Ottoman archives but just look at the Orieantalist studies or ultra secularist studies who believed that that past is our most hateful enemy. Such include Fatma Muge Gocek, *Rise of the Bourgeoisie, Demise of Empire: Ottoman Westernization and Social Change* (NY, OUP, 1996). Or older ones such as Deniz Kandiyoti Studies, such as "Introduction," "End of Empire: Islam, Nationalism and Women in Turkey" in *Women, Islam and the State* (London, Macmillan, 1991), Deniz Kandiyoti (ed.) without looking at the Ottoman archives or archive studies and mainly using the Western resources presented the idea of Turkish seculars rather than the Turkish nation's views. That is one of the main reasons that the West could not realize what is going on inside of Turkey. See especially in the book, article II, by Deniz Kandiyoti, "End of Empire: Islam, Nationalism, and Women in Turkey". These authors try to show the innocence of Turkish secular reforms in statements such as "although was not legally banned, a vigorous propaganda campaign led by Ataturk himself exhorted women to adopt modern styles of dress, and dissenters were dealt with severely." Kandiyoti shows her source at dipnote 1; "Caporal mentions trials and short prison sentences for those spreading counterpropaganda." B. Caporal, *Kemalizm ve Kemalizm Sonrasinda Turk Kadini* [*Kemalism and after Kemalism Turkish Woman*] (Ankara, TIBY, 1982) p. 649. At 23 and 44.

Kandiyoti dismisses two truths; one is that there was a law Kilik ve Kiyafet Kanunu (The Law of Clothing Style) enacted in 1925 that ordered individuals to wear clothing in the Western style and moreover, many dissenters of the reforms were hanged by the Istiklal Mahkemeleri [Freedom Courts] that were established and lived in the early years of the Republic to deal with the cases of the dissenters of the Republic.

See Sadik Albayrak, *Devrimler ve Gerici Tepkiler* [*Revolutions and Reactionary Movements*] (Istanbul, Arastirma Y, 1989,) Tahir-ul Mevlevi, *Matbuat Alemindeki Hayatim ve Istiklal Mahkemeleri* [*My Life in the Press Sector and Freedom Courts*], Atilla Senturk (ed.), (Istanbul, Nehir, 1991), and Ahmet Nedim, *Ankara Istiklal Mahkemesi Zabitlari (1926)* [*Records of the Ankara Freedom* Court (1926)], (Istanbul, Isaret, 1993).

the protection of all faiths and continued to uphold all religious privileges perhaps better than any modern political system. The prominent Ottoman scholar Kemal Karpat notes that:

"the categorical rejection of everything Ottoman became a behavioural characteristic of the Turkish modernist intelligentsia. Any good aspects of that era had to be appropriated and praised as Turkish or else the student expressing such a favourable view of the past would be branded reactionary and anti-Kemalist. The six hundred years of Ottoman history obviously received low priority, but some dedicated scholars still pursued their work."[226]

It is submitted that the "Ottoman society was a mosaic of cultures and religions and provided a peace and harmony among members of society without distinction between Muslim and non-Muslim, race, and colour."[227] Therefore, this experience should be taken into consideration in order to accommodate religious minorities in the modern world. Finally we should not see our own culture as superior to others and not humiliate them, we should try to understand and not to globalise the others, and otherwise we may not be able to eliminate cultural clashes.[228]

Women in the Ottoman Court

It is claimed that the court records [ser'i sicils] are the best source for the social history of the Middle East [and, therefore, the Ottoman Empire's lands].[229] Family law is the cornerstone

---

[226] See Karpat, *supra note* 150, at 5.

[227] See Akgunduz, *supra note* 198.

[228] See Ahmed Akgunduz, "The First Model for the EU: Ottoman State—2 at http://www.osmanli.org.tr/en/yazi.php?id=135&bolum=30 (accessed on July 25, 2008).

[229] See Gerber, *supra note* 113, at 174. Akgunduz insistently claims the same argument looking at the ser'i sicils rather than following academic clichés.

of Islamic law.[230] Under Islamic law, a Muslim cannot marry an atheist; however a male Muslim can marry a Jewish or Christian woman, but a Muslim woman cannot marry a Jewish or Christian man. Under Isalmic law, the marriage ceremony does not require the presence of a religious figure; however, during the Ottoman time, the kadi [judge] was officially authorised to prepare and authenticate the marriage contracts. After the 16th Century, kadis delegated this function to the Imams who conduct the prayers in the mosques.[231] If one of the parties abandons Islam, the marriage contract is automatically terminated under Sharia law.

As stated above, during the Ottoman era, many non-Muslim women applied to Sharia courts in order to get divorced from their husbands. This was due to the fact that, according to their religious beliefs as either a Christian or a Jew, they could not get divorced or and did not have the right to receive an economic benefit from their husband.[232] When those women went to Sharia courts, the kadis [judges] applied the rules of Islamic law to solve the issue. Therefore in order to fully understand the reasons behind this phenomenon, the wider selection of rights available to women when divorce takes a place under Islamic law will be explored briefly.

Islamic law grants the husband the right to a one-sided divorce; however, in theory and practice, women could also have this right [tafwid al talaq].[233] It was common for women to require that this right be available to them under the marriage contracts that

---

[230] See Paul J. Magnarella, "East Meets West: The Reception of West European Law in the Ottoman Empire and the Modern Turkish Republic" 2 J. Int'l & Prac. (1993) at 284-5.

[231] At 294.

[232] See Kemal Cicek, "Interpreters of the Court in the Ottoman Empire as Seen from the Sharia Court Records of Cyprus" 9 Is. L. & Soc'y (2001-2) 1-15.

[233] See general A. Jawad Haifa, *The Rights of Women in Islam* (NY, St. MartinsP, 1998).

See more criticism about this unilateral right, Anver M. Emon, "Conceiving Islamic Law in a Pluralist Society: History, Politics and Multicultural Jurisprudence" 2006 Sing. J. Legal Stud. (2006) at 336-37.

occurred during the Ottoman era. Islam allows divorce between husband and wife only as a last resort as marriage is a life-long commitment.[234] Divorce can take place under three circumstances; firstly if one of the spouses dies; secondly on the action [talaq] of the husband, wife or both, and; finally with a court's decision.[235] Either before or after the marriage a woman might obtain a right to claim for a divorce from her husband. This right cannot be rescinded by the husband.[236] During the marriage, the husband is responsible to provide shelter and food, etc. [nafaqa], even if the husband is poor and the wife is rich.[237] This is an obligation and a woman can go to court to claim it if the husband dos not adequately provide financial support.[238] This obligation in terms of Islamic law is a contractual obligation, even after the divorce, a husband is required to provide it to his wife.[239] If the husband dies, this obligation passes on to his inheritor.[240] If the husband cannot provide financial support [daily allowance—"nafaqa"] a judge may grant a separation order, according to the school of Safi, Maliki, and Hanbeli, but not of Hanefi.[241] In Islamic law, before the marriage can take place, a husband has to make a payment [mahr] directly to his wife or as arranged by the wife. In doctrine, it has been argued that, to stop the abuse of a husband's privilege in divorce, a woman has the right to be granted a very sizeable mahr, even a court has the

---

[234] See Haifa, *id*, at 71.

[235] *Id*, at 79.

[236] See "Evlilik Birliginin Sona Ermesi" [The Dissolution of Marriage], available at http://www.istanbulmuftulugu.gov.tr/index.php?option=com_content&task=view&id=362&Itemid=320 (accessed on August 5, 2008). It is an official webpage of the Republic of Turkey, Religious Affairs Department, the branch of Istanbul.

[237] See Ismail Kaya, *Islam Dini ve Ilmihali*, [*Religion of Islam and Personal Law*, 3rd ed.] (Istanbul, Madve, 1994) at 441.

[238] *Id*.

[239] At 443.

[240] *Id*. Kaya points out interesting knowledge that is almost unknown by the researchers of Islam, if inheritance comes from the mother's side, her children will get equal shares. At 411.

[241] *Id*.

right to set a high level mahr.[242] During the marriage the husband is responsible for all expenses without any quarrel.[243] In Hanefi jurisprudence, the bride or groom can add specific conditions into the marriage contract such as the wife can get an automatic divorce if the husband is guilty of certain acts such as, for example; domestic violence, insufficient financial support or taking a second wife.[244] The case of Mustafa bin Abdullah illustrates one of the conditions placed in the marriage contract, i.e. the above example of automatic divorce in the case of wife beating.[245]

Moreover, after the divorce, a husband should support his wife until the end of the waiting period [according to Islamic law four purpery cleaning terms].[246] Finally, even if a husband is absent a woman has the right to get nafaqa from the husband's financial

---

[242] See "Evliligin Sonuclari" [Consequences of Marriage], available at http://www.istanbulmuftulugu.gov.tr/index.php?option=com_content&task=view&id=356&Itemid=320 (accessed on August 5, 2008).

[243] *Id.*

[244] See Judith E. Tucker, "Muftis and Matrimony: Islamic Law and Gender in Ottoman Syria and Palestine" 1 Islamic L.&Soc'y (1994) at 266. The author has gathered this information from the Khayr al-din which is one of the classics of the Hanefi School. The author claims that he searched several hundred contracts in the records of Jerusalam, Nablus, and Damascus courts of the 18th Century, but could not find any conditions on any of them. I might argue that if he looked at the Anatolian side of the Ottoman land, he would have found many of them. It illustrates that Islamic rules were developed, formed or shaped according to the community's culture. Thus, today we have to reread classical Islamic from a contemporaneous perspective rather than judging them against present day practices in Islamic countries. See Rehman, *supra note* 85.

[245] At 88.

[246] *Id*, at 270. Wife should not cause the dissolution of marriage; otherwise the nafaqa right will cease. See Omer Nasuhi Bilmen, *Hukuku Islamiye ve Islahati Fikhiye Kamusu* [*The Islamic Law and the Dictionary of Fikih Terminologies*] (Istanbul, Sarmasik, 1999) Volume II, 488-9. The originally eight volume collections that published in 1949 by the law faculty of Istanbul. Ebu Zehra claims that a woman had the right to stay in the house up to one year after the husband dies as a divorce occurs automatically upon the death of one of the parties. See Ebu Zehra, *Usûlü'l-Fıkh* (Ankara, TDY 1986) at 166.

assets via a judge's order. In any such nafaqa case, the nafaqa will be arranged on foot of the wife's social status and her background.[247]

Many prejudices and stereotypes abound in the academic world regarding the role of women in the Ottoman time.[248] Here the classical era Ottoman Sharia court cases that deal with non-Muslim divorce issues will be explored. In 1622, in case IS1/76 (540)[249], the claimant, Eline, was the daughter of Petro; she sued her ex-husband, Sofinos, son of Kominoz, before the Sharia court and stated that;

"My husband divorced me previously and then I asked him to return my properties but then we began to fight. After that a mediator from both of our families convinced us to forget the subject. Both of us agree that after today we are not going to sue each other about the these issues. Moreover my son Katakozno, who is from my ex-husband, stays with me and I will take care of him without requesting any financial support from my husband."

This statement was approved by Sofinos therefore the court recorded it. This case is a good illustration of how non-Muslim

---

[247] *Id*, at 269-70. Tucker deals with how Sharia courts dealt with women's issues in Syria and Palestine in the 17th and 18th Century in the Ottoman era. See Judith E. Tucker, *In the House of the Law: Gender and Islamic Law in Ottoman Syria and Palestine* (Berkeley, UCP, 1998).

[248] See general Elizabeth B. Frierson, "Women in Late Ottoman Intellectual History" 135-161 in *Late Ottoman Society: the Intellectual Legacy*, Elizabeth Ozdalga (ed.), (London, RoutledgeCurzon, 2005).

Faroqhi claims that women were so active in business and cultural life and moreover in the palace of the Ottoman Sultanates. See Suraiya Faroqhi, *Subjects of the Sultan: Culture and Daily Life in the Ottoman Empire* (London, I.B. TaurisP, 2000) at 101-122. Pierce also shows how the women were powerful in the Sultan's palace and had an influence on the State's policies and practices. See Leslie P. Pierce, *The Imperial Harem: Women and Sovereignty in the Ottoman Empire*, (Oxford, OUP, 1993).

[249] This and the following cases were sent to me by Professor Ahmet Akgunduz from the Istanbul Ottoman Court Archives (Seri Sicil) and the Prime Minister's Office Archives which are located in Istanbul. The author wishes to acknowledge his invaluable assistance in providing primary source material.

citizens were appearing before the Sharia courts to get some security as the courts recorded every decision in writing. In 1755, in case B23-127/56, both sides appeared before a Sharia court agreeing on a divorce but with some conditions. The wife showed the court a written document and stated that;

"I had a very serious argument with my husband however according to our beliefs and religious rituals we did not arrange financial supports. However we have had our marriage annulled. Because of this annulment we have come to the agreement that we relinquish all rights to sue on the obligations attached to the marriage."

After this statement, the husband approved its content and the court recorded the wishes of the parties. Again this case shows that the Sharia courts were being used equally by non-Muslims to officially record agreements in writing and thus ensure that they would be binding. As will be shown below, non-Muslims were using also using Sharia courts on a daily basis, with a particular use by non-Muslim women, to exploit the broader rights to get a divorce and receive financial support under Islamic law.

Many non-Muslim divorce cases arrived at Sharia courts because of disputes relating to the settlement of financial issues.[250] This was because of the fact that after the divorce is granted, Islamic law provides to the woman as a right, divorce compensation (mahr-i mueccel) and maintenance allowance (after the divorce waiting time has been completed which can be up to one year). The Sharia court was providing these two rights to all Ottoman citizens, Muslim and non-Muslim women alike.[251] In a case dating from 1728 a Christian woman's husband agreed to grant a divorce to her on the agreement that she would not to claim any divorce compensation or maintenance allowance from him.

---

[250] See Gradeva, *supra note* 196, at 55.
[251] At 56.

Sharia courts also dealt with the cases arising from marriage contracts such as maintenance allowance for a child or children due to the death of the father or divorce from him.[252] Maintenance allowance was actually unknown under Canon law therefore Christian women would go to the Sharia court to get such a maintenance benefit.[253] Another case from 1780 in which both parties were Jewish, the wife sued the husband for divorce before the Sharia court. The husband triply divorced[254] his wife and he paid her the requested money.[255] In a following divorce case in 1781 a Christian woman went to the Sharia court to obtain a divorce from her husband but she voluntarily released her husband from his obligation to pay maintenance allowance and daily allowance. Despite this, the husband agreed to the divorce and also promised to pay child support for seven years.[256]

Sometimes the woman would represent herself at court but she could also be represented by a legal agent.[257] Ottoman era Sharia courts were very strict on requiring evidence to prove the claims put forward in divorce cases. For example a case involving Greek Orthodox Christians came before the court where the husband claimed that they had a "Hull" divorce (granted by the husband at the request of his wife, mainly in return for the wife relinquishing her maintenance rights) as the wife had given up the maintenance allowance to encourage her husband to agree to the divorce. The court stated that the husband did not have sufficient proof and was

---

[252] At 57.

[253] At 62.

[254] Under Islamic divorce procedure, a husband (It is generally the right of a husband unless the wife is granted this right under the marriage contract) wishing to grant/obtain a divorce must say it three times (in total during the marriage, not necessarily at the same time) for it to be binding.

[255] See Najwa Al-Qattan, "Dhimmis in the Muslim Court: Legal Autonomy and Religious Discrimination" 31 Int. J. of MES (1999) at 434.

[256] *Id.*

[257] See Ronald C. Jennings, "Divorce in the Ottoman Sharia Court of Cyprus (1580-1640)" 78 Studia Islamica (1993) at 158.

acting dishonestly as Christians could not have a hull divorce.[258] Jennings sees a "Hull" divorce as a contract negotiated by a wife and husband to meet their particular needs.[259] There is another interesting case dating from 1823 where a Christian man sued his wife before a Sharia court because the wife was denying sexual intercourse to him. The husband claimed that he paid her a dowry however he could not prove his claim and the court ordered him not to harass his wife.[260]

In Ottoman times, the placing of conditions into a marriage contract was widespread.[261] Ottoman women have been shown to be shrewd and very capable of obtaining and enforcing the rights which were available to them. In his classic article Jennings looked at several hundred Ottoman court records and concluded that in the 17th century women were well established in the society as property owners and running businesses and/or charitable organisations.[262]

The above cases strongly illustrate that contrary to the popular belief that minority religions were discriminated against, non-Muslim women found that the Sharia courts complimented and expanded the rights available to them under their own religions. The Ottoman courts provided non-Muslim women with increased protection from poverty by providing for financial support and from domestic violence in the form of, for example, the automatic divorce in the even of beating etc. These cases also go some way to refute any allegations of a revisionist agenda, as the cases have been extracted from contemporary records, which have been overlooked or ignored for so long.

---

[258] At 160.

[259] See Ronald C. Jennings, "Women in the Early 17th Century Ottoman Judicial Records: The Sharia Court of Anatolian Kayseri" 18 J. of Ec. & Soc. His. Of Orient (1975) at 84.

[260] See Al-Qattan, *supra note* 255, at 442.

[261] See general Jennings, *supra note* 259.

[262] At 97, and 111.

1917 'Family Law Act'* [Hukuk-i Aile Kararnamesi]

Up to 1917 almost every area of law had been codified by Ottoman legislation or scholars, thus there was a need to codify the final remaining disparate area of family law.[263] Due to World War I casualties, the Ottoman male population decreased and women began to become established in every area of Ottoman society and it began to look similar to Western society.[264] Women also began to establish many organisations and associations.[265] After 1900, support for feminism in the Ottoman Empire gathered speed.[266] The 'Family Law Act' was prepared under the influence of Westernism—Nationalism—and Islamism.[267] This law was prepared by the commissions which consisted of Jewish, Christian and Muslim religious scholars and thus contained the three religions' rules regarding family law separately.[268] For the first time in an Islamic country the family law provisions in force embraced all Sunni sects (Hanafi, Maliki, Safi and Hanbali) and did not just follow the Hanafi School but also leaned heavily on the Maliki rule, a sect which was more favourable to women.[269] This legislation was the first legislation in Islamic countries to codify family law.[270]

---

* This legislation was enacted on 25th October, 1917. It was translated into French and published in 1918 at the annex of the Revue de Turquie. However, there is no English translation available.

[263] See M. Akif Aydin, *Islam-Osmanli Aile Hukuku* [*Islam-Ottoman Family Law*] (Istanbul, MUIFVY, 1985) at 154-55. The book is a classic in that area. Here afterwards, Aydin's book used for the text of the legislation. The legislation was translated into French and published in "Istanbul 1917" and "Revue de Turquie" (in the Annex of the Issue of August 1918). At 151. However, there is no English translation available.

[264] At 158-9.

[265] See Berkes, *supra note* 159, at 436.

[266] See Aydin, *supra note* 263, at 159-60.

[267] *Id*, at 166-80.

[268] *Id*, at 163-65.

[269] See Halil Cin, *Eski Hukukumuzda Bosanma* [*Divorce in Our Previous Legal System*] (Konya, SUY, 1988) at 125.

[270] See Aydin, *supra note* 263, at 211.

It was the first written document in an Islamic State in which women got the right to obtain a divorce.[271] Most importantly Article 156 of the Act abolished the right/privilege of the non-Muslim court to deal with the cases in family law and just ordered that all family law cases would take place in the State court.[272] In other words this lead to the destruction of the main characteristic of the Millet system as a State judge rather than a religious expert would judge the case based on his interpretation of the non-Muslim religions' family law rules. The legislation also ordered that the parties wishing to obtain a marriage or divorce must first approach the judge to enter them onto the court record. In other words, the delegation of judicial powers in relation to family law ceased. With the harsh criticism of observing Islamists and with large scale protests of non-Muslims the law was repealed in 1919.[273] The non-Muslims said that it was taking away their rights and privileges while the Muslims argued it were attacking their identity.[274]

The legislation is mainly divided into two books, those of marriage and divorce. The first book is divided into six sections and fifteen subsections with a total of one hunderd and one articles. The second book is divided into three sections and five subsections with a total of fifty six articles. In the first book, Articles 1-3 deal with engagement, 4-12 deal with capacity to marry, 13-19 forbidden marriages [under Islam], 20-26; forbidden marriages under Judaism, 27-32; forbidden marriages under Christianity, 33-39; the marriage contract [under Islam], 40-44; the marriage contract under Christianity, 45-51; Kefaet (Under Hanafi law for a marriage to be valid, a woman and man should be equal or close from the social status point when they marry, normally Hanafi jurisprudence tests this equality using six measures; financial assets—art—family tree—Muslim—religious observance—and freedom. The Act recognised only two out of these six equality parameters; financial

---

[271] See Cin, *supra note* 269, at 126.

[272] See Aydin, *supra note* 263, at 222.

[273] *Id*, at 221-2.

[274] *Id*.

assets and art, if the couple are equal, they can marry. However, the other Sunni sects do not look at these equality considerations. Even in the Ottoman Turkish practices, society was not concerned with the issues of equality between a man and woman who were entering a marriage.[275]), 52-58; cancellation and abolishment of a marriage [under Islam], 59-62; cancellation and abolishment of marriage for Jews, 63-68; cancellation and abolishment of marriage for Christians, 69-77; rules for marriage [under Islam], 78-79; rules for marriage for Christians, 80-91; mahr [dowry], 92-101; nafaka (financial allowance, in the legislation only daily financial allowance [nafaka] was inserted).

The second book dealt with divorce. Articles 102-110; dealt with the general rules of [divorce], 111-118; permanent or returnable divorce [talak-i ric'i and bain], 119-131; good divorce [hiyar-i tefrik], giving the right to a divorce to women in Islam. In Hanefi jurisprudence a woman has the right to a divorce only if her husband is inompetent to honour the requirements of marriage. However, the legislation extended this right to advantage of women who now gained rights originating from the other Sunni sects. A woman could now obtain a divorce from her husband because of a disbute between them by means of a court order.], 132-138; divorce for Christians, 139-149; the required waiting period [in Islam after the divorce woman should wait for three consecutive perpetry time if she is not pregnant in order to remarry with someone.], 150-154; divorce nafaka, 155-157; established that rule, if there is no written rule in the legislation, rules for Muslims will be followed also for non-Muslims. Article 156 abolished the non-Muslim religious eccelestical court authority over issues of family law.

---

[275] *Id*, at 193.

For non-Muslims what kind of issues defined the divorce issue? Both of the spouses has the right to get a divorce from the court by judges decision, the reasons for the divorce as listed in the legislation could be;

(i)   adultery (Article 132); or

(ii) mental illness (Article 132/2); or

(iii) convicted of a misdemeanour [up to 5 years imprisonment] (132/3); or

(iv) disappearance of one of the spouses for at least 5 years (132/4); or

(v)   one of the spouses was absent for at least 5 years (132/5); or

(vi) one spouse does not inform the other of an illness of which they have knowledge prior to the marriage (Article 132/6); or

(vii) one spouse endangers the other's life (Article 132/7).

The party who caused the divorce might be prevented for three years from entering a new marriage, if both sides were guilty, the rule applied equally to each under Article 133). Also because of the reasons leading to the divorce, one partner might obtain the separation order from the court rather than getting divorce. But if the other side wished to obtain a divorce the judge would grant that. However, during the separation time, one of the sides might ask for the divorce under Article 134. However if the affected spouse pardons the offending spouse, the divorce case will not proceed (Article 135).

Before the divorce case, each side appoints an arbitrator to solve the issue (s) or a religious leader might solve the problem. If this does not work out, the case will be taken by the court (Article 136). After the divorce takes place, within three months, a spouse must approach their religious leader to hold a ceremony making the divorce official in the eyes of the religion in question and thus the State. Otherwise the divorce will not be officially recognised. After the three month period, and with the finalisation formalities completed, within twenty days, the spouse should apply to the State to enforce the decision (Article 137). Article 148 ruled that after the divorce waiting time for a Jewish woman is ninety days, if she is pregnant until the child reaches the age of two. Article 149 stated that after the divorce is grabted, the waiting time for a Christian woman one year. The 'Family Law Act' also provided for a maintenance allowance and the other financial supports previously available in the Sharia court (Article 155). This legislation's thinking has had a major influence on countries such as Israel, Egypt, Syria, Jordan etc.[276]

With the exception of personal family law cases in Islamic countries, according to Hanafi School, if the one of the party of the case is non-Muslim, the case should be taken by the Sharia court.[277] If it is a family law case, non-Muslims either go by their religious court or the Sharia court. The founder of the Hanafi School, Imam Azam set as a condition that both of the sides should be agreed tsking the case to the Sharia court, however, his students Imam Muhammad and Ebu Yusuf state that if one party declares the wish to go before the Sharia court, this would be enough to take the case before the court.[278]

The 1917 Code of Family Law mixed the all Sunni sects ideas in order to increase the chances of finding solutions with the needs of the time.[279] With regard to divorce issues dealt with by the legislation, the rules that the Hanbeli and Maliki school followed gave flexibility to women to more easily obtain a divorce.[280]

---

[276] See Aydin, *supra note* 263, at 225-6.

[277] See Ahmet Akgunduz, Osmanli Hukuk Sistemi [The Ottoman Legal System] at http://.osmanli.org.tr/yazdirilabilirosmanli.php?id=50 (accessed on July 23, 2008).

[278] *Id.*

[279] See Bedir, *supra note* 87, at 388.

[280] See Evlilik Birliginin Sona Ermesi" [The Dissolution of Marriage], *supra note* 153.

Concluding Remarks

Today, many modern Ottoman historians agree that the Ottoman era was a great century for religious freedom. We should be aware that the Ottoman State Muslim's were not only Turks. Giving much importance to different local customs, the Ottoman Turks successfully separated politics from religion and society was still shaped by Islam.

When one looks to the Balkans and Europe none of these nations lost their religion, language, or identity even when they were under the rule of Ottomans for about 400 years. The Ottoman, which appear to have shown a wider tolerance to the people living under her rule without distinguishing them according to their ethnicity, nationality or colour. Hence the Ottoman could be said to have been the first to introduce "human rights" in a modern sense into the world from the 13ᵗʰ to the 19ᵗʰ centuries.[281] There is a very basic argument or claim made by the Ottoman historians when they point to European or Western Imperialist states when they occupied some countries, even for as little as fifty years, people of those countries lost language, culture, religion or identity. One need only look towards Africa, for example, including Algeria, Tunisia, and Nigeria . . . etc or India. But Ottoman was in many places more than four hundred or almost five hundred years, but which nation under its control lost its language, religion, or identity?

With the separate family law system, firstly the religious group identity was protected and accommodated without assimilating it into the Islamic system. Simultaneously giving individuals in religious groups the opportunity to go to a Sharia court which gave them more rights and opportunities compared to their own religious courts. In other words modern liberal societies can do the

---

[281] See Akgunduz, *supra note* 236, at 17,18 and 119.

same thing, i.e. providing the option to people to avail of a separate family law court. This would enable people a greater choice.

Gerber rightly warns us: "we should distinguish here between two topics. One is the application of Islamic law, the Sharia, in real life in Islamic countries. The other is the history of the law itself as a body of thought."[282] Islam does not produce discrimination for non-Muslims that occurs because of claims as to Islamic States' domestic political environments and constitutional inadequacies.[283] My claim is that with certain limits and given certain conditions the Ottoman Millet System i.e. that providing separate family law is feasible and fruitful for today's liberal world in order to eliminate injustices and accommodate religious minorities.

---

[282] See Gerber, *supra note* 113, at 183.

[283] See general Rehman, *supra note* 168.

The following essay was published as a chapter in the following text: The Ottoman Muslim Turkish Women and Divorce in Balkan Studies III: Living Together & Culture & Education, syf. 530-557, (Skopje-Macedonia, Cyril and Methodius University, 2011).

3

THE OTTOMAN MUSLIM TURKISH
WOMEN AND DIVORCE

> "The West for its part has stubbornly refused to call the Ottoman Empire by its name instead labelling this multi-religious, multi-lingual, multi-ethnic polity as "Turkey" and its rulers as "Turks." . . . Even the republic of Turkey approaches its Ottoman past with ambivalence. The Turkey of Mustafa Kemal Ataturk and his successors were to be a nation-State in the European mould . . . It is, however, unacceptable to pass judgment on the Ottoman past and its possible influence on the present without a fair historical trial."*

Around the world, debate concerning Muslim family law remains pertinent; specifically how and why it should be reformed in terms of justice and equality for Muslim women. The following will attempt to pursue this search for justice and equality with particular attention given to divorce cases involving Turkish Muslim women occurring during Ottoman rule. The focus will be the particular charges the women brought to court and their expectations of the justice system. Supplementary analysis will provide a look at the Family Law Act of 1917 as well. This may provide greater insight into the legal bases of the legislation for divorce. A review of this particular history should give some idea of how common practices reflected the law, and what kind of solutions the law gave way to.

---

* See L. Carl Brown, "The Setting: An Introduction" in *Imperial Legacy: The Ottoman Imprint on the Balkans and the Middle East*, ed. L. Carl Brown, (NY, CUP, 1996) at 5-6

To date, researchers in Turkey have chosen to either amend religious or secular legislation, but have refrained from compromising either in terms of the other. Proponents of both the secular and religious approaches to legislating in terms of women's rights have largely disregarded the benefits of doing so in favor of political obstinacy. This stalemate largely leaves the realization of justice and equality for Turkish women in the hands of court decisions and peripheral reforms.

Taking into account the timeframe involved, a comparison of various divorce trials of Turkish women spanning approximately the last 500 years will be offered closer investigation which may help to clarify any gaps or exemptions in the legislation, and so ultimately in justice for these women. It should be noted that most research is defined in terms of various popular locations in Anatolia rather than a thorough extension of analysis, which will hopefully be remedied in this undertaking. Perhaps the best way to set out would be to consider the affects of location, time and the social status of the women involved in the particular trials herein, with the aim of illustrating how any or all of these variables may or may not have changed over time.

What might first be useful is an overview of Ottoman society and its legal system. This may be carried into a comparison of the theoretical yield of Ottoman and, later, Turkish law, in terms of divorce and women's rights. Only then will it help to take a closer look at the legislation in practice through case examples over the broad period, and establish just how relevant the terms justice and equality have applied to women with regards to the judgments of the courts and the settlements involved.

A) Ottoman Society

It is well known that Ottoman rulers were for the most part very religious individuals who strictly adhered to Islamic law. Despite how this may sound, it has been said that the Ottoman State "was a classic example of the plural society."[284] A look at the nature of this plurality will help to better understand the plight of its female citizenry. One of the world's longest standing empires, reigning for 600 odd years from 1299 to 1923, the Ottoman Empire is difficult to compare as a state to any of modern times. It was predominantly subject to Islamic rule, as per the Hanefi school. Said rule spanned parts of Europe, Africa, and Asia, until it later transformed into the law of the unitary state of the Republic of Turkey in 1923.

A useful facet of Islamic law is that it does not discriminate based on race, nationality or faith. It furthermore rejects nationalism "as a source of public policies."[285] There are certain classifications, however, in terms of citizenship under Islamic law. The three primary groupings were the Ra'iyye, the Teb'a, (or Muslim and non-Muslim), and the Muste'men who were non-Muslim and possessed interim residence status in Islamic country.[286] Additionally, the distinctions were not intended to emphasize a difference between Muslim and non-Muslim rights.[287] The distinction was more of a simply natural categorizing of the people as they distinguished themselves, given the title of citizen as Nufus-i Muslime (of the Muslim population) and Nufus-i Gayrimuslime (of the Non-Muslim Population).

---

[284] See Benjamin Braude & Bernard Lewis, "Introduction" in *Christians and Jews in the Ottoman Empire: the Functioning of a Pluralist Society*, Volume I, Benjamin Braude & Bernard Lewis, eds. (NY, London, Holmes & Meier, 1982) at 1.

[285] See Metin Heper, "The State, Religion, and Pluralism: The Turkish Case in Comparative Perspective" 18 Br. J. of ME St. (1991) at 44.

[286] See Ahmet Akgunduz, Tarihi Acidan Azinliklara Taninan Haklar ve Biz I [From the Historical Perspective: Rights Provided to non-Muslims and We no: 1] at http://.osmanli.org.tr/yazdirilabilirosmanli.php?id=30 (accessed on July 23, 2008). Professor Akgunduz who established the Ottoman Charitable Institution in Istanbul and constructed that webpage and put excerpts mostly from his written works. It made his works available on the Internet.

[287] See Ahmet Akgunduz & Halil Cin, *Turk Hukuk Tarihi (Ozel Hukuk), Cilt II* [*Turkish Legal History (Private Law), Volume II* (Istanbul, Osmanli, 1996) at 332.

Original Turks having come from Middle Asia, Ottoman Turks, as part of a State, first appeared in Anatolia. They largely kept to their own traditions as villagers and farmers settling in rural areas and as urbanites who settled in the cities.[288] Social class in Ottoman society evolved through the distinction of an individual's occupation, religious background, and whether or not they lived in urban or rural areas. Ottoman historians note that no group in the society would possess pre-eminence over any other.[289] Moreover, alienation between social classes didn't display the barriers evident in the Western world.[290] Public officials proved to illustrate that they were appointed based on merit.[291] Only Sultans claimed genealogical lines to aristocracy.[292] Transition between classes was also commonplace.[293] There was no evidence of a concessive group in society.

Under the belief of classical Islam there is no place for bureaucracy and hierarchy in the structure of State and community.[294] In the Ottoman era, social class occurrence was based on a person's profession.[295] There were two main social classes; governors (*Askeri*) and the governed (*Reaya*), anyone who worked for the State was accepted into the governor's class and they were exempt from paying taxes.[296] In other words, they represented the State. Those known as "Saray Halki" were palace people who lived with the

---

[288] See Fuat Koprulu, *Osmanli Devleti'nin Kurulusu* [*Foundation of the Ottoman State*] (Istanbul, 1959) at 51.

[289] See Ziya Kazici, *Osmanli'da Toplum Yapisi* [*Structure of the Ottoman Society*] (Istanbul, Bilge, 2003) at 15. Professor Kazici, a theologian professor at Marmara University in Istanbul has rare books about the Ottoman society.

[290] *Id*, at 12.

[291] *Id*, at 16.

[292] *Id*.

[293] See Ogier Ghiselin de Busbecq, Turkiye'yi Boyle Gordum [I saw Turkey like this], translation of Aysel Kurutluoglu (Istanbul, Tercuman 1001 Temel Eser, undated) at 64.

[294] See Heper, *supra note* 285, at 45.

[295] See Kazici, *supra note* 289, at 21.

[296] *Id*.

Sultans, Ilmiyye or scientists who spent most of their time studying the sciences, Seyfiyye or military personnel, and Kalemiyye or all administrative and civil personnel who worked under State authority.[297] The governed classes were urbanites, rural, and nomadic peoples.[298]

As quickly as the Ottomans acquired new land, they distributed it to the *reaya*, or rural people.[299] Moreover, the State distributed food and provided shelter to those who living in poverty. The practice encouraged voluntary acceptance of Ottoman rule, which contributed to its expansion.[300] The State provided new lands to its military personnel for them to cultivate on behalf of the State.[301] This was called the *Timar System*. To have a *timar* meant that military personnel who demonstrated extraordinary bravery during military campaigns were given land and property rights from the State, or Sultan.[302] The State though still remained in possession of the land. These *timar* owners gave this land to villagers for cultivation who at the end of the year paid 10 % of their earnings to the *timar* owner, or

---

[297] See Kazici, *supra note* 289, at 23.

[298] See Gul Akyilmaz, "Osmanli Devleti'nde Reaya Kavrami ve Devlet Reaya Iliskileri" [The Concept of Reaya and State—Reaya Relationship in the Ottoman State], IV Osmanli (1999) at 41.

[299] The *Timar System* was inherited and developed from pre-Ottoman Turkish and Muslim states. See infra 22. Around the 14th century, with the establishment of the Ottoman State, the *Timar system* was crafted. Around the 18th century the system broke down mainly because of the power loss of the central government and its inability to catch up with industrial revolution. See Erol Ozbilgen, *Butun Yonleriyle Osmanli: Adab-i Osmaniyye* [All Aspects of Ottomans: Rules of Ottoman] (Istanbul, Iz, 2007) at 772-75.

[300] See Necdet Sevinc, *Osmanli'nin Yukselisi ve Cokusu* [The Rise and fall of the Ottoman] (Istanbul, Birharf, 2005) at 76. Sevinc claims that the first collective bargaining agreement was signed between an employer and 24 employees in 1776, according to court records (Kutahya Ser'i Mahkeme Sicilleri). The contract came into effect with the approval of the Kutahya Judge (Kadi), at 241-2. Moreover, the author argues that it was a social care action to establish and protect a society who had no special status privileges.

[301] *Id*, at 77.

[302] *Id*, at 79.

to the military representative. In turn, *timar* owners used profits to cover expenses for military personnel during wartime.[303]

Timar owners supervised land for the State as well. Unlike in a feudal system, the *timar system* was one where the government or State gave land to governors, citizens, and *reaya*, in return for small favours with the land remaining property of the State. This is of course in contrast to the feudal system, with the relationship between lord and serf, or owner and slave.[304] A critical difference is that of the shared ownership of land and absence of slavery in the Ottoman system. T*imar* owners did not have any rights over villagers outside of supervising their earnings and ensuring that they received their commission. Any dispute was taken to court. In addition, T*imar* owners had to establish essential facilities and utilities for the property under their management.[305] As a result, profits made by the *timar sahibi* (*timar* owners) could be used either to purchase the land, or it could be donated by the Sultan to the *timar sahibi*.[306] If villagers cultivated the land for at least three years, they gained property rights on the cultivated areas.[307] As a consequence, a bourgeois class was created through the operations of the State. In contrast, the serf was never able to progress beyond anything but a peasant and the lord was always the owner of

---

[303] *Id.*

[304] See Ziya Kazici, *Islam Tarihi: Osmanli Devleti ve Medeniyeti* [History of Islam: The Civilization and State of the Ottoman] (Istanbul, Bilge, 1995) at 408-16.

[305] See Sevinc, *supra note* 300, at 83.

[306] In doctrine, these lands were also called "military tax farms." See Mehmed Fuad Koprulu, *Some Observations on the Influence of Byzantine Institutions on Ottoman Institutions*, (Ankara, TTK, 1999) at 85. This book originally contains published articles that were published around the 1930s and were translated and edited with an introduction and postscript by Gary Leiser.

For Professor Koprulu (1890-1966), one bibliography listed more than 1,300 articles, reviews, essays, editorials, books, and other writings, at 9. Gary Leiser notes that "Koprulu's task was further complicated by the ideas of certain "academics" who were overly imbued with Turkish nationalism, a problem that still emerges from time to time in Turkish scholarly works." at 5.

[307] See Sevinc, *supra note* 300, at 81.

land or property. As a result, when there were clashes among the citizenry in the Ottoman areas, they weren't clashes between the social classes but among higher administration.[308] As a safeguard, the State even forbade *timar* owners from using any superior authority against villagers.[309]

An understanding of family is critical to the understanding of the Ottoman systems. The Qur'an bestows great value upon mother and father. The reason for the predominance of parental respect among Ottoman Turks is contained in *Sura Isra* (Sons of Israel), versus 23:

"Thy Lord hath decreed, that ye worship none save Him, and (that ye show) kindness to parents. If one of them or both of them attain old age with thee, say not "Fie" unto them nor repulse them, but speak unto them a gracious word." [310]

Men were seen as the head of the household, while women were also deeply respected and, therefore, highly protected.[311] Women then however, not much unlike today, were not considered thinkers in the mainstream. This was, however, the general regard of the Muslims, Armenians, Greeks and Arabs of the day.[312] The Prophet Mohammed had stated; "your best (men) are those who take care of their wives in the best way possible."[313] Strong

---

[308] See general Kazici, *supra note* 289, at 9-18.

[309] See Sevinc, supra note 300, at 84-5.

[310] See Kazici, *supra note* 6, at 178. Professor Kazici notes that in the past there never existed any senior citizens' or retirement residences in Muslim Turkish society. Today's Turkish society, however, has established senior citizens' homes. Moreover, seniors are regarded highly among society and tradition continues as elder ladies or men are referred to as aunts or uncles.

[311] See Kazici, *supra note* 289, at 179.

[312] See Ilber Ortayli, *Osmanliýi Yeniden Kesfetmek* [Re-exploration of the Ottomans] (Istanbul, Timas, 2006) at 30, 37.

[313] See Kazici, *supra note* 289, at 179.

family ties shaped a healthier system.[314] Interestingly enough, Professor Kazici finds many Turkish historians citing the rarity of the practice of polygamy during the Ottoman period and that the society largely opposed these kinds of marriages, despite its permission in Islam.[315] It is near impossible to find any proponent of polygamous marriage in modern Turkey, as opposed to other contemporary Muslim societies. Prior to the adoption of Islam, many women reigned as governors in the former Turkish states; some even served as military personnel.[316] Following the official recognition of Islam, women took up positions mostly in civil authority returned to the home.[317]

Even though religion was important to the Ottomans, many aspects of public life did not involve religion.[318] They did attempt to maintain a distance between the public and private, and thoroughly opposed political goals aimed by religion. So despite any

---

[314] At 188-90. See more Ismail Dogan, Osmanli Ailesi: Sosyolojik Bir Yaklasim [The Ottoman Family: From the Sociological Perspective] (Ankara, Yeni Turkiye, 2001).

Professor Ortayli informs that the district (neighbourhood) had so much importance in Ottoman society. Before anyone or any family could move to any neighbourhood s/he or they had to get permission from people of the district. If any resident or family caused trouble in the neighbourhood, neighbourhood inhabitants had the right to make a claim before a judge so that the trouble makers would move out of the district. For example, Ambassador Edward Barton of Great Britain, who was sent to Istanbul by Queen Elizabeth I, was made to move out from his residency because of neighbour complaints. The reason was that he was hosting noisy parties where they drank too much. See Ortayli, *supra note* 312, at 38.

[315] *Id*, at 181. See more Heim Gerber, "Social and Economic Position of Women in an Ottoman City, Bursa, 1600-1700" 12 Int'l J. of MES (1980).

[316] At 181-2. During the Ottoman era, after the 1839 Tanzimat Reforms, women began to appear in social life after becoming teachers in schools. Their roles began to change in the family as well. See Ortayli, *supra note* 312, at 42.

[317] At 181-2.

[318] See William Ochsenwald, "Islam and the Ottoman Legacy in the Modern Middle East" in *Imperial Legacy: The Ottoman Imprint on the Balkans and the Middle East*, ed. L. Carl Brown, (NY, CUP, 1996) at 267.

misconceptions, the Ottoman society could be used as somewhat of an exemplar or template upon which to build or adjust modern societies that struggle with tolerance and the proper recognition of rights. For this to become more evident, it will require a closer examination of law itself.

B) The Ottoman Legal System[*]

This section outlines the main structure of the Ottoman legal system. Basic rights and legal thought in Islam did not progress through the same stages they did in the Western world. They have been in existence since the beginning of Islam, and with a slightly different interpretation of freedom from the notion in Western understanding.[319] The majority of people associate Sharia law to obligation and Western law to right.[320] Islamic law was formerly known as "Fikih" [321]Fikih consisting of two main sections: the Furu-i Fikih, which categorizes the fikih, and the Usulu-i Fikih, which consists in the theoretical aspect of Sharia and the primary sources for Islamic law.[322] Furu-i Fikih was further divided into

---

[*] During the Ottoman era, the most important thing was the Sharia courts in terms of legal system. Each court recorded their decision on Ser'iye Sicili which was the registration book of the courts. The oldest date goes back to 1455 from Bursa Court Ser'i Sicili. See more about Ser'iye Sicilleri-Osmanli Hukukunda Adliye Teskilatinin Yapisi ve Fonksiyonlari [Seri Sicil-Structures and Functions of the Ottoman Judiciary System] at http://.istanbulmuftulugu.gov.tr/index. php?option=com_content&task=view&id=21 . . . (accessed on August 5, 2008).

[319] See Ahmet Akgunduz, Islam ve Bati Hukukunda Insan Haklarinin Tarihi Gelisimi [Historical Phases of Human Rights in Islam and West] at http://. osmanli.org.tr/yazdirilabilirosmanli.php?id:145 (accessed on July 23, 2008).

[320] See Murteza Bedir, "Fikih to Law: Secularization through Curriculum" 11 Islamic L. & Soc'y (2004) at 379. The author provides this information from Joseph Schacht *An Introduction to Islamic Law* (Oxford, OUP, 1964) at 4. In his article, Bedir argues that the Western notion of law influenced the form of fikih into Islamic law.

[321] At 380.

[322] See general Murteza Bedir, Fikih, Mezhep ve Sunnet [Fikih, Sects, and Sunnah] (Istanbul, Ensar, 2004).

ibadat [acts of worship] and muamelat [interpersonal relations] such as in family law, contract law, criminal law, and so forth.[323]

Freedom in Islam means: for one to do as one will without harming themselves or anyone else in the process, and in accordance to the existing legal system.[324] According to Islam, people are free subjects of Allah.[325] Islamic law asserts that no individual live under tyranny, but that individuals should also renounce absolute freedom as that fit only for animals; that which in humans would leave the soul the slave to the inner man.[326] Moreover, Islam does not concede to the mosque and/or priesthood.[327]

The Sunni jurisdiction of Islamic law does not make any distinction regarding public and private law. It is mainly concerned with rights under Allah [God], and basic human rights.[328] Contemporary Islamic legal scholars even claim that rights under God could be interpreted as public law and human rights as private law.[329] In Islamic law, private acts cannot be brought before the courts unless there is a violation of the right[s] an individual for which a claim has been made to the judiciary.[330] This would place criminal law as

---

[323] See Bedir, *supra note* 320, at 380.

[324] See Akgunduz, *supra note* 319.

[325] *Id.*

[326] See Servet Armagan, *Islam Hukukunda Temel Hak ve Hurriyetler* [*Basic Rights and Freedoms in Islamic Law*] (Ankara, TDB, 1987) at 71.

[327] See Nawaf A. Salam, "The Emergence of Citizenship in Islam" 12 Arab L. Q. (1997) at 131.

See for a discussion of how Islam and secularism are incompatible, Mehrzad Boroujerdi, "Can Be Islam Secularized?" in *In Transition: Essays on Culture and Identity in Middle Eastern Societies*, M. R. Ghanoonparvar & Faridoun Farrokh (eds.), (Texas, A & M IUP, 1994).

[328] See Armagan, *supra note* 326, at 118.

[329] *Id.*

[330] See Abdulaziz Sachedina, Guidance or Governance? A Muslim Conception of "Two-Cities", 68 Geo. Wash. L. Rev. (1999-2000) at 1079. The author gathers this information from Joseph Schacht, *An Introduction to Islamic Law* (Oxford, OUP, 1964) at 189-90.

private law in Islam.[331] The victim and plaintiff were both required to be present at the trial and execution.[332]

Theoretically, it is possible to divide Islamic law into public and private.[333] One eminent Islamic scholar in Turkey, Professor Hayrettin Karaman claims that there is always a private/public law distinction in Fikih [Islamic Law].[334] He also advises that private law in Islam should be considered from the perspective of a continental legal system.[335] Others claim that "the Qur'anic vision of an ideal order is not based on the separation of the private and public"; rather, that it is the finding of your own true way.[336] In other words, public and private life is integrated and with the Qur'an as its reference, individual freedom of conscience is the cornerstone of this communal life.[337] The Qur'an intertwines religion and civil responsibility where Christianity would perhaps distinguish "between the sacred and secular."[338] In Islam, religion is not removed from the public arena. There is also the claim that,

---

[331] At 1094.

[332] *Id.*

[333] See Hayrettin Karaman, Mukayeseli Islam Hukuku, 1. Cilt [Comparative Islamic Law, Volume 1] (Istanbul, Iz, 1999) at 20 hereafter.

[334] At 39.

[335] See general Hayrettin Karaman, Mukayeseli Islam Hukuku, 3. Cilt [Comparative Islamic Law, Volume III] (Istanbul, Iz, 1999)

[336] See Sachedina, *supra note 330*, at 1089.

[337] *Id.*

[338] At 1090.

traditionally, public law is less developed in Islamic law when compared to the Western legal tradition.[339]

As mentioned earlier, private law in Islamic law was responsible for the notion of a relationship between "the individual and the social good."[340] Professor Emon, using Western sources, mistakenly argues that Hanafi jurists sacrifice the individual for the public interest or the community.[341] Islam treats all rights equally, whether or not they could be considered major or minor rights. Without the consent of an individual person, his/her right cannot be sacrificed in the name of society. Bediuzzaman Said Nursi reiterates the notion of Islamic justice in a modern sense, as such: [342]

"Pure justice and relative justice may be explained like this: according to the allusive meaning of the verse,—"if anyone slew

---

[339] See Bedir, *supra note* 320, at 400. The same argument was made by many Ottoman legal historians such as Ebul'ula Mardin who was one of the prominent Turkish legal scholars and thought the Islamic law subject in the law faculty of Istanbul University in the early years of the Republic.

See more Ebul'ula Mardin, "Development of Sharia Under the Ottoman Empire" in Law in the Middle East, Volume I: Origin and Development of Islamic Law, Majid Khadduri & Herbert J. Lienbesny(eds.)(Washington D. C. MEI, 1955). Reprinted in 2008 by the Lawbook Exchange Ltd. See about Ebul'ula Mardin's biography, Turgut Akpinar, *Istanbul Universitesinde 50 Yil Oncesi Bazi Buyuk Hocalarimiz [50 Years Ago Some of Our Eminent Professors in Istanbul University]* (Istanbul, Kitabevi, 2004).

[340] See Anver M. Emon, Huquq Allah and Huquq Al-Ibad: A Legal Heuristic for A Natural Rights Regime, 13Islamic L.&Soc'y (2004) at 327.

[341] At 331-33. See parallel idea from Turkish academia "individualistic interpretations of the Sacred law were not allowed." See Heper, *supra note* 285, at 45.

[342] Bediuzzaman Said Nursi (1877-1960)who is of Kurdish origin but was born and died in Turkey and influenced the Islamic thought in modern world—justifies that true enemies are in the century of "science-reason-and civilization-" materialism and atheism and their source is materialist philosophy. To fight against this problem he chose the jihad of the word in other words non-physical jihad and positive action means that maintenance of public order and security that harmed by the acts of unbelief could be repaired by the healing of the truths of the Qur'an. At, http://.www.nursistudies.com

a person—unless it be for murder or for spreading mischief in the land—it would be as if he slew the whole people, [Holy Qur'an 5:32]"—the rights of an innocent man cannot be cancelled for the sake of all the people. A single individual may not be sacrificed for the good of all. In the view of Almighty God's compassion, right is right, there is no difference between great and small. The small may not be annulled for the great. Without his consent, the life and rights of an individual may not be sacrificed for the good of the community. If he consents to sacrifice them in the name of patriotism, that is a different matter. A particular is sacrificed for the good of the universal; the rights of an individual are not considered in the face of the community. A sort of relative justice is attempted to be applied as the lesser of two evils. But if it is\possible to apply pure justice, relative justice may not be attempted, if it is, it is wrong."³⁴³

In the Ottoman courts, the judge sat on the bench alone, though there were officials who assisted him.³⁴⁴ Judges also served as the mayor and chief of police of their municipality.³⁴⁵ A Kadi [judge] acted as a mediator and brought the sides to an acceptable solution; in other words, bargaining and negotiation was part of Ottoman procedural law.³⁴⁶ Until 1864 and the establishment of the

---

³⁴³ See Bediuzzaman Said Nursi, Letters, The Fifteenth Letter, at 79, at http://www.nur.gen.tr/en.html#leftmenu=Risale&maincontent=Risale&islem=read&KitapAd=Letters&KitapId=21&BolumId=732&Page=79. His writings collected under the name of "The Risale-I Nur Collection" consist of about 6,000 pages. Anybody can access it through the web pages either Turkish or English also other languages. Originally, they were written Ottoman-Arabic or Kurdish language.

³⁴⁴ See Ahmet Bostanci, Urdun'de Muslumanlara ve Gayri Muslimlere Yonelik Dini Yargi Sistemi [Religious Judiciary System for Muslim and Non-Muslims in Jordan] 3 Usul Dergisi (2005) at 107. The author claims that the Jordanian Judiciary system is the continuation of the Ottoman Judiciary system that offers a choice for Muslim and non-Muslim in private family law.

³⁴⁵ See Ahmet Akgunduz, "Application of Islamic Legislation in the Ottoman State: Sharia Courts and Sharia Records" at http://www.osmanli.org.tr/en/the_articles.php?bolum=30&id=338 (accessed on July 28, 2008).

³⁴⁶ See Haim Gerber, *State, Society, and Law in Islam: Ottoman Law in Comparative Perspective* (NY, NYSUP, 1994) at 177 and 179.

Nizamiye Courts, Sharia courts were the only courts available.[347] When we compare the Islamic legal system with other systems of today, it is possible to see a similarity to common law—for instance, in the role of a judge and the jury system. A Kadi (judge) described and developed rules and cases, and also arranged trials with a jury that consisted of five or six trustworthy individuals from the local community.[348] Every court recorded its decisions in special record books, a practise ordered by the Ottoman State.[349]

In the Ottoman era, the main principle for the State and its people was fairness [adalet].[350] "Justice was the protection of the rural and urban producers against abuses of the military elite."[351] Many post-classical Ottoman political studies mention that fairness was the cornerstone of the legitimacy of Ottoman era governance.[352] The Ottomans believed that fairness was the protection of legitimate order and recognized mutual rights and obligations in order to sustain a healthy society.[353] Moreover, around the XVIII Century, the principal allowed particular rebellions to take place against the Sultanate.[354] These occasions illustrated that no one in the country, including the Sultans, were out of reach of the law.[355]

The Ottoman legal system "in practice . . . clearly, distinguished [between] the State and religion, dealing with issues that concerned

---

[347] See Bostanci, *supra note* 344, at 109.

[348] See Sevinc, *supra note* 300, at 93.

[349] See Akgunduz, *supra note* 345, at 63.

[350] See Ozbilgen, *supra note* 299, at 117.

[351] See A. Ergene Bogac, "On Ottoman Justice: Interpretations in Conflict (1600-1800)" 8 Islamic L. & Soc'y (2001) at 52.

[352] At 54.

[353] At 86.

[354] See general Mustafa Akdag, Turk Halkinin Dirlik ve Duzenlik Kavgasi: Celali Isyanlari [Fight of Turkish People for Social and Political Order: Celali Rebellions] (Ankara, BKBY, 1999).

[355] *Id*, at 226.

political power and administration independently from religion."[356] Perhaps even prior to French secularism, Ottoman secularist practice was apparent. A noteworthy distinction being that no sectarian uprisings ever occurred anywhere in Ottoman Europe, save the exceptions of State suppression due to various Shia movements.[357] A common Ottoman approach of the day was that one should "give back to Caesar what is Caesar's and to God what is God's".

This separation of State from religion gave rise to the subsequent order of law followed by the Ottomans, though it was not always adhered to in practice. The hierarchy in the Ottoman legal system was, first, the Qur'an [God's Orders], the Hadis [Prophet Mohammad's Orders and Practices], the Icma [Collective Decisions of Islamic Jurists and Scholars], the Kiyas [Analogy], the Orders of the Sultan that complied with Islamic law, the Regulations of Islamic States, the Legal Codes of Newly Captured Lands that complied with Islamic law, the Legal Customs that complied with Islamic law, the Agreements with Foreign Governments, the Principle of Reciprocity in International law, the Istihsan [leaving general rule and establishing an exceptional rule because of necessity], the Istishab [if there is no absolute rule, then it is permissible], and the Previous Prophets' Sharia.[358] Even if this order defined societal laws, the Ottomans also considered new introductions into its society and altered laws according to changing values while at times adopting other legal customs or establishing a secular-universal school of thought while still maintaining its Sunni philosophy.

---

[356] See Halil Inalcik, "The Meaning of Legacy" in *Imperial Legacy: The Ottoman Imprint on the Balkans and the Middle East*, ed. L. Carl Brown, (NY, CUP, 1996) at 21.

[357] See general Taha Akyol, *Osmanli'da ve Iran'da Mezhep ve Devlet* [Mezhep and State in the Ottoman and Iran] (Istanbul, Milliyet, 1999).

[358] See Ozbilgen, *supra note* 299, at 117. See more Cin & Akgunduz, *supra note* 319, at 159-64. See more additional info about those terminological words and their explanations, Mehmet Erdogan, Fikih ve Hukuk Terimleri Sozlugu [Dictionary of Terminology of Islamic Law and Law] (Istanbul, Ragbet, 1998).

Among the four main Sunni mezhebs (sects), the Hanefi school of thought was considered by the Ottoman Turks to be the most rational and liberal.[359] This school of thought also helped to rationalize the legal system; particularly in the field of criminal law, where the State chose not to use capital punishment and authorities preferred to offer compensation to the victim's family.[360] This was a particularly modern legal trade-off for the time.

Another precept adopted to bring greater accord to Ottoman law was the Tacit (customary) law, which was a law that greatly influenced and shaped its legal system despite never being practiced outside of Ottoman society with the same effectiveness in other Islamic societies.[361] The Ottoman State therein, became more multi-ethnic, multi-lingual-and multi-religious. If newly attained countries or land had no legal tradition contrary to Islamic law, the Ottoman rulers adopted their practices as new codes of the State.[362] This also helped people maintain possession of identity and tradition. In practice, the orders of the Ottoman Sultanate were always limited either by Sharia law or the local customs.[363] Some customary laws were indeed in direct opposition to Islamic law, but the State still accepted these as their own legal parameters.[364]

---

[359] See Ozbilgen, *supra note* 299, at 122.

[360] See Ilber Ortayli, *Uc Kitada Osmanlilar* [Ottomans on Three Continents] (Istanbul, Timas, 2007) at 113. Professor Ortayli claims that the Ottoman was one of the three greatest empires in the region of the Mediterranean and the latest universal one. See general, Ilber Ortayli, *Son Imparatorluk Osmanli* [Last Empire Ottoman] (Istanbul, Timas, 2006).

[361] During the Ottoman era, judges went through a three step procedure to pass as candidate judge. After finishing medrese, their first duty was to be a consultant and answer people's questions, second, he had to teach at a medrese and finally if he was successful on these two duties he might be able to become a judge. See Ortayli, *supra note* 28, 128. A judge also controlled all officials within his own area. Moreover, judges were routinely supervised by higher judges. *Id*, 128-9.

[362] See Cin & Akgunduz, *supra note* 319, at 166-70.

[363] *Id*, at 197-8. See also Ozbilgen, *supra note* 299, at 123.

[364] See Akyol, *supra note* 357, at 151.

Renowned Ottoman historians Stanford Shaw, Ira Lapidus, and Halil Inalcik have claimed in numerous writings that, the Ottoman State became secular with its adoption of local customs under State law.[365] Akgunduz, however, protests that Sharia law permitted the Sultan Ulul-Emr to make laws, but that this law should have complied with the Sharia.[366] Though it could be argued that Akgunduz's observations concerning the Devsirme system are inaccurate. This was a system that permitted many non-Muslims to access high bureaucratic and administrative positions, all but the position of Sultan itself. This is a clear violation of Classic Islamic legal systems, in which high State positions were only granted to Muslim citizens. It demonstrates clearly the Ottoman disinterest in conflating religion and politics, or in other words: Ottoman secularism.

All decrees and customs accepted into law since the inception of the Ottoman State were registered by a State official called the Nisanci.[367] Said individual was the State's highest legal advisor, as even Seyhul-Islam, and the highest State clergy came to the Nisanci for interpretation of rules.[368] Registrars wrote legal documents after discussions held between legal and religious scholars with the approval of the Sultan. The commands of previous Sultans were followed by their successors except if new situations arose which required an amendment to retain societal trust in the legal system.[369]

Even during the 14th century there was advancement in the legal system far beyond the norm of the time. Until the 18th Century, the Ottoman State was seen in the eyes of European visitors and philosophers as a source of inspiration and the "most modern

---

[365] See Stanford Shaw, *History of the Ottoman Empire and Modern Turkey*, Volume I, (Cambridge, CUP, 1987) at 134. Ira Lapidus, *a History of Islamic Societies*, (Cambridge, CUP, 1988) 319. Halil Inalcik, the Middle East and the Balkans under the Ottoman Empire, (Bloomington, 1987) at 86.

[366] See Ahmet Akgunduz, *Osmanli Kanunnameleri ve Hukuk Tahlilleri* [Legal Rules of the Ottomans and Legal Analysis], Volume I (Istanbul, Fey, 1990) at 60.

[367] See Ozbilgen, *supra note* 299, at 108.

[368] See Akyol, *supra note* 357, at 150.

[369] See Ozbilgen, *supra note* 299, at 127-8.

government" in the world.[370] Worthy of note was how judges' verdicts remained unchanged even by order of the Sultan.[371] Moreover, governors had no jurisdiction over judges appointed by the Sultan's ministry.[372] This made the Ottoman justice system independent from legislators and executive powers. The Ottoman political system resembled, for the most part, that of the modern United States of America, with the legislative and executive branches intertwined, but the judicial branch completely autonomous in its authority.

Like today, judges, defendants and offenders were able to call expert witnesses into courts.[373] One of the most important features of the Ottoman system was that nobody was sentenced to punishment without a judge's order.[374] No other State at the time possessed this type of law. If, during the trial one of the parties provided new evidence, the judge needed to review the case again, and any one party could apply to the Divan-i Human, the State's main council, located in the capital city, where experienced higher court judges could examine the case.[375] It was a right of appeal, made directly to higher court judges. It was a significant development in the way of State law. In accordance with the Ottoman legal system, each party to the case was able to confer with a legal scholar before going to court, which usually helped parties to reach a settlement prior to trial.[376] This is quite similar to a Mediation-Arbitration system in common law.

---

[370] See Asli Cirakman, "From Tyranny to Despotism: The Enlightenments of Unenlightent Image of Turks" 33 Int. J. MES (2001) at 49.

[371] See Halil Inalcik, *Turkey and Europe in History* (Istanbul, Eren, 2006) at 64.

[372] *Id.*

[373] See Sevinc, *supra note* 300, at 93-4.

[374] See Cin & Akgunduz, *supra note* 366, at 270-1. See Ozbilgen, *supra note* 299, at 219.

[375] See Ozbilgen, *supra note* 299, at 183. See also Cin & Akgunduz, *supra note* 366, at 239-40.

[376] See Cin & Akgunduz, *supra note* 366, at 223.

C) Muslim Ottoman Turkish Women in the Courts

Here, we will go over the role of women in Ottoman society. This will help to clarify their position in accordance to the law. What will follow is an examination of various trial records involving women's rights in the Ottoman legal system, and analysis of the 1917 'Family Law Act'* [Hukuk-i Aile Kararnamesi] which set out the rules of divorce for cases involving Muslim women. It is claimed that the court records [Ser'i Sicils], are the best resource for information concerning the social history of the Middle East [and, thereby, of lands belonging to the Ottoman Empire].[377]

Family law is the cornerstone of Islamic law.[378] A Family that is Islamic should adhere to the particular characteristic principles: children should always respect their parents, and fulfil their other duties, all family members are responsible for their community, all family members should constantly develop themselves in terms of science, culture and art, and so forth.[379] Islam prohibits any kind of extramarital sexual interaction.[380] Under Islamic law, a Muslim cannot marry an atheist, though a Muslim male can marry a Jewish or Christian woman, whereas a Muslim woman cannot marry a Jewish or Christian man. Under Islamic law, the marriage ceremony does not require the presence of a religious figure; though, during Ottoman times the kadi [judge] was officially authorised to prepare and authenticate the marriage contracts.

---

* This legislation was enacted on 25th October, 1917.

[377] See Gerber, *supra note* 346, at 174. Akgunduz insistently claims the same argument looking at the ser'i sicils rather than following academic clichés.

[378] See Paul J. Magnarella, "East Meets West: The Reception of West European Law in the Ottoman Empire and the Modern Turkish Republic" 2 J. Int'l & Prac. (1993) at 284-5.

[379] See Ahmet Yaman, Islam Aile Hukuku [Islamic Family Law](Istanbul, MUIFY, 2008) at 20-6.

[380] See Nurettin Uzunoglu, Family, Marriage and Divorce, According to Islamic Law, (Istanbul, TDVY, 2008) at 9.

After the 16th Century, kadis delegated this function to the Imams who conducted prayer in the mosques.[381] If one of the parties had abandoned Islam, the marriage contract would automatically be terminated under Sharia law.

Islamic law grants the husband the right to a one-sided divorce; though, in theory and practice, women could also exercise this right [tafwid al talaq].[382] It was common for women to claim that [tawfid al talaq] be available to them under the marriage contracts that were made during the Ottoman era. Islam allows divorce between husband and wife only as a last resort as marriage is seen as an otherwise life-long commitment.[383] Authorization of divorce given to the husband was and is still criticized in terms of the principle of equality. Islamic jurists offer that the use of tawfid al talaq by women will make men more cautious about marriage and divorce, as women tend to be more traumatized as a result of divorced and so are able to claim greater compensation from a separation.[384]

Divorce can take place under three circumstances; the first is in the event of the death of a spouse; the second is by the request of either the husband or wife, or both; the third is by a judge.[385] The court's order of divorce would be due to—illness or bodily defect, maltreatment or irreconcilable differences, the cutting off of financial support or inadequate provision of financial support, the husband's disappearance or abandonment, or the accusing of a wife of adultery and proving it with four witnesses who have sworn

---

[381] See Yaman, *supra note* 379, at 294.
[382] See general A. Jawad Haifa, *The Rights of Women in Islam* (NY, St. MartinsP, 1998).

See more criticism about this unilateral right, Anver M. Emon, "Conceiving Islamic Law in a Pluralist Society: History, Politics and Multicultural Jurisprudence" 2006 Sing. J. Legal Stud. (2006) at 336-37.
[383] See Haifa, supra note 382, at 71.
[384] See Yaman, *supra note* 379, at 72-3.
[385] *Id*, at 79.

not to have had sexual relations with the plaintiffs wife for at least a period of four months prior to the instance.[386]

A woman possesses the right to divorce her husband at any time. The right cannot be rescinded by the husband.[387] During the marriage, the husband is responsible for providing shelter and food, etc. [nafaqa], even if the husband is poor and the wife is rich.[388] This is an obligation a woman can go to court to file a complaint for if the husband dos not adequately provide financial support.[389] This obligation, even in terms of Islamic law, is a contractual obligation a husband is required to provide to his wife even after they divorce.[390] If the husband dies, this obligation passes on to his next of kin.[391] If the husband cannot provide this support, a judge may grant a separation order in accordance to the school of Safi, Maliki, and Hanbeli, but not to Hanefi.[392] In Islamic law, before the marriage can take place, a husband has to make a payment [mahr] directly to his wife, or as arranged by the wife. In doctrine, it has been argued that, to stop the abuse of a husband's privilege in divorce, a woman has the right to be granted a very sizeable mahr, which even a court has the right to determine.[393] During the marriage the husband is responsible for all expenses without

---

[386] Id, at 86-92.
[387] See "Evlilik Birliginin Sona Ermesi" [The Dissolution of Marriage], available at http://www.istanbulmuftulugu.gov.tr/index.php?option=com_content&task=view&id=362&Itemid=320 (accessed on August 5, 2008). It is an official webpage of the Republic of Turkey, Religious Affairs Department, the branch of Istanbul.
[388] See Ismail Kaya, *Islam Dini ve Ilmihali*, [*Religion of Islam and Personal Law*, 3rd ed.] (Istanbul, Madve, 1994) at 441.
[389] *Id*.
[390] At 443.
[391] *Id*. Kaya points out interesting knowledge that is almost unknown by the researchers of Islam, if inheritance comes from the mother's side, her children will get equal shares. At 411.
[392] *Id*.
[393] See "Evliligin Sonuclari" [Consequences of Marriage], available at http://www.istanbulmuftulugu.gov.tr/index.php?option=com_content&task=view&id=356&Itemid=320 (accessed on August 5, 2008).

question.[394] In Hanefi jurisprudence, the bride or groom can add specific conditions into the marriage contract that would provide for immediate separation; for instance infidelity, or domestic violence, or marrying a second wife.[395] Even if a husband is absent at trial, a woman will receive the nafaqa from the husband's financial assets via a judge's order. In any such nafaqa case, the nafaqa will be arranged on the basis of the wife's social status and background.[396]

Many prejudices and stereotypes abound in the academic world regarding the role of women in during the Ottoman period.[397]

---

[394] *Id.*

[395] See Judith E. Tucker, "Muftis and Matrimony: Islamic Law and Gender in Ottoman Syria and Palestine" 1 Islamic L.&Soc'y (1994) at 266. The author has gathered this information from the Khayr al-din which is one of the classics of the Hanefi School. The author claims that he searched several hundred contracts in the records of Jerusalam, Nablus, and Damascus courts of the 18th Century, but could not find any conditions on any of them. I might argue that if he looked at the Anatolian side of the Ottoman land, he would have found many of them. It illustrates that Islamic rules were developed, formed or shaped according to the community's culture. Thus, today we have to reread classical Islamic from a contemporaneous perspective rather than judging them against present day practices in Islamic countries. See general Javaid Rehman, "Accommodating Religious Identities in an Islamic State: International Law, Freedom of Religion, and the Rights of Religious Minorities" 7 Int. J. Min. & Gr. Rts. (2000).

[396] *Id*, at 269-70. Tucker deals with how Sharia courts dealt with women's issues in Syria and Palestine in the 17th and 18th Century in the Ottoman era. See Judith E. Tucker, *In the House of the Law: Gender and Islamic Law in Ottoman Syria and Palestine* (Berkeley, UCP, 1998).

[397] See general Elizabeth B. Frierson, "Women in Late Ottoman Intellectual History" 135-161 in *Late Ottoman Society: the Intellectual Legacy*, Elizabeth Ozdalga (ed.), (London, RoutledgeCurzon, 2005).

Faroqhi claims that women were so active in business and cultural life and moreover in the palace of the Ottoman Sultanates. See Suraiya Faroqhi, *Subjects of the Sultan: Culture and Daily Life in the Ottoman Empire* (London, I.B. TaurisP, 2000) at 101-122. Pierce also shows how the women were powerful in the Sultan's palace and had an influence on the State's policies and practices. See Leslie P. Pierce, *The Imperial Harem: Women and Sovereignty in the Ottoman Empire*, (Oxford, OUP, 1993).

Muslim divorce cases only arose in Sharia courts because of disputes regarding the settlements.[398] The Sharia court was provided all such rights to all Ottoman citizens, Muslim and non-Muslim women alike.[399] Sharia courts also dealt a lot with cases arising from marriage contracts involving allowances for a child or children when the father passed away.[400]

Often times, a woman would represent herself at court but could also be represented by a legal agent.[401] Ottoman era Sharia courts were very strict on requiring evidence to prove the claims put forward in divorce cases. Jennings sees a "Hull" divorce as a contract negotiated by a wife and husband to meet their particular needs.[402] In Ottoman times, the placing of conditions into a marriage contract was widespread.[403] Ottoman women have been shown to be shrewd and very capable of obtaining and enforcing the rights which were available to them. In his classic article Jennings looked at several hundred Ottoman court records and concluded that in the 17th century women were well established in the society as property owners and running businesses and/ or charitable organisations.[404] According to Ottoman law, the possessions of the husband and the wife were kept separate.[405]

The following are remains of records of various cases involving the exercise of the rights of Ottoman women, particularly pertaining

---

[398] See Rossitsa Gradeva, "Orthodox Christians in the Kadi Courts: The Practice of the Sofia Sheriat Court, Seventeenth Century" 4 Islamic L. & Soc'y (1997) at 55

[399] At 56.

[400] At 57.

[401] See Ronald C. Jennings, "Divorce in the Ottoman Sharia Court of Cyprus (1580-1640)" 78 Studia Islamica (1993) at 158.

[402] See Ronald C. Jennings, "Women in the Early 17th Century Ottoman Judicial Records: The Sharia Court of Anatolian Kayseri" 18 J. of Ec. & Soc. His. of Orient (1975) at 84.

[403] See general Jennings, *id*.

[404] At 97, and 111.

[405] See Bahattin Yediyildiz, Ottoman Society, in supra note 98, at 532.

to financial issues. They are cases from a store of approximately one hundred that come from various cities all over Anatolia.

The following cases are from the archives of the city of Mardin (South East Anatolia). Each recorded trials included at least five witnesses, as per the Ottoman court system.

Date: 31 August 1865, document no: 14/40(book 14, case 40)
Parties: Vesile, daughter of Benu vs. Serif, son of Davud
Claim: Vesile argues that her husband Serif has not paid the daily allowance support. Moreover, he beats her throughout the marriage. She requests a divorce and that her husband pay the daily allowance and iddah (waiting period fee) in terms of financial support.
Court decision: Ruled in favour of wife, divorce ordered, husband is to pay daily allowance and waiting period charges.
Significance: Ruling in favour of wife seeking divorce and financial support. Point of criticism: The domestic abuse was not addressed in the settlement.

Date: 27 September 1865, document no: 36/99
Parties: Molla Mehmet, son of Haso, on behalf Meymo, daughter of Temur vs. Mehmet Halebi, son of Abdal
Claim: The Vekil (legal representation) Molla Mehmet files on Meymo's behalf, claiming her husband proclaimed divorce by orally reciting the proclamation three times. Following the divorce he did not pay "wait period" alimony amounting to 1,500 kurus (cent). Moreover, the husband stole the wife's money and sheep.
Court decision: The husband admitted to the proclamation of divorce but denied the theft. Both parties could not prove their claims, voiding the request for reimbursement. The husband does however cover housing costs for his former wife.
Significance: Women were not required to be in attendance to seek out their rights. Also, they did project legal confidence in attempting to play the favour of the courts without legitimate evidence for all claims.

Date: 12 September 1865, document no: 22/61
Parties: Zuhre, daughter of Said vs. Mustafa, son of Yusuf
Claim: Zuhre requests 484 kurus in alimony, waiting period costs, rent coverage and a divorce.
Court decision: Mustafa concedes to his wife's claims.
Significance: Consensual divorce did occur.

Date: 05 November 1865, document no: 66/175
Parties: Ahmet Eldene, on behalf of his daughter Zemzem vs. Mehmet, son of Seyh Ali
Claim: Zemzem requests 500 kurus in daily allowance, rent coverage and alimony for the waiting period costs.
Court decision: Mehmet concedes to his wife's claims.
Significance: Once again, women could exercise their rights in court in absentia without reservation.
The following cases are from the archives of the city of Bursa (North West Anatolia).

Date: 31 August 1679, document no: B-189, page 182
Parties: Hala, daughter of Ebu-l Kasim vs. Ahmet, son of Mehmet
Claim: Hala argues that the marriage lacks mutual love and respect, and requests an immediate divorce. She foregoes the 800 akce (Ottoman money) in mahr and alimony if the divorce is swift.
Court decision: Hala's demands are met and a divorce is ordered by the presiding judge.
Significance: When a woman could provide witnesses (this case had six), the judge was quick to rule in her favour.

Date: 05 August 1707, document: B-189/412
Parties: Seyyid Ibrahim, son of Seyyid Rustem, on behalf of Serife Abide, daughter of Mehmet vs. Ahmet, son of Abdullah
Claim: Seyyid Ibrahim was commissioned by Serife Abide to represent her in court. The woman asks for living allowance for herself and her son.
Court decision: Judge rules in her favour.

Significance: The common practice of women appointing powerful individuals to represent them in court. The law also permitted for women who had children to be able to request further financial support if they were unable to provide for themselves over the long-term.

The following cases are from the archives of the city of Corum (Middle Anatolia).

Date: 05 August 1908, document no: 16/page 499
Parties: Fatma, daughter of Kel Mehmedoglu vs. Ahmet, son of Ankaralioglu
Claim: After the divorce, Fatma argues that she cannot take care of their four year old son, and requests financial support from her ex-husband.
Court decision: Fatma is granted fifteen kurus (cents) in daily alimony.
Significance: The trial date is very near the demise of the Ottoman State (1922). A classic understanding of Islamic law by the Ottoman courts, this was again a case of custody given to the mother and full financial responsibility on the father.

Date: 24 April 1907, document no: 16/page 305
Parties: Mavis, daughter of Omer vs. Azeboglu Huseyin, son of Ibrahim
Claim: The husband divorced his wife, but refuses to pay mahr-i mueccel in the form of sixty-six kurus. The wife demands the mahr-i mueccel.
Court decision: Through witness support, a divorce took place and so the husband was to pay the mahr-i mueccel.
Significance: Greater support for the fact that witness presence indeed provided a catalyst in the pursuit of financial restitution.

The following case is from the files of the Court of Istanbul.

Date: 17 November 1870, document no: 225/page 278

Parties: Mustafa Rasit, on behalf of his sister, Halide, daughter of Hafiz Mehmet Nuri, vs. Omer Aga, son of Abdullah

Claim: A divorce took place. Before the marriage the husband paid 500 kurus, he actually had to pay 1300 kurus as mahr-i muaccel; therefore he had 800 kurus still to pay. In addition to mahr-i mueccel, the husband was supposed to pay alimony during the ex-wife's pregnancy.

Court decision: The claims were conceded to by the husband.

Significance: Cases did occur in which an absence of witnesses had no bearing of the decision. The court seemed comfortable with ruling in favour of a wife, so long as her demands were in line with Islamic law.

The following cases are excerpts from the Book of Sukuk (Court Verdicts), available in the Ottoman archives located in Suleymaniye, Istanbul, and edited by Dabbagzade Muhammed Efendi. Re-edited by Seyh Muhammed Esat Efendi in October of 832.

At page 10-11

Parties: Halime, daughter of Abdulhalim vs. Ibrahim Efendi, son of Abdurrahim

Claim: The husband divorced his wife; the wife requests forty kurus for mahr-i mueccel. Moreover, the wife asks for rent and waiting period fees as provided for in their nikahname (marriage agreement).

Court decision: The husband denied a divorce had occurred, though witnesses[properly investigated thereafter by the courts] countered the claim resulting a ruling in favour of the wife by the presiding judge.

Significance: Once again, the prevalence of witness testimony.

At page 11-12

Parties: Rukiye, daughter of Ishak vs. Hasan Aga, son of Abdurrezzak

Claim: The husband gave authorization to his to divorce. The wife demands that her use of this authorization be valid and for her mahr-i mueccel and other remunerations. The husband denies giving this right to his wife.

Court decision: Reliable witnesses resulted in a ruling in favour of the wife.

Significance: Witness value. Point of criticism: Reminder that the right to unilaterally effect divorce belonged to the husband in Islamic law even though he could relinquish it.

The following case is from files in Kayseri (Middle Anatolia)

Date: 1546, document no: Kayseri 4/page 132

Parties: Bagdat, daughter of Abdullah vs. Bali, son of Hasan

Claim: The husband took a second wife. The first wife deems it unacceptable and requests a divorce.

Court decision: The husband offered half a vineyard's ownership instead of mahr-i mueccel, and immediate consent to a divorce. The wife accepted and the decision was then approved by the court.

Significance: Despite popular belief, accepting the taking of additional wives was not the inclination even of the Islamic Ottoman courts.

The following is an interesting case out of Harput (Eastern Anatolia)

Date: 1631, document no: Harput 181/page 38
Party: Widowed former wife, Mircan Hatun, daughter of Haci Ali
Claim: Wife requests the sale of homes belonging to her two children, given to them by her deceased husband, in order to support herself and her children financially, as well as a daily allowance.
Court decision: The court ruled in her favour.
Significance: Widows unable to care for themselves and their children could receive property rights and benefits even after the passing of their spouses.

The following cases are from the archives of the district of Uskudar, once the capital of Istanbul during Ottoman times.

Date: May 1514, document no: 1/217
Party: Huseyin, son of Mustafa
Claim: The husband swore before the court not to remarry again, and that if he did, his wife Gulbahar could divorce him. The courts recorded this in their marriage agreement at the behest of his wife.
Significance: Ottoman women could use the courts as a tool for solidifying and/or broadening their legal rights.

Date: March 1516, document no: 1/320
Parties: Sahi, daughter of Ilyas vs. Bayezit, son of Yusuf
Claim: Sahi had professed before her husband and the courts that she would wave her right to waiting period dues, mahr-i mueccel, and all other financial claims if her husband chose to proclaim divorce by recitation. The court recorded the stipulation.
Significance: An ironic proviso, it illustrates that Ottoman women showed idealistic dedication to the marriage at the outset and practical independence in the face of the possibility of divorce.

Date: April 1520, document no: 1/695
Parties: Yusuf, son of Abdullah vs. Dudu, daughter of Abdullah
Claim: The husband acknowledges his wife's house in Uskudar was sold to compensate her for 1,500 akce [At the time, equivalent to 700g of silver].

Significance: The case was not actually concerned with divorce, but for the wife to establish for herself a bit of financial security.

The above cases strongly illustrate that contrary to the popular belief that Muslim women were severely discriminated against. The Sharia courts strictly upheld and even broadened the rights available to them under Islamic law. The Ottoman courts especially provided Muslim women with increased protection against poverty with scores of decisions in their favour when it came to financial support. These cases also go some way to refute any allegations of a revisionist agenda, as the cases have been extracted from contemporary records, which have been overlooked or ignored for so long.

Sancar points that in terms of the "Ottoman court records, it seems fair to conclude that Ottoman women were conscious of their legal rights and that they generally received the support of the courts in their active pursuit of justice."[406]

D) The 1917 Family Law Act

Up to 1917, almost every area of law had been codified by Ottoman legislation or scholars, leaving no further need to codify the remaining

---

[406] Id, at 139.

disparate section of family law.[407] Due to the casualties sustained during World War I, the Ottoman male population was drastically reduced. Women began to establish themselves in every facet of Ottoman society, much like the situation in the West.[408] Women also began to engage in various public organisations and associations.[409] After 1900, support for feminism in the Ottoman Empire gathered momentum.[410] The 'Family Law Act' was brought about through influences of Westernism, Nationalism, and Islamism.[411] The law was prepared by commissions which consisted of Jewish, Christian and Muslim religious scholars and thereby reflected three distinct sets of religious rules concerning family law.[412] For the first time in an Islamic country, family law provisions in effect embraced the interests of all Sunni sects (Hanafi, Maliki, Safi and Hanbali); not just following the Hanafi School but also leaning heavily on the Maliki rule—a sect which was more amiable towards women.[413] Article 104, concerning the invalidation of particular behaviour of a drunken individual, or Article 105, which permitted for more open review of divorce are examples of an Ottoman legal system attempting to come to terms with liberal realities and modern social change.

This legislation was the first legislation in Islamic countries to codify family law.[414] It was the first written Act in an Islamic State in which

---

[407] See M. Akif Aydin, *Islam-Osmanli Aile Hukuku* [*Islam-Ottoman Family Law*] (Istanbul, MUIFVY, 1985) at 154-55. The book is a classic in that area. Here afterwards, Aydin's book used for the text of the legislation. The legislation was translated into French and published in "Istanbul 1917" and "Revue de Turquie" (in the Annex of the Issue of August 1918). At 151. However, there is no English translation available.

[408] At 158-9.

[409] See Niyazi Berkes, *The Development of Secularism in Turkey*, (NY, Routledge, 1998) at 436. This book was originally published in Canada in 1963 by McGill University.

[410] See Aydin, *supra note* 407, at 159-60.

[411] *Id*, at 166-80.

[412] *Id*, at 163-65.

[413] See Halil Cin, *Eski Hukukumuzda Bosanma* [*Divorce in Our Previous Legal System*] (Konya, SUY, 1988) at 125.

[414] See Aydin, *supra note* 407, at 211.

women received the right to obtain a divorce.[415]Article 156 of the Act abolished the right/privilege of the non-Muslim court to deal with the cases in family law and simply ordered that all family law cases would take place in the State courts.[416] This regulation caused the abolishment of the Act, due to pressure placed on the Allied powers by non-Muslim religious leaders to push the Ottoman State to do so. The non-Muslims charged that it would taking away their rights and privileges while Muslims argued it was attacking their identity.[417] Harsh criticism of observing Islamists and large scale protests by non-Muslims saw the law repealed in 1919.[418]

The legislation is divided into two main books, that concerning marriage and the other divorce. The first book consists of six sections and fifteen subsections with a total of one hundred-and-one articles. The second book is divided into three sections and five subsections with a total of fifty-six articles. Articles 1-3 of the first book deal with engagement, while 4-12 deal with the capacity to marry, 13-19 discuss forbidden marriages [under Islam], 20-26; forbidden marriages under Judaism, 27-32; forbidden marriages under Christianity, 33-39; the marriage contract [under Islam], 40-44; the marriage contract under Christianity, 45-51; Kefaet [Hanafi law in which women and men are required to be of similar social status at marriage. Normally Hanafi jurisprudence measures equality from six points of reference; financial assets, art, culture, family tree, Muslim-religious observance, and freedom., 52-58; annulment and abolition of marriage, 59-62; annulment and abolition of marriage for Jews, 63-68; annulment and abolition of marriage for Christians, 69-77; rules for marriage, 78-79; rules for marriage for Christians, 80-91; mahr [dowry], 92-101; and, nafaka[financial allowance], in the legislation only daily financial allowance [nafaka] is cited.

---

[415] See Cin, *supra note* 413, at 126.
[416] See Aydin, *supra note* 407, at 222.
[417] *Id.*
[418] *Id*, at 221-2 and 206.

In the second book concerning divorce, articles 102-110; dealt with general rules of [divorce], 111-118; permanent or reversible divorce [talak-i ric'i and bain], 119-131; good divorce [hiyar-i tefrik, relinquishing the right to divorce to women in Islam. In Hanefi jurisprudence a woman possesses the right to divorce only if her husband is proven incompetent and unable to run the marriage. However, the legislation extended this right to women by adopting it from other Sunni sects. Pursuant to this, even women could obtain divorce from their husbands in disputes brought before a court.], 132-138; divorce for Christians, 139-149; waiting period [In Islam, following divorce, women are required to wait three consecutive menstruation cycles in order to establish that they are not pregnant and can therefore remarry.], 150-154; divorce nafaka, 155-157; which established the rule that where there is no written clarification in the legislation, the rules for Muslims will be adhered to by non-Muslims as well.

It should be noted here that the Ottoman State applied the rules of Islam fully in private law.[419] The 1917 Act regarding divorce and Muslim women offered basic principles of Islamic law concerning divorce, as the right mainly belonged to the husband. However, the legislation did also provide the right to women in particular circumstances (Article 119-131) known through hiyar-i tefrik. Cin wrongly claims that classic Hanafi law is not familiar with this concept. However, it is evident from Ottoman court records that Muslim women did indeed exercise their rights through this utility.

The Act brought into Ottoman society written legal principle that provided Muslim women with the right to divorce that typically lay outside of common court practice. It was a kind of reform exercised through existing codes. Muslim women could apply to the courts for a divorce; in accordance to the following statutes:

---

[419] See Cin, supra note 140, at 122.

Article 119-"when a woman learns her husband is sterile, she can submit a plea to a judge for a divorce. If a woman is sterile, she cannot request a divorce. If a man is found sterile following any act of intercourse, a wife may not enter such a plea."

Article 120-"A woman may not request a divorce with full knowledge of any of her husband's fertility or other serious sexual dysfunctions. However, knowing of such issues prior to marriage does not nullify a woman's right to divorce."

Article 121-"when a woman applies to a court for any irresolvable problems concerning her husbands reproductive capacities, the judge, upon review and investigation, will grant a divorce; after permitting a period of one year for potential medical remedy."

Article 122-"if the husband contracts a contagious illness after marriage, the wife can ask for a divorce. Given there is an opportunity to cure the illness, the judge may postpone a divorce for a period of one year. If no progress is made, the judge will grant a divorce." This is taken from the law of the minority Hanefi School[420]; and attributed to social change.

Article 123-"Following marriage, the development of any kind of mental incapacitation of the husband entitles his wife to request a divorce from the courts, again with the allowance of a period of one year for potential remedy." This was a derivation from very recent Hanefi law.[421]

Article 124-"In cases as concern Articles 119-123, a woman is not required to be in court and may postpone the process as she wishes; making the legal process accord to her prerogative.

---

[420] See Aydin, supra note 407, at 201.

[421] See Aydin, supra note 407, at 201. See Cin, supra note 413, at 129.

Articles 125 through 131 of this Act provide for much of the same and alternative scenarios and avenues in and through which a woman could exercise her legal right to separation.

E) Concluding Remarks

Gerber rightly warns that: "we should distinguish here between two topics. One is the application of Islamic law, the Sharia, in real life in Islamic countries. The other is the history of the law itself as a body of thought."[422] The history of law as a body of thought generally permits more distortions that what is evident in actual fact. Ottoman legislation was obviously not an exemplar of what we might expect of a fully democratic and modern liberal system. The point is that this can be said of perhaps any legal system of the day if we run the under the microscope of expectations of comprehensive legal theory of the modern day. The key is to look for the things that pervade time and history, and culture and religion, and illustrate the common respects that humanity appears to end up with once all of the extraneous baggage of the past is filtered into reasonable standards of life and living of the present day. In some respects the Ottoman system and progress through legislation should be praised. The mere possibility that women were so well protected, at least financially, not by the theory but by the practice of the law during such times and under the rule of such a vast Empire is rather astounding. The weight of the religious onus of the Ottoman Empire and the paternalistic pride that carried it through the centuries would naturally bring about suspicions of authoritarian approaches in all manner of societal governance. And yet to see glimpses of practical change due to the recognition of modern social forces should at least draw some attention if not respect. It is a tragic characteristic of humanity to laugh and criticize and even persecute before arriving at understanding and respect. The fact that 600 years of Ottoman civilization is

---

[422] See Gerber, *supra note 346*, at 183.

highly specialized study illustrates perhaps that the same kind of reservations human beings display when it comes to things much less suspect, such as the sciences, is much more prone to prejudiced chastising than it is to curious interest. Copernicus could arguably be said to have known best the weight of religion, and the kind of patience that had to be endured before one could see it resolve itself with the fact of the day.

The following essay was first published as: The Republic of Turkey and Women in Divorce Cases, Human Rights Review, Volume II, Issue 2, syf. 35-65 (2012).

4

THE REPUBLIC OF TURKEY AND
WOMEN IN DIVORCE CASES

ABSTRACT

The focus of this study is of gender (in) equality in divorce cases within the Turkish Republic era or the Civil Law period. This work examines gender discrimination against women within the framework of international human rights. A short summary of the current Turkish legal system is noted.

Key Words: Republic of Turkey, Women, Gender Equality, Turkish Legal System.

ÖZET

Bu çalışmada; Türkiye Cumhuriyeti yani Medeni Kanun döneminde boşanma davalarında kadın-erkek eşitliği üzerinde durulmuştur. Çalışma, uluslararası insan hakları hukukunda kadına karşı ayrımcılığın engellenmesi noktasına odaklanmıştır. Ayrıca, çalışmanın başlangıç kısmında mevcut Türk hukuk sistemi hakkında kısaca bilgi verilmiştir.

Anahtar Kelimeler: Türkiye Cumhuriyeti, Kadınlar, Cinsiyet Eşitliği, Türk Hukuk Sistemi.

*   *   *

INTRODUCTION

In terms of Islamic law, firstly; the divorce right belongs to the husband, however, a woman can obtain it from her husband and in practice this happened. Moreover, the Ottoman court appears to have been a place of refuge for women. However, the popular belief, even among the academic scholars, is that during the aforementioned era, Muslim women did not have any rights or practiced the rights they did have. The archive documents disprove that belief. Those documents are "concrete evidence about how the pre-modern Islamic legal system functioned and the type of justice people expected."[423] This paper deals with the experience of Turkish woman for gender equality in divorce cases. Therefore, it is true that religion may either shape culture or culture influences religion. Thus the people of society's motives or behaviours are driven by culturally shaped religion or religiously influenced culture.

In this essay I will explore current Republic of Turkey Supreme Court of Appeals (in Turkish "Yargitay") cases in divorce. The founding fathers claimed that they provided freedom to Turkish women. The sample cases will test that claim illustrating that law in theory and practice. After giving a brief explanation about Turkey's current socio-legal history these cases will then be considered. What is the role of Turkish courts in divorce cases? Can they provide equality for Turkish women? Will secular court practices succeed in an Islamic society?

There were significant changes in the political atmosphere of the 19th Century due to the French revolution, rising nationalism and the involvement of Western powers in Ottoman internal affairs due to the loss of Ottoman State power.[424] With the establishment of

---

[423] See Sonbol A., "Women in Shari'ah Courts: A Historical and Methodological Discussion" 27 Fordham Int'l L. J. (2003-4) at 225.

[424] See Malcolm D. Evans, *Religious Liberty and International Law in Europe* (Cambridge, CUP, 1997) at 60-1.

the Republic of Turkey, a unified nationalist State was constructed in 1923. In 1918 just before the fall of the Ottoman Empire [1922] 75 percent of the territories had been lost; in 1878, 85 percent of the population was gone.[425] After winning the War of Independence against the Allied powers, the Republic of Turkey signed the Lausanne Treaty in 1923. The Republic had established a new nationalist secular system; in the words of Smith:

"Turkish nationalism has weighed heaviest on Kurds, Islamist, religious minorities, and the left. A State run Turkish Reformation of Islam fallen in the 1930s; more recent attempts to nationalize Islam have turned the State into a mouthpiece for mainstream Sunni doctrine. The Turkish case suggests that in states with deep societal divisions, the dream of civic nationalism may be a coerced one . . . Religion has been nationalized."[426]

---

[425] See Aksan V. H., "Ottoman to Turk" 61 Int'l J. (2005-2006) at 30. According to the 1844 General Census, the Ottoman State population was 35 million and consisting of 58 % Muslim(20,5 million), 39 % Greek Orthodox [Armenian, Bulgarian and the rest of the Balkans Orthodox included in that number] (13,7 million), 2,5 % Catholic (1 million) and 0,5 % Jews (nearly 200,000).

See Murat Bebiroglu, *Osmanli Devleti'nde Gayrrimuslim Nizamnameleri* [*Non-Muslim Decrees in the Ottoman State*] (Istanbul, Akademi, 2008) at 20-1.

[426] See Smith T. W, "Civic Nationalism and Ethno-Cultural Justice in Turkey" 27 Hum. Rts. Q. (2005) at 436-7. In his article, Smith evidently shows that during the Republic era non-Muslims of Turkey were destroyed by the State policy and practices.

See also Edip Yuksel who is a Kurdish Human Rights Activist and fled from Turkey to USA claims that that the Republic secular ideology, controls, manipulates and exploits religious believes and attack them who are not converted to official version. See Edip Yuksel "Cannibal Democracy, Theocratic Secularism: The Turkish Version" 7 Cardozo J. Int'l & Comp. L. (1999) at 467.

See also the theory of nationalist religion Talal Asad, "Religion, Nation-State, Secularism" in Nation and Religion: Perspectives on Europe and Asia, eds. Peter van der Veer & Hartmut Lehmann (Princeton, PUP, 1999) at 178-196.

I) SOCIO-LEGAL HISTORY OF TURKEY

Modern Turkey has a civil law system similar to that of most other European countries. Legislation is the main source for law and is binding on courts.[427] According to the classifications of European law, Turkish law belongs to the family of Continental European law.[428] This form of law contains separate classes such as Common law, Continental European law, Islamic law, Socialist law, and American law.[429] After the disintegration of the Ottoman Empire and the creation of the Republic of Turkey, the Turkish state aimed to establish its legal and social order according to Western norms.[430] To this end, the framers of the Republic took very radical actions. In 1924, the Turkish Grand National Assembly (TBMM) passed a law to abolish the Sharia (religious) courts (Ser'iye Mahkemeleri). In 1926, the TBMM abolished Islamic law and forced the Swiss Federal Code Civil law system (with adaptations for Turkish society) into the new State's legal system. The German Commercial code was added into Turkish Commercial law. In addition, the Italian Criminal code of 1889 was adapted and put into effect on July 1926.[431] However, a new Turkish Criminal law became effective in June 2005 in order to come in line with the law of the European Union (EU). Turkish law was made to resemble the Continental

---

[427] See Ansay T. and Schneider E. C.(eds.), *Introduction to Turkish Business Law* (Ankara, TK, 2002) at 3.

[428] Oguzman M. K., *Medeni Hukuka Giris [Introduction to Civil Law]* (Istanbul, Filiz, 1990) at 17-25.

[429] Id, at 18-19.

[430] See Ataturk's strategy to establish a Western style state, Paul Dumont, "Hojas For Revolution: The Religious Strategy of Mustafa Kemal Ataturk" 1 J. of the American Institute for the Study of Middle Eastern Civilization (1980) at 17-32.

[431] See Oguzman, supra note 428, at 20-22. See also Gozubuyuk A. S., Giris H.,[Introduction to Law] (Ankara, TK, 2006) at 61.

European Civil law. The Turkish Parliament now enacts new laws and regulations on a daily basis to conform to EU standards.[432]

There is currently great conflict in the legal arena of modern Turkey. In the Second Constitution of the Republic (The Constitution of 1924); Article 2 stated that the state religion was Islam. The fathers of the Republic, however, believed that secularism was to be one of the most important tools of modern Turkish society. Thus in 1928, although the religion of the state was Islam, this was deleted from the Constitution at that time.[433] In 1937, secularism was added into the Turkish constitutional system[434] and today, the modern Turkish state struggles with its secularist traditions in light of an Islamic citizenry.[435] Traditional Turkish state officials prefer to follow the French and German version of secularism, instead of that of the UK, Canadian and American forms. The Turkish state still wishes to design and control thought and religious belief.[436] Some foreign observers of

---

[432] See about Turkey's efforts to become the EU member, Hugg P. R., "The Republic of Turkey in Europe: Reconsidering the Luxembourg Exclusion" 23 Fordham Int'l L. J. (2000) at 606-706. Moreover;

Elizabeth Shakman Hurd, "Negotiating Europe: The Politics of Religion and the Prospects for Turkish Accession" 32 Rev. Int'l Stud. (2006) at 401-418.

Banani D. D., "Reforming History: Turkey's Legal Regime and Its Potential Accession to the European Union" 26 B. C. Int'l & Comp. L. Rev. (2003) at 113-127.

[433] See Boyle K., J. Sheen, eds., *Freedom of Religion and Belief* (London and New York, Routledge, 1997) at 389.

[434] See Gozubuyuk, *supra note* 431, at 61.

[435] See Turkish nation that thinks about secularism and secular practices, Yumni Sezen, Turk Toplumunun Laiklik Anlayisi [Turkish Society's Understanding of Secularism] (Istanbul, MUIFVY, 1993).

Abant Platformu, Din Devlet ve Toplum [Abant Platform: Religion, State and Society] (Istanbul, GYVV, 2000). Even one of the important issues secularism in Turkey, however, it does not fall directly under this chapter or thesis concern.

[436] See more with examples Morris C., *The New Turkey: The Quiet Revolution on the Edge of Europe* (London, Granta Books, 2005) at 60-86.

Turkey believe that the orientation of secularism will be one of the keystones to the future of Turkish society and policy practices."[437] The practicing of hard-line secularism may in itself destroy our democracies since it kills religious freedom in the name of protecting secularism. Moreover, deep-seated defenders of Turkish secularism make the same mistake as Charles Taylor does with Talal Asad's observance[438]:

"The eminent philosopher Charles Taylor is among those who insist that although secularism emerged in response to the political problems of Western Christian society in early modernity-beginning with its devastating wars of religion-it is applicable to non-Christian societies everywhere that have become modern."

Taylor offers that the modern state should make citizenship its main principle identity and in order to unify different identities within itself it should use secularism as the main tool or transcendent mediation ship. However, Asad claims that using secularism is not the way to create social peace and toleration in a modern state.[439] Because Taylor expects that every individual should believe in independent secular ethics and that when there is a conflict persuasion and negotiation will resolve it. Asad argues that:[440]

---

[437] Larrabee F. S., Lesser I. O., *Turkish Foreign Policy in an Age of Uncertainty* (Santa Monica, Rand, 2003) at xiv. See more Szyliowicz J. S., "Religion, Politics and Democracy in Turkey" in ed. Safran W., *The Secular and The Sacred: Nation, Religion and Politics* (London, Frank Cass, 2003) at 188-216.

[438] See Asad T, *The Formations of the Secular: Christianity, Islam, Modernity* (Stanford, SUP, 2003) at 2.

See again Morris C. examples from Turkish secular practices, *supra note* 10, id.

Moreover; Hakan Yavuz M., "Cleansing Islam from the Public Sphere" 54 J. Int'l Aff. (2000) at 21-42.

[439] See Asad T., *The Formations of the Secular: Christianity, Islam, Modernity* (Stanford, SUP, 2003) at 4.

[440] *Id*, at 6, 8.

". . . the nation state is not a generous agent its law does not deal in persuasion . . . A secular state does not guarantee toleration; it puts into play different structures of ambition and fear. The law never seeks to eliminate violence since its object is always to regulate violence."

When this is applied to the modern world it could be said; "Secularism-like religion is such a concept."[441]

What positions are the women of Turkish society in today? When examining this issue depending on the woman's location in a rural area or whether she is in an urban area, they might as well be living in a different world.[442] The new Civil code points out that the husband is no longer the head of the family, however, in practice in the society has done little to change this position.[443]Arat rightly argues that Turkish women were provided civil and political rights equally at the beginning of the Republic, however; still they were restricted "by communal norms and customs" in other words, they were "emancipated but unliberated."[444] In spite of this, the new generation of the 1980's had begun to raise their voices to claim equality and disapprove of the traditional practices.[445]Another Turkish feminist claims that the family law provisions of "the Turkish Civil Code; past and present, demonstrates that although significant progress has been made toward gender equality, certain Islamic laws dealing with female sexuality survive in their entirety, and in contradiction to the general spirit of gender egalitarianism contained in the codes.[446] Yildirim gives those

---

[441] *Id*, at 17. See Turkey how practices secularism like a religion, Ozsunay E., "On the Permissible Scope of Legal Limitations on the Freedom of Religion or Belief in Turkey" 19 Emory Int'l L. Rev. (2005) at 1087-1128.

[442] See Morris C., supra note 436, at 143-4.

[443] Id, at 144.

[444] See Arat Y., "From Emancipation to Liberation: The Changing Role of Women in Turkey's Public Realm" 54 J. Int'l Aff. (2000) at 107.

[445] Id.

[446] See Yildirim S., "Aftermath of a Revolution: A Case Study of Turkish Family Law" 17 Pace Int'l L. Rev. (2005) at 349.

examples from the 1926 Civil Code to prove her claim (Islamic law's influence on the Civil Code) such as: grounds for divorce; adultery; life threatening or psychologically destructive behavior; criminal behavior; abandonment; mental illness, and; irreparable damage to marriage union.[447]Moreover, she adds correctly that the 1926 Civil Code protected the traditional way of the patriarchal family by setting out the structure that the husband was the head of the family; the husband's last name was the family name; the husband was the official representative of the family; the husband was responsible for the wife; the husband had to protect the wife's financial and social interests, and; the husband was also the legal representative for the wife. Moreover, all types of property entering into the family through marriage were under the management of the husband.[448]However, on a positive note, the 1926 Civil Code provided both husband and wife equal entitlement to divorce and divorce grounds were the same for both of them The husband's absolute right to divorce was eliminated and divorce became possible on enumerated grounds by the decision of a judge.[449]

The general tendency of the Supreme Court of Turkey (Yargitay) was that divorce was in the interest of public policy, therefore the judge should have a broad discretion on it.[450] However; in 1988,

---

[447] Id, at 359.

[448] Id, at 359-60.

[449] Id, at 357-8. Yildirim's provided information easily may find at any Turkish family law books, such as;

See Hatemi H., Serozan R. & Arpaci A., Hukuku A. I., [Family Law I] (Istanbul, Filiz Kitabevi, 1993).

See Koprulu B. & Kaneti S., Hukuku A.[Family Law], 2nd ed. (Istanbul, FilizK, 1989)

See Kemal Oguzman M., Dural M., Hukuku A. [Family Law], 13th ed. (Istanbul, FilizK, 2001).

See Sulhi Tekinay S., Aile Hukuku T. [Turkish Family Law], 7th ed. (Istanbul, Beta, 1984).

[450] See Orucu E., "Turkey: Diverse Issues, Continuing Debates" in Andrew Bainham ed., The International Survey of Family Law 1994 (The Hague, MNP, 1994) at 461.

the Parliament of Turkey had introduced a new section into the Article 134 (accepting divorce by mutual consent) of the Civil Code in order "to make divorce easier and to limit the discretion of the judge in divorce cases."[451] Especially in the last ten years, the Turkish legislature had attempted to reform family law issues to the benefit of woman such as;

—that there is no head of the family and spouses work together for the family unit . . . and help each other (Civil Code Article 185)

—the family home is chosen together (Article 186) and woman's work at home is now accepted as a contribution to the family expenses (Article 187), It was previously held that the woman was a helper to her husband and took care of the home, (Article 153)

—the woman still takes on her husband's surname, but she can add her surname onto her husband's (Article 187). In 1997, there was a case before the Constitutional Court challenging this article, the wife wished to use only her maiden name, however, the Court did not strike down the then Article 153 (now Article 187).

—the family unit can be represented by either the husband or the wife for daily life matters (Article 188)

—the husband or wife may work outside of the home and there is no need to obtain permission from the other (Article 192). In 1990, the Constitutional Court rejected the previous stated version of the Article which set down that the wife needs to obtain permission from her husband to work outside of the home . . . etc.[452]

In 2002, the new Civil Code was enacted in Turkey; one major change was revising the language removing all Arabic words and

---

[451] Id.

[452] See Orucu E., "Turkey: Family Law Enters the New Century" in Bainham A. ed., The International Survey of Family Law 2004 Edition (Bristol, FL, 2004) at 472-4.

replacing them with their Turkish equivalents. The majority of the provisional changes were to family law provisions with the aim of providing more gender equality.[453] Yildirim points out[454] that still there is a surviving article in the 2002 version Civil Code from the 1926 Civil Code that is linked to female sexuality; she argues that in the age of technology using the medical tests now available we may determine maternity more easily, this kind of prohibition is rooted in female sexuality in Islam.[455] Article 132 of the Civil Code 2002 states;

"If the marriage has ended, the woman cannot marry for three hundred days starting from the end of the marriage. This period may end when she gives birth. The court may lift this prohibition upon finding the woman is not pregnant, or the divorced spouses want to re-marry each other."

Lastly, in that subsection, I would like to give some basic information about the Turkish court system. The Turkish Judiciary system set out that the civil court system is composed of:

a) General First Instance Courts (criminal courts; magistrate, general criminal, and heavy penal courts, civil courts; civil courts of peace, general civil courts, and commercial courts);

b) Specialized First Instance Courts (juvenile courts, land registration courts, labor courts, intellectual property courts, and family law courts.) The Supreme Court of Appeals (the Court of Cassation in Turkish "Yargitay")

---

[453] See Yildirim, supra note 446, at 364. Actually, some of those changes were given in previous paragraph.

[454] Id, at 365-6.

[455] Id, at 366. She notes that if woman remarried during the waiting period, her new marriage is not void in the 2002 Civil Code such as took the same way in the 1926 Civil Code (Article 154). What it can be said about this argument Islam might not establish this kind of rule just for pregnancy; it could be giving plenty time to people re-think about marriage that is not a game, it should be respected to each other. Another reason could be giving enough time to heal marriage wounds . . . etc.

is the last instance for reviewing decisions and judgments given by criminal and civil courts;

c) The administrative court system (composed of: i) Administrative courts; ii) Tax courts; and iii) Regional administrative courts). The *Council* of State (in Turkish "Danistay") is the last appellant court for administrative and tax court decisions.

d) The Military Judiciary System is that the First instance courts are military courts, military disciplinary courts. The Military High Court of Appeals in Turkish "Askeri Yargitay") is the last instance for these courts. In addition, there is a military high administrative court, which is the first and last instance court for the military personnel administrative cases; and

e) The Constitutional Court examines the constitutionality, in respect of both form and substance of laws, decrees having force of law and the rules of procedure of the Turkish Parliament.[456] The following subsection will explore deeply current divorce cases from the Supreme Court decisions; mainly it will be focusing on the gender equality issues of those cases.

II. DIVORCE IN CURRENT TURKISH LAW WITH SAMPLE CASES

Article 41 of the Constitution of Turkey, establishes that the family is the basic institution of Turkish society. However, there is a clear distinction between families that live in rural areas; the traditional religiously oriented large family model and the other that live in urban areas; the nuclear family, under the influence

---

[456] See Ansay & Wallace, supra note 427, at 14-6.

of globalization.[457] The Civil Code of Turkey was adopted from the Swiss Code that was designed for small families, therefore the Civil Code of Turkey brought contradictions for the families which give importance to moral and religious practices. Although, the Supreme Court and the Constitutional Court had tried to fill the gaps for society and also comply with current international conventions that Turkey had signed and ratified, some gaps still remain.[458] Here I will look at the cases, especially those which show the failure of gender equality. It can be said, as stated above, that formal equality may be established between a man and a woman, but substantive equality whether officially constructed in Turkey may still be unattainable. In other words, it may claim that the law in theory provides this while in practice it is not applied. Since 1923 with the establishment of the Republic of Turkey, there were a lot of changes and amendments to the Turkish legal system in order to catch up with the modern Western system, but Turkey is still adapting new rules to aid accession into the EU.

III. DIVORCE GROUNDS

The Civil Code 2002 provides for divorce in Articles 161 to 182, formerly provided for under Articles 129-150. However, in Turkish academic literature, the reasons for divorce are divided into: a) the sole ground (i-v below) and b) the general ground (vi below).[459] In this section, I follow the structure of the Civil Code. Divorce may be decided on the following grounds:

---

[457] Id.

[458] Ansay at 111-2.

[459] See Dural M. & Oguz T., and Alper Gumus M., Turk Ozel Hukuku III Aile Hukuku [Turkish Private Law III (Volume): Family Law] (Istanbul, FilizK, 2008).

A) Adultery (the Article 161)

Adultery is labelled as one of the sole grounds for divorce in academic literature. Any sexual intercourse with a person other than his/her spouse by a married person is defined as adultery.[460]Adultery is a violation of the duty of fidelity in the marriage that is a legal obligation to spouses, even if it happens only once.[461] If both of the spouses commit adultery, any of them may take the divorce case before the court.[462]

Prior to 1996, there was a tragic comic practice in Turkish law; the Turkish Criminal Code 441 was stating that a husband's adultery occurs if the husband lives with another unmarried woman even in his marital home or somewhere else <u>known to others</u> (Conditional adultery for husband). However, the Criminal Code 440 was required that the wife's adultery takes place only if she had sexual intercourse with a man (Basic Adultery for woman). In other words, sexual intercourse was sufficient for wife, but for husband there were additional conditions for the claim to succeed. In 1996, the Constitutional Court rejected the Criminal Code 441 claiming that there was no legitimate reason to give superiority to an adulterous husband as that was the violation of Article 10 of the Constitution which prohibits discrimination based on gender . . . etc. Terms of imprisonment were for both either the husband or wife from six months to three years.[463] Currently, in Turkish Criminal Law, adultery is not a punishable action due to standardisation with the European Union. Moreover, homosexual relations are not accepted as adultery, however, the spouse may use the provisions of Article 163, dishonourable life to gain a divorce decision.[464] In doctrine,

---

[460] See Hatemi/Serozan, at 220.

[461] See Turgut Akinturk Aile Hukuku [Family Law] (Ankara, YetkinK, 1996) at 211-2.

[462] See Oztan B., Hukuku A. [Family Law] (Ankara, 2005) at 376 or Tekinay, supra note 449, at 200.

[463] See Dural . . . etc., supra note 459, at 102-3.

[464] See Dural, at 102.

it has been argued flirting or the other kind of relationship is not adultery, but it could be a way to determine if there is sexual intercourse, therefore the judge may allow a divorce decision.[465] However, the Supreme Court disagrees with this proposal.

Action of divorce may be suited within six months after the determining of the adultery. The general prescription is for five years (the Article 161). The spouses may forgive each other, if the party cannot have a divorce suit right (the Article 161/3). This is different from the consent given to adultery that is regulated in the Swiss Civil Code, because forgiveness of the petitioner is given after the adultery, while consent is the approval of the action before it has been committed.[466] It is not only the Turkish legal system but also Turkish tradition and moral values that deny the concept of approval of adultery.

Sample Cases

If one of the spouses is captured in a photograph in an informal way other than with the wife or husband, or seen with someone half naked, or seen together in a quiet place such as a forest this evidence of the adultery can be accepted to show the grounds upon which the divorce can be granted in the eyes of the Supreme Court.[467] It seems at some level in some Western societies it is hard to grasp that some of these reasons could be accepted as evidence of the adultery. However, in the view of Turkish society, those actions easily mean that there is a high possibility for the adultery or sexual intercourse. In another case, the Supreme Court held that in a case where the husband had proved that the wife had committed adultery but

---

[465] See Dural, at 103.

[466] See Guven K., General Principles of Turkish Law, 3rd ed. (Ankara, BilgeY, 2007) at 48.

[467] Y2HD.23.09.1993, 7903-7941. [In the Turkish legal system, the case is identified this way. The first part shows the section of the Supreme Court which produced the decision, the second part gives the date, the third part is the application number and the number of the decision.]

the wife claimed that she had been forgiven by him but she could not prove it, the lower court had refused the divorce. The Supreme Court ordered that the adultery was proved and then forgiveness was claimed, but not proved. Therefore, the lower court had to proceed and grant the divorce.[468] The Supreme Court has produced some interesting cases, if the woman's uterus was removed during an operation, the husband should be patient about it, because this reason was not valid as grounds for divorce[469]. However in a case where the wife was raped, it is not adultery but there could be grounds to grant a divorce based on severe incompatibility. This is because even though a husband tolerates the situation, Turkish society does not accept this situation and the husband will lose his credibility in society.[470] This is still used as a precedent in the court, a position that should urgently be addressed as it is a clear violation of gender equality. It is evident that Turkey may establish gender equality in terms of the public sphere, but not in the private sphere. It is not good enough merely to structure formal equality. This should be followed by the important task of constructing substantive equality.

B) Attempt Against Life, Extreme Cruelty and Behaviour Against Honour (the Article 162)

Any act by one of the spouses, indicating intention to kill the other is seen as an attempt to kill. Any actions of a spouse inflicting grievous bodily injury or mental suffering of the other spouse is known as extreme cruelty. These are the inhuman treatments of a spouse. For example to refuse to save the spouse who attempted in suiciding, beating, swearing are the most routinely granted grounds for divorce in practice.[471]Another new clause added by this provision is "serious insult." Such as; calling the spouse an idiot, maniac, slut, non virgin, dishonourable, or you cannot handle anything,

---

[468] Y2HD.27.06.2005,7976-10033.

[469] Y2HD.2.6.1977,4349-4616

[470] Y2HD.1.3.1976,1414-1767.

[471] See Guven, supra note 466, at 48.

you cannot be a man or woman . . . etc.[472] Under this doctrine, the following also fall under this provision; leaving the spouse hungry, passing on contagious sicknesses over sexual intercourse, leaving the spouse as naked on the marble area, locking the spouse into a room, forcing participation in abnormal sexual intercourse.[473] Moreover, under this provision, to prove there is attempting against life of the spouse, the aim of killing must be identified.[474] Unfortunately, there is a belief in Turkish doctrine that a verbal threat to the spouse even a very serious one is not accepted as an attempt against life.[475] The first, Turkish doctrine should be reformed on this issue, then the local and Supreme Court practices will follow it. We should take into consideration the differences between men and women. Woman should be protected against violence in private spheres. In addition, the new version of the Criminal Court 2004, Article 232 orders that if a person commits extreme cruelty against those who live in the same cohabitation, punishment should range from two months to two years.

Sample Cases

The Supreme Court cases established the principles under this provision as follows: one beating is enough[476], calling the spouse dishonourable in the market[477], stating "my wife is not virgin" in

---

[472] See Tekinay, supra note 449, at 221.
[473] See Hifzi Veldet Velidedeoglu, Ailenin Cilesi Bosanma [Family's Suffering: Divorce] (Istanbul, FilizK, 1976) at 199. Ferit Hakki Saymen & Halid Kemal Elbir, Turk Medeni Hukuku: Aile Hukuku [Turkish Civil Law: Family Law] (Istanbul, FilizK, 1960) at 247. Aydin Zevkliler & Ayse Havutcu, Medeni Hukuk: Temel Bilgiler [Civil Law: Basic Knowledge] (Ankara, YetkinK, 2004) at 932. Bilge Oztan, Aile Hukuku [Family Law] (Ankara, YetkinK, 2005) at 230. See Akinturk, supra note 39, at 215.
[474] See Tekinay, supra note 449, at 218-9.
[475] See Omer Ugur Genccan, Bosanma, Tazminat ve Nafaka Hukuku [The Law of Divorce, Compensation, and Alimony] (Ankara, Yetkin, 2008) at 131.
[476] Y2HD.4.3.1996,1432-2070.
[477] Y2HD.26.05.1986,4702-5431.

a café.[478] If a case is taken under this provision, the judge cannot use the other divorce provisions to establish a divorce verdict.[479] It is a rule in Turkish private law that the judge cannot take into consideration reasons other than the parties have claimed unless required by law. Here also these practices show that no discrimination against woman occurs under this provision.

C) Felonies and Dishonourable Life (the Article 163)

The conviction of a spouse for a humiliating crime, such as theft (excluding "political crimes") and dishonourable conduct, such as habitual drunkenness are grounds for divorce. If one of the parties commits a crime which causes infamy, the other spouse may request to be divorced. Felonies are considered crimes against reputation. For that reason a suit of divorce cannot be granted in the case of simple crimes (misdemeanours) such as traffic offences. Those are accepted as felonies under this provision are: embezzling, malversatio, subornation, bribery, theft, fraud, counterfeit, abusing confidence or trust to bad ends and bankruptcy.[480] Under the doctrine, those actions are identified that break the basis of the marriage's moral values[481]. Dishonourable life is the way of living against public ethics. Public disgrace or dishonour means the dishonourable life of an alcoholic, gambler, drug addict, homosexual, sodomite or bestial.[482] The judge will look at society's moral values, not the type of felony, thus it is under the judge's discretion whether the action whether could be grounds for divorce.[483] However, according to the provision, because of this article, spouses may open a divorce suit at any time if one of the spouses committed a felony or engaged a dishonourable life.

---

[478] Y2HD.19.04.1951,2561-2993.

[479] Y2HD.12.03.2008,21691-3289.

[480] See Namik Yalcinkaya & Sakir Kaleli, Bosanma Hukuku [Divorce Law] (Ankara, Yetkin, 1987) at 732.

[481] See Tekinay, supra note 449, at 222.

[482] See Guven, supra note 466, at 49. Y2HD.03.05.2004,5027-5634.

[483] See Oguzman & Dural, supra note 449, at 118.

Sample Cases

The spouse may have committed a felony but the suing party must prove that because of felony, the marriage is no longer bearable.[484] Mostly, in Turkey, it is the husband that commits these kind of felonies. I believe that if the judge finds that a felony is against public/social values, there should be no additional proof needed as to the viability of the marriage. The judge may grant a divorce verdict. It is interesting that in another case, the Supreme Court held that the woman committed theft; therefore the lower court had to grant the divorce.[485] It is evident that this is a clear violation of gender equality. Generally, the Supreme Court looking at the viability of the marriage under this provision must be proved, but when the issue comes to women, the Supreme Court believes that they do not require this condition as the societal beliefs are good enough for them. The husband takes care of the family, therefore the husband is considered superior to the wife. Once again, establishing verbal or legal equality in the public realm does not give us a solution for constructing equality in practice.

D) Desertion (the Article 164)

Desertion is the abandonment of a wife by a husband or vice versa, with unreasonable grounds intending never to return and to refuse performance of marital obligations arising from marriage. Not every desertion justifies the divorce. Desertion is a ground for divorce, it depends on justified reasons. Grounds such as military service, appointment as a public agent to another place, to be treated in hospital do not justify the suit of divorce against the spouse concerned.[486] If one forces the other to leave or prevents him/her returning home without good cause, the prevented party

---

[484] Y2HD.01.12.2004,13099-14288.

[485] Y2HD.23.01.2001,15378-1057.

[486] See Zevkliler & Havutcu, supra note 486, at 937. Oguzman & Dural, supra note 449, at 120.

is considered not to have deserted.[487] In practice, women are facing these kinds of experiences.[488] The suing party should wait for four months from the date of the forced or prevented time. The spouse whose wife or husband has left his cohabitated home without any legal cause for a period of more than six months (previously three months), may ask him or her to return within two months, by means of an order of the court. If it is to no effect, divorce may be requested.

For a divorce decision based on desertion; the suing party should show that: the other party had left the cohabitation place; the sued party intended to end the cohabitation; desertion did not occur because of a legal reason such as military service or hospitalisation; and it should be sent to the sued party "the court warning" after the fourth month of the desertion. The court warning sent states that failure to return to the cohabitation place within two months will lead to the suit opening. The deserted spouse cannot sue the other party (the Article 164). Most of the time, due to the economic weakness of women in Turkey, men force the woman from the cohabitation place in order to have a divorce suit against his wife based on desertion.[489]Without substantive equality, the formal one is not working. Thus, Turkish legislature and civil society urgently need to produce solutions for establishing and maintaining substantive equality between man and woman, especially for the married couples.

---

[487] See Pinar Ozlem Demir, Yeni Medeni Kanunda Evli Kadinlarin Hukuki Durumu Ile Ilgili Yenilik ve Degisiklikler [In the New Civil Law Novelties and Amendments on Married Woman Status] (Istanbul, Beta, 2004) at 8.
[488] Id.
[489] It is a common knowledge about Turkish society of today. See supra note 553.

Sample Cases

Under this provision, the Supreme Court has produced very interesting cases. Particularly, decreeing that the cohabitation place should be chosen by the spouses or under the discretion of the Family law court. If the spouses did not choose the cohabitation place in the divorce processes based on desertion together, "the court warning order" states that the return order is invalid.[490] This is beneficial to women as before the new version of the Civil Code, the husband always chose the living place for the marriage, now it is up to both. It give some power to the woman to sue her case from where she lives. In another case, the Supreme Court held that before "the court warning" if there is physical violence or verbal threat, "the court warning order" is not acceptable, thus the lower court should alter its verdict.[491] Where the wife was beaten before "the court warning order," the Supreme Court held that the warning is not valid.[492] During the term of (two months) "court warning order" the suing party (the husband) made a phone call to the other party: "do not come back, I will make this place unliveable for you." The Supreme Court sees that it is not acceptable for those words to wish the continuation of the marriage, thus the husband is not acting cordially. That is why "the court warning order" is invalid.[493] The Supreme Court also agrees that if there is legitimate reason, the spouse cannot go back to the cohabitation place even there is a "court warning order" to return the living place, but the sued party must prove such a legitimate reason.[494]

Furthermore, the Supreme Court does not accept as valid "the court warning order" if the spouse (almost always a man in

---

[490] Y2HD.29.05.2007,7462-9398.

[491] Y2HD.19.03.2007,16364-4353.

[492] Y2HD.14.01.2003,13613-193.

[493] Y2HD.08.03.2005,16976-3475.

[494] Y2HD.25.09.2006,5662-12407.

practice) began to live with another person.[495]Also the Court sees this action (living with another woman) as putting the wife "under pressure". Therefore, again, the court warning is not void.[496] The Court practice has established that when the suing party gathers "the court warning order" should send or deposit some money into the sued party's account. That money should be enough to cover return to the cohabitation place.[497] Lastly, there were many cases before the Court where husbands were forcing wives to leave the cohabitation place and then after four months, they were seeking "the court warning order" to invite their wives to the living place and threaten them not to return. The Supreme Court holds that this threat it is a legitimate reason for wives to leave the cohabitation place.[498]

It is shown that divorce based on desertion is possible when after four months pass and then the suing party obtains "the court warning order" by the statement of return to the cohabitation place within two months. After two months, there could be a divorce suit against the other party based on the desertion. The lower court will look at only the procedural and time conditions if they pass the test, the judge does not have any discretion, divorce verdict will be delivered. Once more here I would like to point out that even court practices shows that legal enforcement cannot stop violence against a married woman who deserted or is in the beginning of the divorce process. The husbands' threats to his wife still are mostly ignored, but in many cases, these threats are followed by beatings, wounding or killings.[499] Thus, women should be protected in these private spheres.

---

[495] Y2HD.20.12.2006,11758-18035.

[496] YHGK.06.11.2002,2/824-896. It is a precedent case that produced by the all sections involvement of the Supreme Court.

[497] Y2HD.03.07.2006,10193-10659.

[498] Y2HD.17.05.2004,5596-6318. Y2HD.19.03.2007,16364-4353.

[499] See supra note 553.

E) Incurable Insanity (the Article 165)

According to Article 165, in order to bring a case before the court some conditions are required: one of the spouse develops a mental illness; the illness is incurable; and because of this mental illness marriage life is unbearable. Moreover, the mental illness should appear after marriage. The situation should be proved by an official health report. The previous version of this Article (Article 133) had stricter conditions: to have a divorce case based on mental illness at least three years must pass after the illness appeared. Considering Turkish society lifestyle, as the woman manages the home life, cooking, cleaning etc. she would have to nurse her mentally ill husband for three years before she can apply for divorce. But the new version of the Article has added that the suing party should prove the marriage life is unbearable. This should be removed as a condition as the suing party provides the court with an official health report that concludes the illness is incurable. If she or he would like to be loyal to the partner, she/he can do it. But the law should not force people to do something if they do not want to do it with their free will.

In doctrine and practice schizophrenia and paranoia has accepted as incurable mental illness.[500] Someone can think that way, if the spouse is mentally ill rather than proving the unbearable condition, can the healthy partner use Article 166 (severe incompatibility, general ground for divorce) claiming that because of illness the marriage broke down? The Supreme Court strictly ordered that . . . because the sued party is retarded, the party is not acting with his free will, thus there can not be a divorce case against him. The case can be established only by the Article 165 that based on incurable insanity.[501] It is the nature of private law in civil law systems. Lastly, those actions are accepted as unbearable for the marriage if the

---

[500] See Akinturk, supra note 461, at 240.

[501] Y2HD.06.02.2008,4261-1013. For the parallel decision, Y2HD.14.11.2007,2194-15644.

retarded party attacks the other partner or children of her/his, or causes murder of the child.[502]

Sample Cases

The Supreme Court unfortunately held that even if the spouse has an incurable mental illness, if the suing party cannot prove an unbearable condition exists because of this illness, the case will be turn downed.[503]Actually Supreme Court practices might defeat that unbearable condition easily as the official health report already serves that the ill person is in a situation that can not be cured. It would be some kind of torture to force someone to live with the ill partner. Urgently, legislatures should remove this condition or the Supreme Court can eliminate that by its verdicts. It may claim that basically the partner has incurable illness, there is no extra condition required. In another case, the Supreme Court has repeated itself, the official health report should include that this illness is incurable and makes the marriage unbearable.[504]

F) Severe Incompatibility (Irretrievable or Matrimonial Breakdown) (the Article 166)

This is the only general ground for divorce in Turkish law. That gives the judge process to his/her own discretion on the case. Those cases deemed as incompatibility between individuals. A conflict between the spouses may not be decided a ground strong enough to be divorced, while for another one it is unbearable sort of life. If the harmony and the happiness of the spouses have been lost absolutely, it may be decided that they are incompatible. Previously, the spouse responsible for the breakdown was not entitled to sue for divorce

---

[502] See Ali Ihsan Ozugur, Bosanma, Ayrilik ve Evlenmenin Iptali Davalari [Cases of Divorce, Separation, and Cancelation of Marriage] (Ankara, Adalet, 2008) at 178.

[503] Y2HD.17.03.2005,2242-4252.

[504] Y2HD.14.09.2005,8749-9940.

before the court. Now, any party can bring the divorce before the court. With the exception of the other party, at least cause some breakdown for the marriage. According to the Article, not every conflict justifies granting divorce, only the severe ones.

The suing party should prove two things; one is that there is an event that caused the matrimonial breakdown; and two that because of this event the marriage is unbearable. Any event causes the unbearably falls under this provision.[505] For example, those actions that causes severe incompatibility and makes unbearable of marriage[506]: over jealousy; not cooking; even once beating the spouse; forcing to leave the cohabitation place; threatening; letting in someone in to the cohabitation place rather than the spouse for sexual intercourse; first night the wife was found not to be a virgin; verbally always putting down the spouse; in quiet places seen with other man or woman; woman seen night times in the streets as habit or going unknown places; leaving the house without telling the spouse; telling the third person of disliking his/her partner; drunkenness as habit; gambling as habit; having sexual relationship with other persons; changing the door locks without telling the partner; not to care of the partner when she/he is ill . . . etc. If such behaviour causes the partner not to bear the marriage any more, the judge may decide that the marriage falls under severe incompatibility, thus will grant the divorce. The most important thing about these actions are that the partner knows and does them intentionally with his/her free will.[507]

In two normative cases, the family relations are deemed to be injured fundamentally:

a) If a previous action for divorce on various grounds has been rejected by the court but the spouses could not come together to perform a family and have lived separately for at least three years, the action depending on the

---

[505] See Ozugur, supra note 502, at 183.
[506] Id.
[507] Id, at 184.

accusation of incompatibility, should be accepted by the court (the Article 166/4).

b) Divorce by mutual agreement; in case of a contract in contemplation of divorce, the judge must divorce the spouses. Divorce by the consent of the spouses married for at least one year, is demanded by the parties together or the case is accepted by the other party, tendering a contract, which regulates the legal consequences of divorce. The court is only authorised to examine the conditions according to the benefit of the children and parties. If the court is sure about the agreement has been accepted with the free wills of the spouses, the case has to be accepted (the Article 166/3 regulates the divorce by mutual agreement).

Sample Cases

This kind of divorce ground is the most popular one and has used extensively in Turkish court practices.[508] Therefore, the Supreme Court has produced many parallel cases about that provision. Mostly, they are of benefit to woman. Such as, if the husband verbally assaulted his wife and used physical violence against her, he cannot have a divorce case under this provision, because he solely caused the breakdown of the marriage.[509] On its own "sterility" cannot be grounds for divorce.[510] In another case, the wife has epilepsy which also alone cannot be grounds for divorce.[511] The suing party has the right to sue her husband because the husband used violence against her and forced her to leave the home, thus the lower court should deliver a divorce verdict.[512] Where the husband bears the full fault because he had sexual intercourse with another woman, his case based on matrimonial breakdown had to

---

[508] See Genccan, supra note 475, at 287-8.

[509] Y2HD.17.07.2007,21979-11425.

[510] Y2HD.27.02.2003,1119-2551.

[511] Y2HD.11.05.1998,4799-5677.

[512] Y2HD.20.06.2007,21292-10446.

be refused by the lower court.[513] The wife's divorce case could not be accepted by the lower court, because she lives with another man and bears the full fault.[514] If the spouse carries full fault, the divorce suit cannot be taken into the court by him or her.[515] It is evident that who bears the full fault cannot depend on this provision to sue his/her partner.

In another case the Supreme Court correctly held that the wife has a right to sue her husband based on the provision of Article 166, because during the pregnancy term, her husband did not look after her.[516] The Supreme Court expects that the event should cause on the other party unbearable marriage. If the party cannot prove that the event has caused an unbearable marriage, the divorce case cannot be processed, thus the lower court should refuse the case.[517] In another case, the Supreme Court acted to protect a woman; if the husband abuses alcohol and beats his wife, he carries full fault, therefore the wife's divorce case had to be accepted and a divorce granted.[518] However, if the Supreme Court sees that the spouse has kleptomania, the court cannot establish a divorce verdict as it is an illness, this cancels punishment as it is not happening because of free will.[519]

If there is an event that causes breaking of trust/confidence that is the reason for divorce under this provision.[520] In an interesting case, the Law General Committee of the Supreme Court held (stare decis case) that the wife's diary had found by the husband in the cohabitation place, it can be used against her.[521] It could be vice versa, the husband's diary can be used against him. However, from

---

[513] Y2HD.18.06.2007,20905-10304.
[514] Y2HD.28.05.2007,19698-8950.
[515] Y2HD.19.03.2007,16136-4320.
[516] Y2HD.14.03.2007,16079-4039.
[517] Y2HD.21.03.2005,2417-4442.
[518] Y2HD.16.06.2003,7780-8765.
[519] Y2HD.04.03.1991,1184-3883.
[520] Y2HD.08.04.2003,2415-5129.
[521] YGHK.25.09.2002,2/617-648.

the procedural law perspective, this stare decis (precedent) verdict should be eliminated from the practice of Turkish courts. Because, if people has began to believe whatever they write down even in their home, one day it might be used against them by their partner. Definitely, it may damage confidence or trust between the husband and wife.

IV) THE SEPARATION ORDER

This subsection, I will look at the separation order in divorce cases. If the spouse has the right to bring a divorce case before the court may demand judicial separation from the judge. The judge may order it if there is possibility for the spouses that they could live together in the future. But, if the suing party has asked for the separation order, the judge can not give divorce verdict. However, if the suing party has brought before the court a divorce suit, and divorce reason has approved by the court, the judge either deliver a divorce verdict or separation order. Judicial separation may be obtained on almost the same grounds as divorce, and the court relieves the petitioner from the duty of cohabitation. Both the husband and wife relationship continues despite judicial separation. The judge may decide from one year to three years for separation (the Article 171/1). It is interesting to note that during the judicial separation if the husband dies, the wife may have a claim against for maintenance against her death husband's estate, but the husband does not have this right (the Article 170-172). It is one of positive discrimination for the benefit of wife. We should note that it is very rare practice to obtain judicial separation in Turkey.[522]

---

[522] See Ansay & Schneider, supra note 427.

Sample Cases

The Supreme Court believes that if there is no chance that the partners in a marriage union will live together in a cohabitation place, the lower court judge should deliver divorce verdict instead of separation order.[523]In another case, the Supreme Court rightly has argued that if the divorce conditions have not been proved, it can not be a separation order, and if there is no any chance spouses will not live together again and divorce conditions are fulfilled, the judge cannot give a separation order. [he has to deliver divorce verdict].[524] In the end of the separation order, if the spouses did not come back to live together, one of them may go to the court and ask for divorce verdict.[525] Lastly, I would like to point out the case; that the determination of the duration of the separation order is under the judge's discretion.[526]Actually, the Turkish private law system provides judges discretions in many areas[527]; however, judges should be elected among well experienced law practitioners.

V) THE LEGAL CONSEQUENCES OF DIVORCE

In that subsection, it will be explored outcomes of divorce in Turkish legal system. In order to establish a substantive equality between men and women in a system, we also should look at the consequences of divorce. The legal system might be a good one for divorce, however after the divorce, one of the essential issues to provide justice in terms of substantive equality, there could be a

---

[523] Y2HD.07.06.2007,20660-9576.

[524] Y2HD.20.03.2006,19665-3692.

[525] Y2HD.26.05.2005,6078-8314.

[526] Y2HD.03.10.1983,6664-7034.

[527] See general Ansay & Schneider, supra note 5. Currently, if someone has graduated from the law faculty in Turkey, s/he takes the exam by given the justice ministry and if s/he passes, there is a one and a half year internship in the courts. Around the age 22-25 they sit on the bench as a full judge. What I propose, those newly has graduated, they have to stay at least 10 years in practice environment and then parliament may appoint them.

disadvantage for woman because of divorce verdict. Especially, in Turkish example when a woman is economically weak, a divorce verdict might not give what woman expects from the court.

a) During the marriage the parties should cohabitate in a place or home that arranged by them (the Article 186). When there is demand for divorce or the separation order; both husband and wife entitled to choose a separate domicile if the court permits that under fair reasons such as health-popularity-or business affairs (the Article 197). Previous version of the Civil Code was stating that the husband may choose the cohabitation place. With this new version of the provision in the Civil Code has recognizes equality between husband and wife. It is another noble step in terms of establishing substantive equality in private realm. The Supreme Court held that none of the spouses as alone can terminate the contract of the cohabitation place or can sell or limit the other spouse rights on it, in fact, even they had lived separately around two years.[528]

b) According to the Article 187 a married woman has to take the family name of her husband, after the divorce she may use her maiden name. As earlier stated she can use her maiden name before her husband's last name upon her written request. This article urgently should be revised from the Turkish law. It is clear evidence of violation of gender equality; providing superiority to husband over the wife using the last name of the husband. As an individual person a woman may able to choose either her maiden name or husband's surname or mixing them. If the wife has legal interest in carrying of ex-husband's family name and this will not cause damage to the husband, she has the right to use it by the court decision, until it

---

[528] Y2HD.23.05.2005,5698-7970.

has been demanded to be cancelled by the husband (the Article 173). Actually, this provision provides positive discrimination to the woman. The previous version Code was ordering that when there is a divorce the wife had to use her maiden name that was causing confusion as a mother in having a different last name than her children.

c) The Article 185 orders that with the marriage both of parties are under the duty of co-habitance, support, assistance and fidelity. Those duties could be in monetary or moral ways. During the divorce or separation process when the judge look at the case s/he carefully scrutinize both of the spouses "living places-living expenses-and protection and taking care of the children" situations and then s/he delivers interim decisions about those issues (the Article 169). In Turkish legal system that alimony called "tedbir nafakasi" [interim alimony]. In the lower court practices, even the wife has equal earning to her husband's earnings that the lower courts had settled interim alimony for wives. However, the Supreme Court disagrees with the lower court practices and demands that if the wife has equal earning to her husband, the court can not deliver interim alimony for the wife during the process of divorce or separation.[529] Especially, those cases happen when the spouses work as government agent such as civil servant or teachers, they have almost equal earnings. The lower courts of Turkey still thinks woman is dependent on her husband, but the reality is changing in Turkey that women take more employment in job sector more than twenty years ago in Turkey. Thus, judges have to carefully follow up what is occurring in the country. In the following interesting cases, the Supreme Court again has corrected lower court verdicts; during the divorce

---

[529] Y2HD.17.07.2007,10900-11439.   Y2HD.14.03.2007,16953-4029. Y2HD.20.06.2006,3984-9852. Y2HD.06.06.2006,1796-8951.

process, the wife has began to live with another woman, thus the court can not deliver interim alimony for benefit of woman . . . during the case the wife was engaged with another woman, therefore she does not deserve interim alimony.[530] The Supreme Courts also pointed out that since 01.01.2002 [process date of the New Civil Code] the wife should participate into marriage union expenses, if she has economic power.[531]

During the divorce case or after the divorce, any of the parties may ask for "poorness alimony" [yoksulluk nafakasi] to the other side if s/he is going to become under wealth because of divorce (the Article 175). Poorness alimony can be for unlimited time if the spouse is destitute on condition s/he is not more faulty party (the Article 175). Alimony ends upon death, marriage to another, living with another as if married, or leading a dishonourable life (the Article 176). The Supreme Court practices also have maintained that if the spouse is in full fault, s/he can not demand poorness alimony from the partner.[532] The other verdict of the Supreme Court has repeated the words of the Article 176; the wife has began to live with another man like they are married, thus the lower court cannot deliver poorness alimony for the benefit of woman. The verdict should be altered.[533] Lastly, in many cases, the Supreme Court has turned down the verdicts of the lower courts; if the woman did not demand the poorness alimony, the lower court can not order the payment of the poorness alimony for the benefit of

---

[530] Y2HD.28.03.2006,17446-4283. Y2HD.10.03.2003,1034-3249.
[531] Y2HD.23.06.2003,8243-9207.   Y2HD.06.02.2003,550-1771. Y2HD.22.02.2006,17614-2091.
[532] Y2HD.27.03.2007,10664-5007.   Y2HD.21.03.2007,16393-4557. Y2HD.23.02.2006,17799-2154.
[533] Y2HD.06.04.2006,20637-4977.

woman. The court can not go beyond the wife's demand in that issue.[534]

The other alimony is given when there is divorce or separation who has the parental authority on children ask the other spouse participate for the expenses of children that called "participation alimony"[istirak nafakasi]. In other words, it is allowance of participation, after the divorce or during the separation time one spouse has parental authority, the other one should contribute to expenses of raising the children (the Article 182/2). The Supreme Court decisions rightly stresses out that participation alimony should been determined based on current economic conditions and economic and social statues of parties.[535] The Court also pointed that if the child is adult (18 years and over), the parent can not demand participation alimony on behalf of him/her.[536] Who has the parental authority or child is under her/his custody did not demand participation alimony from the court, but the court should determine and order payment of participation alimony for the child.[537] In an interesting case that smells stereotype that altered by the Supreme Court; always man has economic power in Turkish society. The lower court has refused the father of children's demand for participation alimony from the ex-wife that children (2) were under custody of the father after divorce. The Supreme Court has delivered that the father has parental authority that children are under custody of their father, when the mother has economic

---

[534] Y2HD.21.03.2007,16407-4535. Y2HD.29.03.2006,20109-4376. Y2HD.15.03.2006,19039-3480. Y2HD.06.10.2005,11074-13633.

[535] Y2HD.19.07.2007,11626-11591. Y2HD.04.10.2005,10976-13448.

[536] Y2HD.27.02.2006,17593-2325. Y2HD.20.10.2003,12662-13902.

[537] Y2HD.24.02.2005,695-2771.

power she has to pay participation alimony for her children.[538]

Material damages are awarded for existing or expected interests. There has to be a divorce verdict-who demands award s/he should be less faulty or no fault position-because of divorce s/he should face to damages-and there has to be reason between damages and award (the Article 174). The Supreme Court has repeated in many cases, if the suing party was no faulty or less faulty was found by the court in divorce case, s/he can demand award because of material damages.[539] If the court found out the parties' faults are equal none of them can demand award for material damages.[540] Once again, the Supreme Court expects that from the lower courts; awards should be based on according to parties' economic power, social statues, and current economic environment.[541]

Moral damages are awarded if the party is faultless or less faulty and if his/her personal rights are damaged (the Article 174/2) after the divorce. If one of the spouses verbally has insulted the other spouse during the marriage time, after the marriage s/he can demand award for moral damages.[542] During the marriage time, the husband did not take care of his wife such as not to take her to the hospital when she is sick, moreover he verbally insulted her and forced her to leave the home, thus he has to pay for moral damages.[543] The Supreme Court again pointed out that if the spouses are equal at fault, there is no moral

---

[538] Y2HD.20.01.2003,14614-587.

[539] Y2HD.19.07.2007,22200-11546.   Y2HD.08.12.2004,13708-14683. Y2HD.11.12.2003,15370-16627.

[540] Y2HD.09.07.2007,10079-10759. Y2HD.16.04.2007,17952-6371.

[541] Y2HD.31.05.2005,4324-8483.

[542] Y2HD.19.07.2007,22190-11538.

[543] Y2HD.16.07.2007,21690-11365.

damages award such as same for material damages.[544] The Supreme Court or lower court practices how have determine the equal fault for spouses that for example one of the spouse had sexual intercourse with someone and the other one did the same thing, or both of them verbally assaulted each other. The courts call those situations that they are in an equal fault position. In an interesting case, the husband had prevented his wife from seeing her family (mother, father, brothers and sisters), the Supreme Court held that the wife had to be awarded for moral damages because of her husband's behaviour.[545]

Finally, all law suits lapse after one year from the finalisation of the divorce verdict where previously there was no time limits.

d) By the marriage children are legitimized who are born during the marriage, even three hundred days after the termination of marriage (the Article 285). Both of spouses have parental authority upon children, this authority has exercised together (the Article 336). If they are not married, the mother represents the child (the Article 337). By separation or divorce the parental authority is given one of the parties by the court decision, after the hearing both of the parents (the Article 182/1). In case of death, the other party has the parental authority alone. Remarkably after the signing and ratifying children rights conventions by Turkey, the Supreme Court has carefully reviewed the custodian cases and search for the best interest of the child. Such as, if the child has reached the mature ability, the court should listen to the child before giving her/his custody to one of the parent.[546] Interestingly, in some cases the Supreme Court stated that

---

[544] Y2HD.16.07.2007,10134-11238.

[545] Y2HD.30.04.2007,5380-7164.

[546] Y2HD.20.11.2006,7797-15997.

the child is fifteen years old, she had to listen before her custody given to any of her parent, otherwise it is against the law [of Turkey] and international conventions.[547] The Supreme Court also began to break social clichés of Turkey on some cases; the twin children were under custody of mother, she was married, because of that her custody rights on children can not be terminated.[548] Generally, the Supreme Court enthusiastically prefers to give the child custody/parental authority to mother when there is divorce between the spouses.[549]

e) The marriage between the spouses and their blood relatives entitles an affinity, after the divorce this relation continues (the Article 129/2).

f) By the marriage settlement, spouses may regulate their property relations before or after the marriage; either they choose: a)separated property system(the Article 242-243); b)shared separated property system (the Article 244-255); c) common property system (the Article 256-281); or d) earned property system (the Article 202/1, 218-241). If there is no marriage settlement, the law accepts that system of fusion of the acquired property that basically depends on the participation of the property and income acquired during the marriage (earned property system). Divorce and annulment of marriage cease the contractual matrimonial property systems.

---

[547] Y2HD.08.11.2005,12496-15273.
[548] Y2HD.13.01.2004,16607-179.
[549] Y2HD.01.07.2003,6847-9975.   Y2HD.05.12.2006,10351-16974.
Y2HD.09.11.2006,8304-15357.

VI) THE LEGAL PROCEDURE ON DIVORCE CASES

Lastly in this subsection we will look at the legal procedure for divorce cases. Before the 2002 version of the Civil Code, the general rule was the divorce suit may be opened in the family union's place that always was in favour of the husband; the married woman was her husband's abode, in reality where the husband lived. The new Code has maintained either the district court of the place of the last six months where the spouses lived or the suing spouse lived. Now, the new system, the court is the abode of the spouse bringing the divorce case into the court. It means in interest of woman.

The court of family is on duty to deal with divorce cases. They established in January 2003[550]as a special court to deal the cases that arises court from family law issues. Previously, those cases were handled by the general civil court (Asliye Hukuk Mahkemesi). What brought those courts into the Turkish legal system; before looking at the core of the case, the judge must look at what the problems are of the spouses and children and then try to solve issues with peace if there is possibility-finally, there are specialist who serve under those courts such as psychologist, pedagogue and social worker when the case needs those ones by the order of the judge they involve the case to help the judge and parties.[551] Especially, those specialists have begun to help judges in the issue

---

[550] The Official Gazette, No: 24997, published on January 18, 2003.

[551] See general Nese Dogan Yuksel, "Nereden Cikti Aile Mahkemelerindeki Bu Uzmanlar" [Where Did They Come Those Specialists Who Are in the Family Court] Istanbul Bar Journal (March 2007), Special Issue on Family Law, at 131-146.

of determination of the child custody or parental authority after the divorce or during the separation order.[552]

CONCLUDING REMARKS

Actually whats happening in Turkey? Those cases show that generally, Turkish law has constructed formal equality between man and woman in divorce issues, but particularly, some areas still should be eliminated from the practices of the court, in the name of gender equality. It is very normal to see in a daily basis on news; women beaten or killed during divorce process or after

---

[552] See those cases held by the Supreme Court is turning down the lower court verdicts because of not involve of those specialists in the determination of the parent who will has the parental authority or child custody.

Y2HD, 19.10.2006,6855-14355-Y2HD,08.04.2008,2369-4863-Y2HD,07.06.2005,6527-8789-Y2HD,28.12.2006,12224-18581-Y2HD.20.03.2007,10111-4490 . . . etc.

the divorce decision.[553] Law in books or court are different than in real life practice. The rule of law does not work properly, Turkish women demand substantive equality, formal one does not provide solution for their problems. We should note that as earlier stated with the establishment of the Republic in Turkey, the roots of Islam officially has been tried to be suppressed from the society. The founding fathers of the Republic made the system depend on nationalism. Women of Turkey have been represented as a new face of the Republic to all over the world. It has been rightly stated that "women's roles have been defined as inextricably linked with the family and domestic sphere."[554] In other words, in early stages of the nation building women have been portrayed as one of the main free figures of the Republic. Moreover, their role was seen culturally as preservation of national identity in society. It is acceptable that

---

[553] See "Esinden Bosanan Kadinin Cesedi Bulundu" [Divorced Woman Body Found] at http://www.hurriyet.com.tr/gundem/12438893.asp (accessed on September 1, 2009).

See "Bosanan Kadinlar Hangi Zorluklari Yasiyor?" [What Do Kind of Hardship Face Divorced Women?] at http://www.turkhukuksitesi.com/showthread.php?+=6935 (accessed on September 1, 2009).

See "Bosanma Nedenleri Arastirmasi Basladi" [Research Had Begun: Reason of Divorce] at http://www.aile.gov.tr/bosanma (accessed on September 1, 2009).

See Ishak Ozkan & Omer Boke, "Bosanma Ile Sonlanan Evliliklerde Kadinin Hedef Oldugu Saldirganlik" [Marriage Had Ended Divorce: Violence Against Woman] at http://www.aile.selcuk.edu.tr/text/makale1.htm (accessed on September 1, 2009).

It is interesting to note that all family law books in Turkey briefly points out that there is violence against woman because of demanding divorce, however, almost none of them deals in a deep way to resolve this serious issue. Actually, Turkish law books generally tend to deal with law in books or theory not in practice. It seems tradition in Turkish legal environment. Some of rare articles deal with these kind of issues. It is evident that the real question should be that one Turkey how can establish rule of law in the country by providing safeguard in public or private realm for its own citizen?

[554] See Siobhan Mullally, Gender, Culture and Human Rights: Reclaiming Universalism (Oxford, HartP, 2006) at 123. The author makes that claim for the context of Irish Constitution. However, after scrutinizing Turkish divorce cases, I may argue that same result is valid for Turkish case.

Turkey has structured at some level gender equality in public sphere, but not in private realm. Therefore, Turkish legislatures should formulate in a nationalistic state structuring of substantive equality between man and woman beyond the formal equality.

The following essay was first published as: The Modern World and Minorities, in Constitutional Law Readings for Turkey, Fatih Öztürk, Filiz Kitabevi, 2008, Istanbul, pg. 1-36.

5

A Theory of Liberal Minority Rights of Will Kymlicka

Since the establishment of the Republic of Turkey, rights of minorities, specifically religious ones, have continually been violated due to an exaggerated fear of losing the principle of secularism in its democracy; and the consequent fear of a dismantling of the Turkish political identity. The ambiguous efforts at censoring or suppressing such fears on the part of authorities in Turkey, directed against the ultimate taboo of struggling to bring this unfound conservative fear to light, is the primary concern of this thesis and, as such, the primary problem it will attempt to bring to resolution. The scope of this issue is contained within attempting to find accommodation for religious minorities in the Turkish democratic context.

Why religious protections are necessary in any governmental system which maintains a priority to protecting minorities is because religion, though a privately rooted subject, contains elements which inescapably spill over into the public realm. Though the fundamentals of religious belief and where they should lay are deeply controversial, taking for instance the multi-dimensional problem of Abraham's in Kierkegaard's *Fear and Trembling*, secularist exclusion from governmental systems does not and cannot possibly exclude the tendencies of religious belief to influence the public by virtue of individual ethical direction.[555]

---

[555] Kierkegaard, as *Johannes De Silentio* in *Fear and Trembling* (Cambridge, CUP, 2006), illustrates a problem in the paradox that evolves from confining religious belief in the individual as it isolates itself from general ethics as in the internal struggle of Abraham's over having to sacrifice his son Isaac, in accordance to the Biblical reference. In Islam, not Isaac but Ismail is the potential sacrifice.

We must in essence, as offered up by Kierkegaard, concede the possibility that there must be acknowledgement of a relationship between the public realm and religion, as opposed to the paradoxical conception of them as completely distinct.

Various theoretical aspects of minority rights, but specifically religious minority rights and what they are in modern liberal democracies, must be clear at the outset; the main focus here being how well a liberal democracy can theoretically provide accommodation for the just treatment of religious minorities. The position that will be supported is that indeed such accommodation is insufficient or ineffective in considering the philosophical background in the political and legal framework.

Certain academically relevant theoretical positions on individual versus collective rights should be taken into consideration in order to establish any theoretical grounding for our purpose. An initial observation that is critical to understanding religious minority rights is that we must assume they are a brand of collective right. Despite various philosophical arguments, religion clearly extends itself in practice as an establishment of peoples together in a group or collective and, furthermore, whose guiding principles are at least universal to the group in some sense.

From these precepts will an evaluation on a narrower scale begin, in a comparison and consideration of the systems of rights in Turkey and France; both ultimately found standing firm on a principle of secularity which limits religion very strictly to the private sphere. Turkey and France are taken here in the analysis on the smaller scale since they provide as counterparts in another aspect as well: being directly involved in religion despite the strict secular position. The Turkish government, for instance, still regulates mosque construction and distribution while France maintains an interestingly similar relationship with Catholicism.[556] It is clear that the collective nature of religion is what keeps it an issue intertwined with the affairs of these two governments, and essentially all governments.

Will Kymlicka's "differentiated citizenship rights", or minorities and rights in a liberal democracy will provide a starting point for the current undertaking. Kymlicka's systematic approach to developing his liberal minority theory will be examined and crystallized so that its practical implications can be clarified. Kymlicka's theory has for the last ten years remained a most persuasive one in the sphere of minority rights. Its pertinence here is relevant precisely because Turkey has tried to establish a liberal democracy of a kind, though unsuccessfully, for the last eighty years while constantly riddled with concerns on such rights. Kymlicka provides an approach to a solution to Turkish minority rights problems but in a somewhat unintended inverse manner, or through his theory's weakness. The weakness is that, as in most liberal thought, the requisite political space for religious minorities is lacking. This creates a significant vacuum of protection for religious minority rights, especially when one extrapolates the concern into broader perspective and in light of the events of 11 September 2001 and the global atmosphere thereafter.

The very real question penetrates in the fact that liberal democracies may be providing sufficient protection for ethnic and linguistic minorities, but not for religious ones. The French model of secularism or its Turkish counterpart, the latter incidentally a poor copy of the former, unfortunately provide exemplary models of the deficiency. Anglo-Saxon soft secularism, as is predominant in the United Kingdom or the United States, could provide a more accommodating solution for liberal democracies. It should be noteworthy that conceptions of religious political space should not

---

[556] See William Kidd, and Sian Reynolds (eds.), *Contemporary French Cultural Studies* (Arnold, London, 2000). Special reference to section 8 on this issue.

be thought of as equal across religions, for secularism in the West began as reaction to the Church, which wanted public control, while in Islam there is a clearly inverse example, with the exception of Iran, Islam does not permit religious leaders any real legal control over the state.[557]

In the Ottoman era even, a number of religious leaders lost their position due to their disagreements with the Sultans over the expansion of ecclesiastic political powers. Islamic nations did not admit of the kind of antagonism or war against the religious leaders or mosques in the political sphere as was and still remains prevalent in the traditional Western understanding. It is, however, a clearer understanding of what Kymlicka poses in his theoretical evaluations that is critical to the difference in the traditional western liberal democratic perspective on religious minorities, setting it apart from others but not leading us far enough; as is to be shown.

What may be demonstrated hereafter is that liberal democracies have continually failed to accommodate religious minorities; as evident from an analysis of Lucas Swaine's text *Liberal Conscience.* Swaine will be presented as purporting that most of the present day challenges are rooted in the opposition to liberal values of theocrats, with the assertion that theocrats are the most difficult minorities to appease in any liberal state. He will also be shown as rigorously affirming that liberal democracies have consistently failed to protect religious minority rights in accordance with existing practices and policies. Along these lines, it will be concluded that modern

---

[557] See general Taha Akyol, *Osmanlı'da ve İran'da Mezhep ve* Devlet [*State and Sect in the Ottoman Era and Iran*], 2nd ed., (Milliyet, İstanbul, 1999). Mr. Akyol is a well-known Turkish author and journalist. He writes daily sections for the Milliyet newspaper, a slightly centre-left publication. Mr. Akyol himself has been in the public eye as a slightly right wing nationalist author for more than 30 years. He writes most extensively on sociological perspectives concerning the state-individualism-nationalism—triad and it's relation to religion.

liberal democracies are presently incapable of effectively protecting religious minority rights and that an independent system of rights altogether is required in order to cure this deficiency.

A) Individual vs. Collective Rights

The views herein that concern the necessity of collective rights are most often perceived as a little radical, legally speaking, particularly with respect to the position that will be put forward here, which will affirm that not even a minority language can survive without the existence of collective rights, as per the debate with individual rights. And if language can sorely be expected to survive without such rights, it can hardly be expected that a religion, something built on particular understandings based in language, could survive. For just as one would be pressed to conceive of the existence of a language for a single individual, one would be equally pressed to conceive of the existence of an ethnicity or religion in like wise. These are all inherently social notions. The point being that there is obviously no coherent way to discuss protecting the survival of a group without necessitating a discussion of collective rights.

Proponents of this position are found with Patrick Thornberry, as he defines existence as a tool for collectivity without which there is no group or members and that this existence is based on a shared consciousness coming from "language, culture or religion, a shared sense of history, and a common destiny". He further maintains that without this "group existence" it is possible to maintain that individuals live, but not that any group does.[558] Another friend to this view is Segesvary who adds that

> "there can be no individual without a group or
> community; there can be no community without

---

[558] See Patrick, Thornberry, *International Law and Rights of Minorities* (Oxford: Clarendon, 1992) at 57.

> individuals who are not only the actors in social
> and cultural life but the bearers of the community's
> belief—and value-systems, of its traditionally
> transmitted symbolic order. But the community is
> not only the sum of the individuals who constitute
> it; it is more because its institutions, mental and
> symbolic orders and traditional values represent the
> accumulated experiences and cultural treasures of
> past generations."[559]

This, of course, naturally arouses the suspicion of whether or not collective and individual rights can coexist?[560] But then all rights consist in two dimensions, so provoking artificial tension between individual and collective rights is misleading.[561] It appears to be inherently human that all rights consist in this duality. It may just be that particular rights appear to have a more individual or collective leaning. If we take for example the freedom of conscience, when I speak to defend my opinions it is an individualistic right; though when I speak to defend the opinions of a group I belong to, it becomes the collective I speak on behalf of through my consent to joining that group. The duality raises problems as such: for instance, belonging to the country Turkey— so being Turkish—while not conceding personally to all of the opinions and actions of my government.

So rather than discussing coexistence, which is moot, the focus here will be on how we strike a balance when a conflict arises. As in

---

[559] See Victor Segesvary, "Group Rights: the Definition of Group Rights in the Contemporary Legal Debate Based on Socio-Cultural Analysis" 3 International Journal on Group Rights (1995) at 93.

[560] See Leighton McDonald, "Can Collective and Individual Rights Coexist?" 22 Melbourne U. L. Rev. 310 (1998). The author claims that "coexistence is impossible on account of a "pervasive irreconcilability" between collective and individual rights and that any constitutional recognition of both types of rights would give the court's a near impossible task." At 313.

[561] See Douglas Sanders, "Collective Rights" 13 Human Rights Quarterly (1991) at 383.

the example above in citizenship, there is a significant concern in whether group identity should be upheld in any and all conflicting cases while ignoring personal autonomy, or vice-versa, and whether or not case by case analyses of any situation can arrive at a compromise. It certainly doesn't seem a viable option to jump out of citizenship whenever we don't agree with our government. Now though liberal democracy generally tends to defend individual autonomy, since there is no immediate threat that citizens will renounce their citizenship—a somewhat awkwardly anti-social, uncomfortable, but not theoretically impossible, maneuver—communitarians argue that group rights are paramount to personal autonomy in order to protect minorities. Of course the liberal fear here is of group tyranny over the individual. Indeed, the most important base right is personal autonomy. However, a simple right of freedom of exit from the group leaves this fear irrelevant. Of course such claims, like all other legal claims, would rightly be presided over in normal legal proceedings, i.e. if the individual wants to file a claim or suit against the group or vice versa. In any case, there is a very simple outlet to overriding the fear of an individual's rights being trampled by a group.

Tantamount to this, Will Kymlicka claims that there is a misconception in the liberal principle of freedom and that equality is inconsistent with group-differentiated rights.[562] He poses that it is normal to assume that collective rights are exercised by a group, which is clearly far from the complete truth, as many group-differentiated rights are exercised by individuals.[563] He then elaborates by defining "**internal restrictions**" as "the claim of a group against its own members" and "**external restrictions**" as "the claim of a group against the larger society."[564] He correctly designates these rights collective rights, or tools for stability but

---

[562] See Will Kymlicka, Multicultural Citizenship: A Liberal Theory of Minority Rights (New York: Oxford, 1995) at 35.
[563] *Id.*
[564] *Id*, p.4.

at the same time, instability.[565] He adds that external protections instigate inter-group tensions which may leave open the possibility of producing unfairness towards various groups.[566] He stresses that internal restriction occurs in culturally homogeneous countries while, conversely, external protections are required in multinational or poly-ethnic states.[567] His main argument maintains that "liberals can and should endorse certain external protections, where they promote fairness between groups, but should reject internal restrictions which limit the right of group members to question and revise traditional authorities and practices."[568] Bhikhu Parekh challenges the position in suggesting that individual rights or autonomy can actually be used to harm or even eliminate minority groups.[569] The challenge is serious, as Kymlicka does not permit internal restrictions a place in liberal principles. Of course the adherence to liberal principles is an internal restriction in itself, as someone who does not wish to concede such principles is suffering precisely the tyranny over his or her individual rights within the system that is alleged to protect them.

There appears to be a need for a separate institution or system aimed at reducing or resolving these particular kinds of conflicts, which is where Shachar's system of judicial distribution might prove useful. It would appear, therein, that we must assert either that we should flat out accept or reject internal restrictions automatically. Additionally, the respective institutions should be erected in case of conflicts that arise thereafter, with each case examining primarily who the ultimate right should belong to: the individual or the group. Of course, while priority is first the right

---

[565] *Id.*

[566] *Id*, at 36.

[567] *Id*, at 37.

[568] *Id*, at p. 2.

[569] See Bhikhu Parekh, *Rethinking Multiculturalism: Cultural Diversity and Political Theory*, 2nd ed. (New York, Palgrave, 2006) at 211.See more Ayelet Shachar, "Two Critiques of Multiculturalism," 23 Cardozo L. Rev. (2001) 253, at 262-67, Shachar makes critics of Parekh's theory.

of the individual, it does not imply, however, that a group may not restrict or limit its members' practices. What will be argued as essential in the function between group and individual rights in the end is that individuals have not only the right to exit the group but also to challenge traditional group practices.

The provision of both rights effectively ensures that a group may impose internal restriction in the aim of preserving its culture without imposing harm upon its members since they ultimately will have the choice to concede or propose change or stasis, rather than only having the option of disengaging themselves from the group. That is, since the makeup of the group belongs to the entirety of the group and not the individual, as all groups are formed out of a unanimous consensus of foundation. This will permit for the protection of any group whose core values and traditions are threatened by members with uninformed, undisciplined, extreme, or just simply amicably diverging views. This will prevent any extreme duress to the individual or group, as the individual always has the alternative of withdrawal while the group is not stripped of the essential tenets, customs, traditions, or other foundations upon which it was established. This entails of course that any state concurrently and carefully protect the duality in this inverse relation of the system of individual and group rights.

Kymlicka believes that a protection of the minority group rights could be used for arbitrarily excessive internal restrictions by powerful members or authorities of group, but especially in religious groups; citing that most often than not those restrictions are aimed against women or children. Jane Norton counters Kymlicka's sentiments well, however, by affirming that "the rights of women are better protected while minimizing the burden placed on religious practice". She adds, furthermore, that it is unclear as to whether or not "there can ever be a reconciliation of the rights of religious communities and the rights of women", claiming that it is only within the sphere of the community itself that this can be effectively reconciled.[570] The only real question that arises in the reconciliation of a system of the protection of individual and group rights, as such, is how much a liberal state could tolerate illiberal practices or groups.

Interestingly enough, in academia when there is a talk about internal restrictions, religious minority groups are the entities that come to mind most frequently, as opposed to ethnic or linguistic ones. It may appear more obviously true that a system of normative values is derived more directly from religion than anything else, though one must be more careful in a closer analysis of variables such as culture, and the complex interconnection of variables culture itself assumes; particularly, for instance, in the case of a country like Turkey; where the citizenry illustrates more a reflection of its culture than its religion. An obvious example is that of the honor killings of out-of-line daughters which today are still rampant in the Eastern provinces, something clearly intolerable in any individual understanding of Islam but, tragically, a prominent Southeastern Kurdish tribal custom. However, in modern and even scholarly interpretation, this kind of thing is too often tragically misconstrued to coincide with the fact that Turkey is an overwhelmingly Muslim nation.

Kymlicka does clearly point out one thing, that is that it is believed, as he does, that "some group-differentiated rights are in fact exercised by individuals, and in any event the question of *whether the rights exercised by individuals or collectives are not the fundamental issue.* The important issue is why certain rights are group-differentiated—and therefore, why the members of certain groups should have rights regarding land, language, representation, etc. that the members of other groups do not have."[571] Parekh,

---

[570] See Jane Norton, "Insular Religious Communities and the Rights of Internal Minorities: A Dilemma for Liberalism" 9 Auckland U. L. Rev. (2000-2003) at 433-34.
[571] See more Richard Spoulding, "Peoples as National Minorities: A Review of Will Kymlicka's Arguments for Aboriginal Rights from a Self-Determination Perspective" 47 Univ. of Toronto L. J. 35. (1997) at 46.

on the other hand, acutely notices that Kymlicka does not show a proper respect of illiberal cultures "in their authentic otherness" because he defends minority rights as long as the establishment of these groups is consistent with liberal principles.[572] In Kymlicka's model there is as previously mentioned the failure to account for liberalism as its own special group, which can be restrictive to or tyrannical over other groups contained within it. For like any other ideology, it cannot lay claim to a universal answer to the principles of truth in either the foundations or future of any individual or group, and this is the challenge that will be taken up here.

B) Will Kymlicka's Liberal Theory of Minority Rights

Here, Kymlicka's theory (following an outline of Kymlicka's *Multicultural Citizenship*), which mainly derives from the experience of Canadian multiculturalism, will be analyzed in greater detail. Over the last ten years, Kymlicka has become a leading scholar in the field of multiculturalism. He insists that universal human right standards may not able to solve or provide an adequate solution to the protection of individual autonomy in a multicultural society.[573] In his own words:

> "Traditional human rights standards are simply unable to resolve some of the most important and controversial questions relating to cultural minorities . . . The problem is not that traditional human rights doctrines give us the wrong answer to these questions. It is rather that they often give no answer at all."[574]

---

[572] See Parekh, *supra note 569*, at 108.
[573] See Kymlicka, *supra note 562*, at 4.
[574] *Id* and 5.

This sentiment illustrates exactly that no prevailing modern liberal universal rights system has been able to provide answers on how to effectively protect cultural minorities, attributing the primary failure to their predominantly majoritarian character. We can hereby understand why a theory for an independent system of protections for minority rights is required.[575] On the flip side of this, Kymlicka also warns that "recognizing minority rights has obvious dangers."[576] He recognizes that minority rights are, and have been in the past, open to abuse. The Nazi regime is an example, but not a one that sits entirely alone, as radicals and nationalists all over the world have taken advantage, of course not on the same scale.[577] Kymlicka asserts and reasserts that a liberal theory of minority rights will demonstrate how minority rights will survive in concurrence with universal human rights, and "how minority rights are limited by the principles of individual liberty, democracy, and social justice", anchoring a minority rights theory in liberalism.[578] However, the question remains as to whether or not there is real consensus among liberal theorists about just what exactly liberal values are?

---

[575] *Id.*

[576] *Id*, at 6.

[577] *Id.*

[578] On this view, Brian Barry strongly disagree with Kymlicka, Bhikhu Parekh, and M. Walzer, a liberal state can insist that all groups should respect and follow liberal values as personal autonomy and equality. Barry claims that liberalism is oppressive because it expects and wants from the groups act with the principles of liberal values. And he also argues "ordinary democracy encourages deliberation to the degree that is possible or desirable by pressing all groups to make arguments that are accessible to other people. See Brian Barry, "Second Thoughts-and Some First Thoughts Reviewed," in Paul Kelly, ed., *Multiculturalism Reconsidered: Culture and Equality and Its Critics* (Oxford, Polity, 2002) at 212, 232-3. Currently, Barry is one of the attackers of multiculturalism. See his book, *Culture and Equality* (Cambridge, Polity, 2001).

The Politics of Multiculturalism

Cultural diversity takes place because of "national minorities," as Kymlicka calls them; ". . . self-governing, territorially concentrated cultures . . . typically wish to maintain themselves as distinct societies alongside the majority culture, and various forms of autonomy or self-government to ensure their survival as distinct societies."[579]

He claims that a "nation" is an "historical community more or less institutionally complete, occupying a given territory or homeland, sharing a distinct language and culture."[580] From this point of view one could pose that prior to the settling of Israel, Jews were not a nation; an implication that this paper will take issue with. In accordance to the same line of argument, the Kurds of Iran, Iraq, Syria, Turkey and other regions of the Middle East, who, again according to this authors outline, are indeed a nation, would not then be permitted any similar kind of status. Kymlicka observes or claims that if a state contains more than one nation, it is a multination state, with essentially smaller cultures to be called national minorities.[581]

Kymlicka rejects the "Anglo-conformity" which prevailed up to the 1960's in Australia, Canada, and the United States, entailing the official position that immigrants should be left their unique heritage, but concurrently be completely assimilated into the existing cultural norms.[582] The general understanding was that assimilation be a policy tool aimed at the maintenance of political stability.[583] Kymlicka legitimates the position somewhat, however, affirming that "immigrants are not nations, and they do not

---

[579] Kymlicka, *supra note* 562, at 10.

[580] *Id.*

[581] *Id.*

[582] *Id.*, at 14.

[583] *Id.*

occupy homelands."[584] He also implies legitimacy in colonial occupation, outlining that colonists did not define themselves as immigrants and so were not required to adjust themselves to the new territory.[585] The bottom line in all this appears to be a definitional matter of property, where without the ownership thereof, there can be no stake to any claim of recognition on the part of any minority. Parekh, of course, finds this position quite strange, in that Kymlicka appears to promote the preconception that it is okay to refrain from permitting voluntary immigrants due recognition.[586] Joseph H. Carens rightly challenges along these lines as well, positing that "if people's native societal cultures are so important to them, why should not immigrants be able to bring their societal cultures with them and establish them in their new home?"[587] There is nothing to explain the frame of mind then, of an individual fleeing from oppression as conceiving being treated as a second rate citizens when fleeing from the same discriminatory tyranny. This is especially applicable when one considers modern day Muslims, as they may be fleeing from oppression in the Middle East to the West where whether or not their treatment as a citizen is questionably less discriminatory.

Three Forms of Group-Differentiated Rights

a) <u>Self-Government Rights</u> are the rights of national groups to ". . . some form of political autonomy or territorial jurisdiction, so as to ensure the full and free development

---

[584] *Id*, at p. 5.

[585] See Eric Metcalfe, "Illiberal Citizenship? A Critique of Will Kymlicka's Liberal Theory of Minority Rights," 22 Queen's L. J. 175.

[586] See Parekh, *supra note* 569, at 103. In his footnote, at the same page, Parekh became agreement with Kymlicka and he states that "I do not think it is wrong for liberal states to insist that immigration entails accepting the legitimacy of state enforcement of liberal principles, so long as immigrants know this in advance, and nonetheless voluntarily choose to come."

[587] See Joseph H. Carens, "*Culture, Citizenship, and Community: A Contextual Exploration of Justice as Evenhandedness*" (Oxford, OUP, 2000) at 55.

of their cultures and the best interests of their people."[588] Federalism may function as a system to divide powers between central and local government, however, the core issue is striking the correct balance between centralization and decentralization.[589] Kymlicka offers the Canadian example, in that "federalism can only serve as a mechanism for self-government if the national minority forms a majority in one of the federal subunits, as the Quebecois do in Quebec."[590] Applying this understanding inter-continentally, the Kurdish population of Turkey could be seen to not only theoretically but realistically possess the same distinction in Turkey. This would follow with the respective inclusions of control over education, language, culture, and even immigration policy.[591] And these rights, of course, are not temporary but as much permanent as they would appear to be inherent.[592] The bottom line is the provision for the basis of a minority possessing the ability to exist outside of an authority of the majority, in effect to exist under its own authority and in its own culture, at base providing it a sense of the legitimacy of its distinct societal and cultural differences.[593]

b) Poly-ethnic Rights: The collapse of policies adhering to Anglo-conformity has permitted immigrant groups to successfully challenge for new policies, especially in particular instances to habituate anti-racist practices.[594] The respective rights aim to "help ethnic groups and

---

[588] *Id*, at 27.

[589] *Id*, at 28.

[590] *Id*, at 29.

[591] *Id*, at 28, p. 2.

[592] *Id*, at 30.

[593] See Eric Metcalfe, "Illiberal Citizenship? A Critique of Will Kymlicka's Liberal Theory of Minority Rights," 22 Queen's L. J. 175 (1996) at 181-2.

[594] See Kymlicka, *supra note* 562, at 31.

religious minorities express their cultural particularity and pride without it hampering their success in the economic and political institutions of the dominant society."[595] An example is the provision of funding for cultural practices, and targeted exemptions from laws and regulations which obstruct or put at a disadvantage certain religious practices, such as for Orthodox Jews and the right to wear the yarmulke during military service in the United States.[596] c) <u>Special Representation Rights:</u> In recent years there has been increased demand from either national minorities or ethnic groups to be provided various ranges of rights dependent on "the idea of special representation rights."[597] One way Kymlicka suggests satisfying such demands is reforming political parties in order to eliminate barriers which may possibly restrict the various minority groups, whether a particular category of woman, ethnic minority, or impoverished, by proposing more proportionally representative ones.[598] Another option may

---

[595] *Id.*

[596] *Id*, at 31.

[597] *Id*, at 32.

[598] *Id.* Feminist perspective points out multiculturalism permits to groups violations of women rights. For example, in Asia some of traditionalist culture allow husbands to burn their wives and who commit those practices are not punished. Also Western perspectives based on white middle class views. Moreover, public and private spheres are male dominated around the World.

See William H. Meyer, "Towards a Global Culture: Human Rights, Group Rights and Cultural Relativism," 3 International Journal on Group Rights (1996) 184-5.

Susan Moller Okin claims that multiculturalism and feminism cannot stand together and culturalism is bad for women. See her book, *Is Multiculturalism Bad for Women?* (Princeton, PUP, 1999).

Feminism is a fight against male sex dominant culture, it is debatable universal or local characters burden on it. Political struggle for recognition totally related and achievable with the understanding of gender relations. See Jurgen Habermas, "Struggles for Recognition in the Democratic Constitutional State," in Amy Gutman, ed., *Multiculturalism: Examining the Politics of Recognition* (Princeton, PUPress, 1994) at 117.

be providing a quota for a certain number of seats, as they would be reserved for disadvantaged groups.[599] Kymlicka poses, however, that the aforementioned outlets may be manipulated and produce "grounds of oppression" though they may prove effective for ensuring self-government if uncorrupted.[600] In the end, Kymlicka stresses that "an economically successful immigrant group may seek poly-ethnic rights, but have no basis for claiming either special representation or self-government, etc."[601] Here Parekh catches Kymlicka with another serious charge, displeased with the hierarchy for minority rights that the latter appears to have developed, asserting "it is difficult to see what general principles inform this hierarchy of rights". He asserts further that Kymlicka appeals to such disparate criteria as "territorial concentration [national minorities], history of independent existence, institutional completeness, past commitments, consent, the level of poverty in the immigrant's country, and the receiving country's degree of responsibility for it."[602] Parekh's ultimate counterclaim here is that "there is no obvious reason, why we should accept the liberal premise in the first instance."[603] Seyla Benhabib also picks up on Kymlicka's hierarchical tendencies, challenging his distinction between groups based in political legitimacy [mainly governing power, though in all fairness Kymlicka does not deny justice, democratic inclusion, public culture and historical memory].[604]

---

[599] See Kymlicka, *supra note* 562, at 32.

[600] *Id*, p. 6.

[601] *Id*.

[602] See Parekh, *supra note* 569, at 109.

[603] *Id*, at 111.

[604] See Seyla Benhabib, *The Claims of Culture: Equality and Diversity in the Global Era* (Princeton, PUP, 2002) at 64-8.

Freedom and Culture

The core of Kymlicka's analysis rests in minority rights steered more by the principle of liberal autonomy rather than equality.[605] The line of thought is also evident in his connecting of culture and freedom.[606] What he puts forward, in his own terminology, is a picture of what he calls "societal culture, whose practices and institutions cover the full range of human activities, encompassing both public and private life," and links these with national groups.[607]

What he defines as such is "a culture which provides its members with meaningful ways of life across the full range of human activities", in which he includes particulars such as "social, educational, religious, recreational, and economic life, encompassing both public and private spheres"; which cultures, he outlines, tend to be territorially concentrated and based on a shared language.[608] Language turns out to be the key tool for societal culture. Kymlicka stresses further that societal cultures' aim are to become national cultures.[609] Despite this, he continues pointing out that people have been known to move between cultures, though this is an exceptional situation.[610] Kymlicka here distances himself from communitarians. He posits that most of the time communitarians explain our links to sub-national groups such as "churches, neighborhoods, family, unions, etc.—rather than to larger society which covers these sub-groups.[611]

---

[605] See Robert Justin Lipkin, "Can Liberalism Justify Multiculturalism," 45 Buffalo L. Rev. (1997) 39.

[606] See Kymlicka, *supra note* 562, at 75.

[607] *Id* and 76.

[608] Id, at 76, p. 4.

[609] *Id*, at 80.

[610] *Id*, at 84.

[611] *Id*, at 92.

Communitarians of course submit to limiting individual rights under the precept that is not a harmful due to the overarching support for shared values which would more than compensate for any less significant freedoms relinquished.[612] Most communitarians also hold that "politics of the common good" is applicable to minorities on a local rather than a national level. Thus, communitarians do not find it useful to assume for themselves a national identity as a requisite to asserting their political views, since nations share language and history, and so individuals can disagree about the meaning of life or "the ultimate ends in life."[613]

Opposition to this entrenches itself in Kymlicka's understanding in terms of its limiting of individual autonomy at the sub-national level as a possible root of dissatisfaction, and oppressive overtones for the members of a group who criticize traditional practices.[614] Kymlicka asks proponents of such systems how liberals should respond to cultures that illustrate such an illiberal tradition or focus. Some nations and nationalist movements are deeply illiberal, and he answers his own question by claiming that such nations should not be dissolved for being illiberal but should be liberalized

---

[612] *Id.* However, Chandran Kukathas makes distinction between his views and Kymlicka's, with his own words, "there is a clear distinction between Kymlicka's views and my own. The differences stem, ultimately from two views of liberalism. In Kymlicka's view, I think, a liberal society is one in which certain ideals of equality and individual autonomy associated with Kant, Mill, and Rawls, are generally upheld. Another view is that a liberal society is one in which different ways of life can coexist, even if some of those ways of life do not value equality and autonomy. The distinction might be expressed more sharply by saying that the second view does not hold that a liberal society must be composed of (more or less) "liberal" communities. I hold to the second view, for I see, liberalism as offering a solution to the political problem of pluralism and social conflict rather than a comprehensive moral ideal. This is not to say that this liberalism has no moral basis, only that this basis is not the ideal of individual autonomy." See Chandran Kukathas, "Cultural Rights Again: A Rejoinder to Kymlicka" 20 Political Theory (1992) 680.

[613] *Id.*

[614] *Id*, p. 4.

so as not to eradicate the culture itself but to merely adjust it to liberal systematization.[615] Robert Justin Lipkin astutely criticizes that point arguing the following:

> "Kymlicka's position fails because it is arbitrarily restricted only to those cultures committed to the deliberativist paradigm. In short, Kymlicka's imperative, like other versions of liberalism, is antithetical to one of the chief paradigmatic cases of a culture, namely, dedicated cultures. Some dedicated cultures reject the legitimacy of internal protections, intra-group freedoms, and civil liberties for their members, and other dedicated cultures do not even permit inter-group equality between and among different cultures. Kymlicka's liberalism cannot tolerate these forms of internal and external restrictions for all types of cultures. Thus, Kymlicka's version of liberalism can explain and justify tolerating only those cultures that are sufficiently like liberal cultures because they embrace the deliberativist ideal.[616]

Interestingly, Kymlicka argues that national minorities have societal cultures yet that immigrants do not and that it is possible to settle immigrant groups collectively and to empower them so that they become, in effect, national minorities.[617] He also appears to slip by the implication that immigrants can have no societal idea of the good, as it is something they cannot contribute to under the given liberal framework above. So as an immigrant in such a situation, I could only choose to take up one of the positions of the existing national minorities on this point. This clearly untenable argument is rectified by Carens position that outcomes for individuals should be a product of choice rather than of circumstance; a version of the liberal neutrality ideal. His concern is that the relative security of a person's access to her own societal culture is a function of

---

[615] *Id*, at 94-5.
[616] See Lipkin, *supra note* 605, at 39-40.
[617] See Kymlicka, *supra note* 562, at 101.

circumstances rather than choice, aside from voluntary immigrants, which is ultimately incoherent."[618]

This position assumes entirely that one who persists in her own culture's greatness is necessarily negating other cultures, which is by no means necessary logically or otherwise. In Kymlicka's vision, one might expect immigrants to become members of national societies in their new country.[619] We can here point out the circumstantial paradox in, say, if an individual from France wished to settle in Quebec (assuming 100,000 other French did the same) and, according to Kymlicka, could not enjoy societal culture nor claim self-government and special representation rights, while these are exactly the rights and freedoms the French Quebecois enjoy. The historical situation throws a monkey wrench into the works of minority rights this way, for then we are to separate rights even among those who are the same peoples merely by where they happened to have landed geographically and at what time; almost like basing rights on a first-come first-served basis when no one really knew where to "go first" would be most beneficial.

This presumption clearly bases itself here in historical gains, which, in this author's point of view, should bear no further relevance to liberal belief. It is a distortion of the focus of rights relaying it from the individual to mere geography. This is a little disturbing to say the least, and as Charles Taylor poses, perhaps it should be that "the politics of equal dignity is based on the idea that all humans are *equally* worthy of respect."[620]

---

[618] See Carens, *supra note* 587, at 61.

[619] See Kymlicka, *supra note* 562, at 114.

[620] See Charles Taylor, "The Politics of Recognition," in Gutman, *supra note* 46, at 41.

Justice and Minority Rights

States are inescapably aimed at supporting certain dominant cultural identities, which clearly results in an atmosphere of innate discrimination against other cultures.[621] How do governments approach the relevant policies then? How effectively "decisions on languages, internal boundaries, public holidays, and state symbols" are made is indeed the question at hand.[622] The issue of statutory public holidays is an interesting diverging point, which questions the neutrality of liberal principle. Carens offers us in response that "the ideal of cultural neutrality is an illusion" and that there are particular issues "on which the state cannot avoid making decisions that have a significant impact on culture, and, if the polity contains people from different cultures, that advantage some and disadvantage others."[623] Both Carens (Toronto) and Kymlicka (Kingston) reside in Canada, making this observation even more acute; as during the Christmas holiday Jewish and Muslim parents take their kids to the play ground on days the rest of the nation celebrates their holiday. The obvious circumstantial consequences are not altogether unpleasantly daunting, that is—taking one's child to the playground, but the subtle exclusion from a society-shared holiday is poignant. Kymlicka points out that support by a state of a majority culture by using a majority language in school and public institutions should not provide as grounds for denial of minority languages based on "the separation of state and ethnicity."[624] Unfortunately, France and Turkey have used this argument to deny language rights for their own minorities. What France and Turkey uphold is that real survival right belongs only to the majority, or unitary state in these particular cases, in a single culture: the French or the Turkish. Kymlicka notes that language rights conflicts cause a certain degree of political instability as the

---

[621] Kymlicka, *supra note* 562, at 108.

[622] *Id.*

[623] See Carens, *supra note* 587, at 53.

[624] See Kymlicka, *supra note* 562, at 111.

evidence is resounding in Canada, Belgium, Spain, Sri Lanka, the Baltics, Bulgaria, and Turkey, as well as various other nations.[625]

Kymlicka here inserts the issue of federalism as a way to distribute self-government rights, which applies, however, only if forming a federation was voluntarily done by all parties involved. There is no problem if agreements are put in place for a federal state where voluntariness is not at issue. If incorporation was involuntary, it should follow that, under international law, national minorities should possess the right to stake a claim to establishing a voluntary federation.[626] Another issue is that Kymlicka accepts that former generations still possess validity transference for today's or tomorrow's generations. He claims that the Quebecois voluntarily agreed to join the Canadian federation while securing language and education rights control in the provincial government.[627] He does not, however, discuss today's generation, which is obviously compelled to adjust to the historical roots of the situation. His world especially lacks a place for religious minorities, which today's liberal democracies face more and more challenges from.

Finally, however, he confesses that if we defend group-differentiated rights we are forced not only to depend upon historical agreements but equality arguments as well.[628] He appears to assert a merely tangential, or secondary, role of equality to minority rights concerns alongside historical agreements. This project will attempt to illustrate that providing rights for national minorities should in fact be based primarily in respect of equality, if only by the consideration that a single individual is as right-worthy as the next. In the end, however, the differences between what right should qualify for the minority will be shown as determined, and predetermined, by the majority; whose primary distinction from the former is only that they possess the numbers combined

---

[625] *Id.*

[626] *Id.*, at 117.

[627] *Id.*, at 118.

[628] *Id.*, at 120.

with the legal and economic powers to delegate what rights should be distributed and to whom. The inclination to concede a greater weight to historical relevance than to equality first and foremost results in a disparity that causes newly developed beliefs to be considered substandard to existing belief systems. Only by considering equivalent weight in the value of various minorities, as may be more or less historically rooted, can we avoid subjectively oppressing one minority in favor of another, which necessitates autonomous governing. In order to eliminate this disparity, the majority must look to extend through equality, the relevant rights to the respective minorities.

Ensuring a Voice for Minorities

How can we solve conflicts involving minority rights then? Well, Kymlicka's answer is on "a case by case basis, in light of the particular history of a group, its status in the larger society, and the choices and circumstances of its members", and furthermore that "they must be resolved politically, by good-faith negotiations and the give and take of democratic politics."[629] Kymlicka suggests that over the last few years there has been a tendency for systems to set a quota for a certain number of seats in parliaments for ethnic, national, and racial minorities who are under-represented.[630] This appears to want to avoid any special recognition for religious minorities and view religion as particularly irrelevant when it comes to minority rights. This seems a rather fear-induced oversight, however, given the relevance of the protection required for particular religious minorities not only in the contemporary international situation but historically as well; for what other variable bound the Jews but religion in Nazi Germany before the holocaust—needless to say, a political situation that could have used a stronger safeguard.

---

[629] *Id*, at 131.
[630] *Id*, at 132.

He does make strides as concerns his assessment of the ineffectiveness of modern democracies, however, as he eventually questions why it is that only marginalized regions, as opposed to marginalized peoples, should only enjoy special representation in the senate.[631] He also makes poignant notes on the dominating objectivity of the middle class white male.[632] Moreover, he asserts perhaps his most interesting question in whether or not it actually is that any one individual can effectively represent anyone else, in what is maintained in his designation of the "challenge of empathy".[633] What are also agreeable in Kymlicka's discussions are the necessary characteristics for full representation by a group who "shares their gender, class, occupation, ethnicity, language" or "mirror representation."[634] An interesting side note in this listing is the absence again of a religious group distinction, though he recognizes that truly effective representation cannot occur due to particular barriers in political mechanisms.[635] So though Kymlicka leads us in the right direction, he fails on the follow-through which is the aim herein, in that we must attempt to push through these "particular barriers"; which includes the inability of religious groups to govern autonomously. Another important question is the one of adequate representation in numbers, and the concern over quotas and what suffices as an adequate number of these as well.[636] The first step to a solution appears to be in this, or that there should be a representation with respect to the populations as a whole in the nation with a minimum threshold guaranteeing adequate voice in representation.[637] Something that is especially true with regards to Turkey's religious minorities; who have faced better than 80 years without sufficient representation, as promised in the Treaty of Lausanne.

---

[631] *Id*, at 137.

[632] *Id*, at 138-9.

[633] *Id*, at 141.

[634] *Id*, at 138.

[635] *Id*, 141.

[636] *Id*.

[637] *Id*, at p. 4.

Toleration and Its Limits

So Kymlicka carries on that liberal principles lay down "freedom within the minority group, and equality between the minority and majority group.[638] He additionally asserts that "a liberal conception of minority rights cannot accommodate all the demands of all minority groups," with his classic disclaimer that some cultural minorities limit individual freedom and autonomy.[639] He offers the example of how some minority groups limit or block education rights for girls or deny votes or holding office for women.[640] Again here, Kymlicka is definitively rejecting internal restrictions on behalf of liberal values. He notices that any theory inconsistent with permitting substantial civil rights to its members is incompatible with liberal standards.[641] Through this, he refuses the millet system allegedly because of its restriction of civil rights over group members.[642]

With respect to this particular system, it appears Kymlicka is misinformed or has some distorted misconceptions about the millet system, because it is a system of governance that clearly denotes a right of individuals to challenge their own group's authority before the courts. The Ottoman archives clearly and consistently exhibit that the state is obliged not to leave individuals at the hands of group authorities where individual autonomy is threatened in the eye of the beholder.[643] Another Western misconstruing concerns the disregard for the actually exemplary model of the Ottoman millet

---

[638] *Id*, at 152.

[639] *Id*, at 153.

[640] *Id*. Chandran Kukathas believes that non-liberal groups should be left alone and state should not help them in any way. According to Kukathas liberal view, liberal tolerance should accept some internal restrictions, but must not provide external protection. See more at 155.

[641] *Id*, at 164.

[642] *Id*, at 165.

[643] See general Ahmet Akgunduz & Said Ozturk, *700. Yilinda Bilinmeyen Osmanli [Unknown Ottoman on the 700ᵗʰ Anniversary]* (Istanbul, Osmanli, 1999).

system due to the grossly inauthentic knowledge said to be acquired from the Ottoman archives, which is restricted to limited sources in English; and those in actuality confessing to the approximate 500 years of success of the Ottoman millet in protecting and preserving it's minority rights.[644]

The Ties That Bind

How then can today's democracies promote national integration? Kymlicka stresses that the most effective ways are through the welfare state; which provides free education, health care, and the requisite social security programs.[645] How successful these are is debatable. Democracy should indeed serve equally for all of citizens in order to distribute social justice effectively. In a multination state, "common citizenship" promotes majority nation culture.[646] If the state attempts to suppress minority cultures on behalf of the majority culture, it may well be cause for the destabilizing of democratic virtues at their core.[647] This we provided as what may indeed be the case as we had set out with reference to Kymlicka's inability to go beyond the "particular barriers" of politics as above, and in our arguments against giving heavier weight to historical grounding over equivalent rights among groups. Kymlicka believes that states should accommodate self-government demands, and that if they are denied in the name of common citizenship, it "will simply promote alienation and secessionist movements."[648] This particular view in practice is illustrated well by the Turkish example with respect to the Kurdish population. Ironically, Kymlicka rightly points out the great danger of states denying peoples their universal rights. He adds that we can remember how Norway seceded from Sweden in 1905, as well as the possibility

---

[644] *Id.*

[645] *Id*, at 180.

[646] *Id*, at 183.

[647] Id.

[648] *Id*, at 185.

of the province of Quebec doing the same and positing that "it is difficult to see why liberals should automatically oppose such peaceful, liberal secessions?", since "After all, liberalism is fundamentally concerned, not with the fate of states, but with the freedom and well-being of individuals, and secession need not harm individual rights."[649] This is of course important to keep in mind for those like Kymlicka who might implicitly be suggesting by exclusion, in their enumerations of autonomy-worthy traits of peoples, the religious element, since the exclusion appears to imply that the religious factor might be cause for non-peaceful secession in some manner, and thus should be kept distanced from the relevance to any right to autonomous governing.

What then is the basis of social unity in a multination state? Parekh somewhat agrees with Kymlicka that a multicultural society cannot survive without having "a common sense of belonging among its citizens."[650] He arrives at a conclusion similar to Kymlicka's in that, "although multicultural societies are difficult to manage, they need not become a political nightmare and might even become exciting if we exuviate our long traditional preoccupation with a culturally homogeneous and tightly structured polity and allow them instead to intimate their own appropriate institutional forms, modes of governance, and moral and political virtues."[651] Parekh reasserts that "religious [as Kymlicka all but rejects this basis], cultural, and ethnic communities, women, and others should therefore be able to bring to the public agenda their respective views and experiences,

---

[649] *Id.* When a government systematically discriminate one group with unethical policies and provides economic, social, and cultural benefits to the other groups, disadvantaged group has moral right to leave the union how the U. S. did against the British Empire. See Adeno Addis, "Individualism, Communitarianism, and the Rights of Ethnic Minorities" 67 Notre Dame L. Rev. (1992) 624.

[650] See Parekh, *supra note* 569, at 341.

[651] *Id*, at 344.

which they can best do only if they speak in their own voices."[652] If, however, we don't concede the religious element as a potential voice and adhere to Kymlicka in doing this, we thereby negate the voice and input of religious minorities.

One claim is that the ability to achieve this depends on shared values such that satisfy a unified conception of liberal justice; but this only begs the question of what exactly liberal justice is.[653] If it is defined by the confines of a nation state, shared identity might come from history, language, and even religion. Kymlicka calls Charles Taylor's theory for help, "deep diversity," since "we must accommodate not only a diversity of cultural groups, but also a diversity of ways in which the members of these groups belong to the larger polity", asserting further that "it is the only formula on which a united Polyethnic, multination state can be built."[654] In order to stick together a multination state, citizens should value deep diversity, particularly ethnic groups and national cultures in the country where they live.[655] Amy Gutman supports the same idea, offering that:

> "multicultural societies and communities that stand for
> the freedom and equality of all people rest upon mutual
> respect for reasonable intellectual, political, and cultural

---

[652] See Bhikhu Parekh, "Redistribution or Recognition? A Misguided Debate" in Stephen May, Tariq Modood, and Judith Squires, eds., *Ethnicity, Nationalism, and Minority Rights* (Cambridge, CUP, 2004) at 207. His article rightly observes that ". . . identities are valued, recognized, respected, and cherished when they meet the society's criteria of success, and in ours these are economic and political. Groups at the bottom of the economic and social hierarchy therefore need to fight for justice and equality and become powerful if their identities are to be respected, not superficially, out of goodwill or in response to moral blackmail, but s their due. The politics of recognition remains impotent unless it is embedded in the politics of redistribution." At 208.

[653] See Kymlicka, *supra note* 562, at 187-8.

[654] *Id*, at 189-0.

[655] *Id*, at 191.

> differences. Mutual respect requires a widespread willingness and ability to articulate our disagreements, to defend them before people with whom we disagree, to discern the difference between respectable and disrespectable agreement, and to be open to changing our own minds when faced with well-reasoned criticism. The moral promise of multiculturalism depends on the exercise of these deliberative virtues."[656]

Pursuant to this, what is citizenship for liberal theorists then? Of course, it is a legal status which sets rights and responsibilities and identifies with the individual members in a politic system.[657] The conclusion for Kymlicka then, or at least the remaining problem is for liberal theory to develop a way to properly account for the unifying elements of a modern unitary democratic multination society.[658]

Conclusions

To round out Kymlicka's general conclusion, one could say that he insists that minority rights not allow a group dominative capacity over another group, nor a group the same over it's own members, adding that liberals should seek to ensure the equality within and between groups as minority rights will continue to be central to the future progress of liberal tradition throughout the world.[659] He consistently and deliberately omits the relevance of the religious minority however, which if we can't submit as Parekh and Kierkegaard might suggest we consider, as intricately relevant to the ethic of society; neglects the conscience of a substantial number of individuals.

---

[656] See Amy Gutman, "Introduction," in Gutman, *supra note* 93, at 24.
[657] *Id*, at 192.
[658] *Id.*
[659] See John Tomasi, "Kymlicka, Liberalism, and Respect for Cultural Minorities" 105 Ethics (1995) 580. The author claims that "Kymlicka has not shown that liberalism's fundamental principles require a recognition of cultural rights." At 594.

At the root of things, Kymlicka correctly observes that immigration and national minorities are the two main sources of cultural diversity in modern liberal democracies; though he rejects "the benign neglect of liberal principle" in which majority culture controls the state and looks at people first and foremost as individuals, including all members of minority cultures. He adds that liberalism should be the champion of minority rights as long as they are consistent with and respect individual autonomy.

This wants to say that liberal theory accepts group-differentiated rights with "external protections," which means to protect minorities against outside pressure, which comes from the larger society or other individuals or groups, with the precursor that "internal restrictions", or the denial of basic civil and political rights within a group, are not an issue. Kymlicka solemnly believes internal restrictions are inconsistent with freedom by liberal principles. Kymlicka gives priority to individuals as a means, or precondition, to providing it for groups. In essence, this is the major point of issue that has been the theme herein. Actually, the underlying issue is whether or not religious groups, illiberal by definition, can exist within liberal democracies as a recognized entity, how they should be accommodated, and what ought to be done to make for tangibly recognizable tolerance of said groups in the public realm.

C) Failure of Liberal Democracies or Lucas Swaine's "Liberal Conscience"

We will here examine how liberal democracies fail to effectively protect religious minorities; as is the primary focus of Lucas Swaine's recent book "the Liberal Conscience."[660] The cornerstone of Swaine's argumentation appears to be that religious individuals

---

[660] See Lucas Swaine, "*The Liberal Conscience: Politics and Principle in a World of Religious Pluralism*" (New York, Columbia UP, 2006).

are in essence in conflict with liberalism due to the very nature of their beliefs and practices. He outlines in his own terminology the "theocrats" which he labels the individuals of religious groups who deny "freedom of expression, separation of church and state, freedom of association, and women's equality."[661]

This is at best a highly contentious statement for two reasons: the first is that there is a serious danger of generalization, and the second is that many religious groups concede the ultimate autonomy of the individual. The position is one that may be pertinent with regards to abuses in the intrusion on the secularism of state and over women's rights, but the sentiment is still a precarious one that requires delicate handling in the application of the phraseology. Swaine does astutely observe, however, that liberalism is currently under fire for exactly the kind of disregard and disrespect of religious diversity, which perhaps plagues his own sentiment, and being partisan in lacking a broader perspective on diversified moral valuation.[662] He observes that liberal democracies fail to protect theocrats and suggests that "now is the time to renew the liberal project, to expand its legitimacy across the globe."[663] In true liberal fashion he argues that theocratic groups must be engaged in a way that would include them in the structural integrity of liberalism.[664] He asserts additionally, however, that the legal liberal frameworks of the day are insufficient to accommodate religious diversity, and can only do so by conceding such communities a kind of "quasi sovereignty." Swaine persistently makes the condemnation that liberals have failed to provide adequate reasons for religious groups to affirm liberal institutions given the failings to provide clear and reasonable grounds to subsume the governance of such groups.[665] He offers the salient warning that "liberalism need not be just another partisan theory

---

[661] *Id*, at xiii.
[662] *Id*, at xiv.
[663] *Id*, at xv.
[664] *Id*, at xiv.
[665] *Id*, at 2.

of how to live."[666] Regardless of what denials ensue, the positing of a particular always carries the undertone of implication as the potentially ideal universal. The issue is how any system may accommodate differences or diversity based on justice without violating neither individual nor group rights. For at it's base, liberalism itself is more a theory for the protection of a certain way of thinking of a group, not an individual; which only separates itself from more communistic thinking by drawing a very arbitrary line, as there is clearly no liberal democratic society that proclaims that no individual is under any obligation at all to the collective.

Swaine defines theocracy as "a mode of governance prioritizing a religious conception of the good that is strict and comprehensive in its range of teachings."[667] He further identifies that theocrats are distinguished as either "ambitious" or "retiring", where the former are prone to engaging in political life in order to eliminate stricter practices or laws entangled is conceptions of the religious good, while the latter withdraw themselves from political and even from public life so they may live in small communities.[668] Examples given of the first group are offered as Muslims who have settled in America or other Western nations, while examples of the second nature as in the Ammish, Mormons, or Native Indians originating from the western pueblos of New Mexico.[669] What is interesting to note is that despite their relative distance or inability to directly affect politics in Western nations, Swain designates the Muslim communities as ambitious while outlining the clearly politically engaged and influential active polygamist Mormons as retiring. The oversight of accounting for almost 12 million Mormons living in America and clearly exhibiting direct influence in local government and state courts is a curious assigning of attributes to say the least, especially while only 4 million Muslims in America are seen by Swaine to be more ambitious, while at the same time they remain

---

[666] *Id*, at xix.

[667] *Id*, at 7.

[668] *Id*, at 9.

[669] *Id*.

effectively lacking or even negligible on the American political scene.

Swaine emphasizes time and time again the stereotypical generalizations; that ambitious theocrats are fighting for "prohibition of abortion—strictly religious values enforcement in public life—censorship of irreligious speech—legal sanctions against minority faith—and the penalization or criminalization of homosexuality."[670] The reality illustrates a very surprising contrast, however, when one considers that very authentically essential and basic Islamic history and law contradict Swaine's stereotypical charges.

Unfortunately, what one would think would not require undue repetition will come up in this project quite frequently as the undercurrent that emphasizing what isn't nearly as important as how it is emphasized; and in this case, in a tone repeatedly challenging the relatively fresh and ill-informed knowledge of true religious histories of practice as opposed to negatively charged speculation. Unfortunately, the post 9/11 environment has brought on countless, if not entirely, superficial analyses and projections in the academic world of Islamic culture, for one.

In any analysis of the sort, one has to consider at base the mostly Sunni influence of Islam worldwide, as well as it's variations against the mostly Iranian Shia Islam or Saudi Arabian Wahhabi Islam. Scrutiny of Indian or Pakistani Muslim culture will not give an accurate notion of either worldwide Islam or a reliable picture of its governance and structural laws. The most important point is where religion becomes confused in inter-cultural or international and regional comparisons or overarching generalizations. Who can say exactly where Ayatollahs come from? There is no single definition of the proper practice of a Prophet life. How many are aware that Islamic law permits abortion, or that, as even Imam-I Gazali, one

---

[670] *Id*, at 10.

of the greatest Islamic legal scholars, has admitted that if a woman merely does not desire that her beauty diminish she may abort a child prior to the second trimester (reference, ihya-I ulum-ud din, I will mark page numbers). And though this project does not strictly confine itself to Islamic society, or misinterpretation thereof, in a liberal world; the intention behind this strong contemporary example is to aim our concentration down the scientific path. That is, we clearly require, especially given contemporary world society and its conundrums, a genuine and sincere analysis not only of what we are looking at, but how we are looking at it.

Reverting back to Swaine, religious minorities in Turkey are considered ambitious rather than retiring, whereas Jews and Christians tend to hide their identities due to fear of nationalists and the deep state. So on first glance the latter groups appear retiring theocrats, which is clearly not the case.

Swaine furthermore gives four moral reasons why liberal democracies fail to accommodate religious diversity in today's world:

1) "liberal government lacks a well-devised and justifiable schema for treating theocrats dwelling in liberal democracies" (there is no recognized legal standard on how to treat religious minorities properly),

2) "liberal government should, but does not, have proper and identifiable grounds in hand for governing theocrats" (even liberals claimed but could not provide grounds for interfering with religious practices),

3) "liberal government is in the habit of coercing theocrats where they break the law, it would seem that government owes them an explanation for why it does so" (liberals should explain why they need to regulate theocratic practices),

4) "and finally, explanation to this effect, and for a particular standard under which to treat theocrats and theocratic communities, should be provided in terms that theocrats should accept."[671]

Swaine's observations are astutely well configured. He rightly states that each liberal democracy should provide a place to hear ambitious theocrats' concerns about social or political practices if they will affect people's moral or religious beliefs.[672] He also correctly asks whether liberal government has any legitimate reason to administer religious minorities.[673] The practices of Liberal states aimed against religious or moral beliefs should be well justifiable.[674] In order to consist in such justifiability of course, the liberal position would require explanation consistent to understanding in theocratic terms, or at least attempted to be posited in such. It is through a kind of attempt to translate religion into liberalism through a deliberative medium that illustrates Swaine is at least attempting to establish a line of connection, rather than sublimation of one or the other, between religious groups and the State. This will also crystallize the priority of the theocrats before the public and state with respect to their own groupings.

Ultimately, Swaine stresses that because of the four moral failures we need a separate system to protect so-called theocrats in liberal states. He provides the conclusion that only providing a legal structure which allows semi-sovereign status to theocratic groups will properly protect these groups in today's democracies.[675] However, he again makes clear the voluntariness of the individual to admit themselves to any group and that religious authority only applies to such members, and certainly does not make allowances

---

[671] *Id*, at 16-20, and 29.

[672] *Id*, at 16, p.2.

[673] *Id*, at 16, p.3.

[674] *Id*, at 18.

[675] *Id*, at 72.

in the extremes that would excessively limit individual members' rights.[676]

Why Swaine refrains from admitting to the necessity of providing full sovereignty is due to the obvious perceived threat of instability that arises with factions that may become overly ambitious and potentially seek secession from the society, which could be accompanied by more intricate problems that would not only affect the seceding group, but may adversely affect the group seceded from, or cross-sectional loyalties or custom; not to mention the threat of the seceding group redefining it's impositions upon the individual in a manner no longer obliged concretely to the ultimately imposing authority of the liberal society it used to be maintained under the umbrella of.[677]

With semi sovereignty liberal society may able to limit illiberal practices. Swaine converges on Kymlicka when it comes to an all important umbrella of liberalism, though he provides preconditions for his system in order to avoid various "corrosive effects" on the whole of a liberal society.[678] In addition, Swaine concedes that semi sovereignty will permit religious groups their own criminal penal system with the quid pro quo of regulation over extreme or unusual punishment.[679] As it is, Swaine seems to offer a step in the right direction and beyond what Kymlicka offers up first. He offers the Ottoman Millet System as an exemplar for his approach.[680] This is a variation on Shachar in a manner similar to how a semi-sovereign system exists in Federal states as in contrast to Unitary states in terms of the governments scope on autonomous control; where autonomy is full in the unitary state, as with a minority group in Shachar's view, and only partial in a Federal State, as in Swaine's view.

---

[676] *Id*, at 76.

[677] *Id*, at 91.

[678] *Id*, at 94-104.

[679] *Id*, at 99.

[680] *Id*, at 92.

Of course adding a step in the right direction doesn't find the best answer if we don't force ourselves to continue in that direction. What needs to be asserted with more flare is the stepping away from a strictly liberal outline and encapsulation of societies who willingly and voluntarily commit themselves to groups who cherish societal values over individual ones, or the illiberal groups we have mentioned herein.

E) Concluding Remarks

This project has herein dealt with the theoretical concerns at hand. The first step was outlining exactly why minority rights cannot be protected without conceding collective rights. Then a close look was taken on Kymlicka's model of multiculturalism which appears to have failed in some critical respects, but primarily in failing to establish a necessary distinction of systems of rights. Pursuant to this, it follows that Lucas Swaine's liberal conscience show us why liberal democracies have failed to protect religious minorities in a contemporary theoretical context. His proposal was "quasi sovereignty", which amounted to a nearly acceptable step towards separating the distinct systems of rule over the individual. Finally, Ayelet Shachar's models were enumerated and examined as a resolution or continuance on the path to what is seen in this project as the natural stepping towards separation of systems of governance of religious and state. Without which, liberal democracies are perilously doomed to failing to provide stability in the modern era of increasing minority rights driven politics. However, it will be asserted that the task is ultimately left incomplete, and that the assignment here is to complete what Shachar leaves as unsatisfactory to the protection of religious groups; that being the unconditional primacy of the right of the individual. The drawback will be satisfied in this project by asserting a greater onus on the individual and group to be clearer on their relationship and responsibilities, so that neither is damaged by any inconsistency in understanding.

The following essay was first published as: Critics of Will Kymlicka's Liberal Minority Rights: Failure to Protect Religious Minorities, e-akademi (Hukuk, Ekonomi ve Siyasal Bilimler Aylık İnternet Dergisi, Ocak 2012, Sayı: 119.

6

CRITICS OF WILL KYMLICKA'S LIBERAL MINORITY RIGHTS THEORY: FAILURE TO PROTECT RELIGIOUS MINORITIES

Abstract

In this paper, an evaluation or various criticisms of Kymlicka from the perspective of Shachar, Parekh, and Benhabib, political scientists and legal scholars, will be made in order to understand and present a clear view on Kymlicka's liberal minority rights theory. Kymlicka's theory has for more than fifteen years remained most persuasive in the realm of minority rights.

Initially, the importance of the protection of minority human rights in modern liberal democracies was defined. Second, I questioned Will Kymlicka's liberal minority rights and whether it could be successful. Under the subsection of Ayelet Shachar and Joint-Governance; according to Shachar, Kymlicka's claims to protect religious minority rights are not successful. In the subsection of Parekh and Rethinking Multiculturalism, Parekh is negative regarding Kymlicka's theory on the proposals about immigrants. Then, under the subsection of Seyla Benhabib and Claims of Culture; Benhabib's critics will be explored. How it is insufficient in terms of Kymlicka's theory from the perspective of gender equality. Lastly, I will explore the meaning of religious freedom within the discourse of secularism.

In conclusion, Kymlicka's multicultural citizenship, or in other words minority rights, could be successful in order to protect ethnic and linguistic groups, yet is questionable in the protection of religious minority groups.

Introduction

In fact, Kymlicka's theory does not provide the requisite political space for religious minorities, and therefore in his weakness that resolution will be sought after here. In broader perspective, it is to say that today's liberal democracies are in crisis in terms of the protection of religious minorities, especially post 9/11. However, I will abandon Kymlicka at this juncture and instead resolve the discrepancy in leaning towards Ayelet Shachar's point concerning the real question around religious minorities. This real question surrounds the fact that liberal democracies may provide enough protection for ethnic and linguistic minorities but not for religious ones. The French model of secularism or its Turkish counterpart, incidentally a poor copy of the former, may provide quite lacking in this regard. Anglo-Saxon soft secularism, for instance as in the U. K. or the U. S., could provide a more compatible solution for liberal democracies. Of course, one should note that secularism began and developed in the Western world as a reaction to church or ecclesiastical superiority, or perhaps even tyranny. It would be a mistake of transference, which appears to be the case, however, as it was when the Western world takes a look at the religious issues in Islamic states. One would be mistaken to simplify the approach to religion as such, to think the issue is the same around the world and in all religions. However, the exception of Iran (consisting in mostly Shia Islam) does not allow the religious leaders to control the state. In the Ottoman era, many religious leaders lost their position because of disagreement with the Sultans concerning the expansion of ecclesiastical expansion of political powers. Islamic nations did not admit of the kind of antagonism or war against the religious leaders or mosques in the political sphere as it is in the traditional Western understanding. In the end, Kymlicka's theoretical evaluation is crucial for understanding this difference and a real liberal democratic state

A) Ayelet Shachar and Joint Governance

Schachar claims that Kymlicka's group-differentiated rights theory is a good beginning, which provides different rights for different groups, but that Kymlicka does not provide an attempt to discover institutional models for these groups.[681] Shachar rightly challenges that "Kymlicka pays relatively little attention to" religious minorities, effectively dissolving them arbitrarily into ethnic or merely immigrant groupings which leave them with only a claim to poly-ethnic rights.[682] However, Shachar acutely observes that central debate of multiculturalism is occupied primarily by religious minority issues.[683] Where I also distinct myself from Kymlicka. This a point especially salient in today's world, in pronounced democracies such as France, Britain, the U. S. and Germany with regards to Jews and Muslims.

Shachar critics Kymlicka concerning his misperception in which minority cultures impose internal restrictions on their members are undeserving of equal protection.[684] In addition, Shachar criticizes Kymlicka's argument that if a group is illiberal the majority is unable to prevent violations of individual rights, astutely challenging that a system should be established which blocks crucial internal restrictions on members of the group.[685] Shachar also rightly observes that Kymlicka fails to answer properly why minority groups involve "unfair in-group practices," and why those groups need state accommodation for these practices.[686] She offers her theory of "joint governance," as an alternative model, in which:

---

[681] See Ayelet Shachar, **Multicultural Jurisdictions: Cultural Differences and Women's Rights** (Cambridge, Cambridge University Press, 2001) at 9.
[682] Id, at 26.
[683] Id.
[684] Id, at 30.
[685] Id, at 31.
[686] Id, at 42.

"the challenges of multiculturalism by recognizing that some persons will belong to more than one political community, and will bear rights and obligations that derive from more than one source of legal authority . . . it is based on the awareness that the paradox of multicultural vulnerability arises from three sets of intersecting and conflicting interests: those of the state, those of the group, and those of the individual who belongs to both. [687]

Shachar's theory based on "transformative accommodation," which:

"aims to establish an ongoing dialogue between different sources of authority as a means of eventually improving the situation of traditionally vulnerable group members without removing them from *nomoi* [minority] groups . . . transformative accommodation stand three core principles. They are: 1. the "sub-matter" allocation of authority; 2. the "no monopoly" rule; and 3. the establishment of clearly delineated choice options . . . Like the federal-style accommodation design, transformative accommodation does not grant jurisdiction in an "all or nothing" fashion. [It] significantly restricts the power of the state. At the same time, however, it also imposes limits on the *nomoi* group: it denies it a monopoly over its members in each of these social arenas . . . the central question becomes *how* the state must intervene to protect the interests of individuals put at risk by their *nomos*, while still allowing their group maximum jurisdictional autonomy."[688]

Shachar shows us in her book's appendix, how the transformative accommodation model works in the arenas of immigration law,

---

[687] Id, at 88-9.
[688] Id, at 118, 126, 143-4.

education, and criminal justice.[689] Her model reminds me the Ottoman millet system in fact.

B) Bhikhu Parekh and Rethinking Multiculturalism

Parekh's first disagreement with Kymlicka seems to concern immigrants. He finds it quite strange that Kymlicka's theoretical arguments include somewhat of a preconception that those who immigrate are subject to lesser law merely because they migrate voluntarily.[690] There is nothing to explain how it is then that those fleeing from oppression would conceive of being treated as second rate citizens when fleeing from the same, for why would they flee expecting lesser treatment?

Parekh claims that Kymlicka does not show a proper respect of illiberal cultures "in their authentic otherness" because Kymlicka defends minority rights as long as these groups are consistent with liberal principles.[691] Another serious charge made by Barekh is that Kymlicka establishes a hierarchy for minority rights, and he rightly challenges that "it is difficult to see what general principles inform this hierarchy of rights. He asserts further that Kymlicka appeals to such disparate criteria as "territorial concentration [national minorities], history of independent existence, institutional completeness, past commitments, consent, the level of poverty in the immigrant's country, and the receiving country's degree of responsibility for it."[692] Moreover, Barekh claims "there is no

---

[689] Id, 151-165

[690] See Bhikhu Parekh, **Rethinking Multiculturalism: Cultural Diversity and Political Theory**, 2nd ed. (New York, Palgrave, 2006) at 103. In his footnote, at the same page, Parekh became agreement with Kymlicka and he states that "I do not think it is wrong for liberal states to insist that immigration entails accepting the legitimacy of state enforcement of liberal principles, so long as immigrants know this in advance, and nonetheless voluntarily choose to come."

[691] Id, at 108.

[692] Id, at 109.

obvious reason, why we should accept the liberal premise in the first instance."[693]

He somewhat agrees with Kymlicka that a multicultural society cannot survive without having "a common sense of belonging among its citizens."[694] He arrives at a conclusion similar to Kymlicka's in that, "although multicultural societies are difficult to manage, they need not become a political nightmare and might even become exciting if we exuviate our long traditional preoccupation with a culturally homogeneous and tightly structured polity and allow them instead to intimate their own appropriate institutional forms, modes of governance, and moral and political virtues."[695] Parekh, like Kymlicka, claims that "religious [Kymlicka almost deny religious basis], cultural, and ethnic communities, women, and others should therefore be able to bring to the public agenda their respective views and experiences, which they can best do only if they speak in their own voices."[696]

Parekh's main challenges against Kymlicka, is that individual rights or autonomy can be used to harm or eliminate minority groups.[697] It is a serious challenge, as Kymlicka does not accept

---

[693] Id, at 111.

[694] Id, at 341.

[695] Id, at 344.

[696] See Bhikhu Parekh, "Redistribution or Recognition? A Misguided Debate" in Stephen May, Tariq Modood, and Judith Squires, eds., *Ethnicity, Nationalism, and Minority Rights* (Cambridge, CUP, 2004) at 207. His article rightly observes that ". . . identities are valued, recognized, respected, and cherished when they meet the society's criteria of success, and in ours these are economic and political. Groups at the bottom of the economic and social hierarchy therefore need to fight for justice and equality and become powerful if their identities are to be respected, not superficially, out of goodwill or in response to moral blackmail, but s their due. The politics of recognition remains impotent unless it is embedded in the politics of redistribution." At 208.

[697] Id, at 211. See more Ayelet Shachar, "Two Critiques of Multiculturalism," 23 Cardozo L. Rev. (2001) 253, at 262-67, Shachar makes critics of Parekh's theory.

internal restrictions in the name of liberal principles. For how are we to go about violating individual autonomy if in an instance the individual does not adhere to liberal principles where the group does? I believe that there has to be an institution or system aimed at reducing these particular kinds of conflicts, which is where Shachar's system might come in useful in terms of justice distribution. It will be asserted by the author here that we should in fact either flat out accept or deny internal restrictions automatically. Second, there should be the establishment of institutions to solve internal cases that do arise. Third, each case must be examined with respect to who holds the ultimate right, the individual or the group. Of course, our priority should first be individuals and then groups. This does not require however that a group cannot restrict or limit its members' practices. In the end, I will assert that individuals have the right to challenge traditional group practices alongside exit rights. The provision of both rights effectively ensures that a group may impose internal restriction in the aim of preserving its culture without imposing harm upon its members since they ultimately will have the choice to disengage themselves from the group. The issue belongs to the group. Thereby, also, will any group that is too extremely internally restrictive self-destruct by the pure nature of the individuals' will not to be harmed. The state duty is providing these two rights concurrently; the challenge and exit right, while checking the internal restrictions for implications of any manner of harm against its own members.

C) Seyla Benhabib and the Claims of Culture

Siobhan Mullally observes that Benhabib's goal is to defend universalism via an exploration of gender and community.[698] Benhabib argues that "cultures are formed through complex dialogues with other cultures."[699] She notes accurately that "multicultural justice emerges at the interests of such [cultural] conflicts and paradoxes; there are no easy ways to reconcile either in theory or in practice rights of individual liberty with rights of collective cultural self-expression."[700] Culture is an identity for Benhabib, and thusly that states went through culture wars because of identity politics.[701] She illustrates her primary concern in that, "there is a profound and unavoidable connection between cultural diversity and gender-related differences."[702] This provides a distinction of angles between Kymlicka and Benhabib. According

---

[698] See Siobhan Mullally, **Reclaiming Universalism: Gender, Cultural Diversity and Human Rights** (Hard, Oxford, 2006) at 69. Mullaly rightly states "the negotiation of cultural conflicts is a key test for any defense of universalism." The critical point is that how a universalist theory deal with cultural conflicts.

In her book, at the chapter 5, Mullally lays down her attitude very clearly; "I ask whether discourse ethics can reconcile feminism with the universalistic discourse of human rights and provide the critical resources necessary for a truly global feminist movement." At 70. However, Benhabib states that universalism is not ethnocentric. See Seyla Benhabib, **The Claims of Culture: Equality and Diversity in the Global Era** (Princeton, PUP, 2002) at xi. In her book's introduction, she summarizes her ideas with a great effort.

Jennifer Saul rightly challenges that "it is possible to be feminist while respecting cultural traditions." She deals with her argument in her book, under the chapter 9, Feminism and Respect for Cultures.

See Jennifer Saul, **Feminism: Issues & Arguments** (New York, Oxford, 2003) 261-292.

[699] See Benhabib, at ix.

[700] Id, at x.

[701] Id, at 1.

[702] Id, at xi.

to Kymlicka cultural diversity arises out of national minorities and ethnic groups.

A point on which Benhabib and Kymlicka appear to converge is in recognizing cultural identities as very important from the point of universal justice.[703] However, Benhabib correctly adds that "conflicts around the rights of women and children who are members of minority cultural nations or immigrant groups within liberal democracies unable to us to see most clearly the moral and political choices involved in advocating the preservation of traditional cultural identities over and above individual rights."[704] She makes another important point which seems especially relevant to Turkish society in that, "the great majority of Muslim people all over the world, as well as others in whose midst they live are caught in a democratic learning experiment."[705]

In Benhabib's conception, not far off from Kymlicka in this respect, democratic theories should provide and assist minority group claims regarding equality and justice for self-determination in cultural terms.[706] Benhabib accepts Hagerman's dual-track approach to multiculturalism, which is first, "the official public sphere of representative institutions," including legislature-judiciary-executive, bureaucracies and political parties, and second; "the unofficial public sphere," providing places for social movements including civil, cultural, religious, ethnic, artistic, and political associations, etc. She also recognizes "the certain forms of legal and political pluralism, including multiple jurisdictional systems and regional parliaments, may be compatible with deliberative democratic universalism."[707]

---

[703] Id, at xii.

[704] Id.

[705] Id, at xiii.

[706] Id, at 19.

[707] Id, at 21. See more Joan B. Landes, "Jurgen Habermas, the Structural Transformation of the Public Sphere: A Feminist Inquiry" 12 Praxis International (1992) 106.

What Benhabib claims through Mullally's interpretation is that, "there are no such societal cultures [in terms of Kymlicka's beliefs]? There is no single organizing principle that encompasses both public and private spheres for distinct cultural groups." Mull ally also criticizes Kymlicka for permitting too readily an "access to a range of meaningful options [via societal culture theory]" rightly pointing out that "some cultures do not provide their members with a range of options, and do not permit their members to revise their conceptions of the good."[708]

Lastly Benhabib rightly challenges Kymlicka's distinction between groups which are based on political legitimacy [mainly governing power, however, Kymlicka does not deny justice, democratic inclusion, public culture and historical memory] arguing then, that in today's world providing rights for minorities or our treatment of groups be based on justice, democratic inclusion and exclusion.[709]

D) Religious Freedom: Secularism v. Religion

In this section, I will explore the meaning of religion within the discourse of secularism. Religious freedom is a fundamental right of citizens of modern world democracies. The understanding of the need to protect minorities in the modern world began with the protection of religious minorities in the early XVIIth Century. Then in the early XXth Century this also expanded to the protection of linguistic and ethnic minorities, especially with the establishment of the League of Nations and bilateral treaties between these countries. However, in today's world, due to a

---

[708] See Mullally, supra note 698, at 86. See more about Kymlicka's societal culture and Benhabib's critics regarding this issue. See Benhabib, at 59-60. Benhabib rightly challenges "there cannot be such a single principle of societal culture, and also that at any point in time there are competing collective narratives and significations that range across institutions and form the dialogue of cultures."

[709] Id, at 64-8.

fear of religious radicalism, many of us believe that if we provide more religious freedom for a religious group, even if the majority of the population belongs to it, we are in danger of losing our democracies. In particular there is a fear of theocratic states. However, modern democratic states are also prone to becoming fundamentalist in their secularism. Secularism itself behaves like a religion. I will argue that practicing hard-line secularism may in itself destroy our democracies, since it kills religious freedom in the name of protecting secularism. This misunderstanding of secularism, especially in Turkey and France destroys the peace and social consensus within society. As James Massey rightly observes "religious freedom is the condition and guardian of all other freedoms. Even individuals without any religious convictions, but who have faith in democracy, acknowledge this relationship."[710] Around the world, there is the misconception that "diversity of opinion" causes religious conflicts among the groups. However the reality is that such conflicts occur because of "the absence of tolerance and understanding."[711] Massey supports this by quoting the Indian thinker, Humayun Kabir, when he says "we cannot have a democracy, without minorities, without distinct and different groups . . . Where there is no democracy, the question of minorities as such cannot arise."[712] This could be the case with Turkish democracy. Here I will try to show that our current fears does not have real basis, but rather that it is based on our past fears and stereotypes.

Another multiculturalism intellectual, Tariq Modood, claims that "most theorists of difference and multiculturalism exhibit very little

---

[710] See James Massey, **Minorities and Religious Freedom in a Democracy** (New Delhi, Manohar Publishers, 2003) at 9. His book deals very insight to look at India and its religious minorities.

[711] Id, at 10. John Rex challenges that religious conflicts are not happening every time because of religions. Most of the time reason seem that ethnicity, political conflict, and nationalism. See John Rex, Ethnic Minorities in the Modern Nation State: Working Papers in the Theory of Multiculturalism and Political Integration (London, McMillan Press, 1996) at 200.

[712] Id, at 17.

sympathy for religious groups; religious groups are usually absent in their theorizing and there is usually a presumption in favor of secularism."[713] He warns us that we should not block religious groups from political debates on multiculturalism. Secularism should be careful to maintain dialogue between religious and non-religious groups.[714] He adds that this ignorance predominates in the Western world about Muslims. I claim that, generally speaking, the same ignorance takes place in Islamic countries about Jews or Christians. More specifically, it occurs in Turkey.

The Western world believes that Islam does not separate politics and Mosques. Modood rightly claims that this is one of the biases against Islam in Europe.[715] Most of the Western world accepts the bad example of Iranian Islam rather than recognizing that Ottoman practices took place successfully for seven centuries. Interestingly, the Ottoman State fought against Iranian Islamic practices. Modood argues that we can distinguish theocracy from mainstream Islam. Radical or ideological secularism could be that which claims absolute separation between state and religion, which is in practice at a moderate level in the Western Europe except France.[716] Unfortunately, at the moment, Germany as well as some other European countries began to follow the example of France, especially after 9/11. The main reason for this seems to be that the U. S. media is prejudiced against Islam and the cultures of Islamic countries. Modood insists that even in Europe religion defines and shapes the dimensions of European secularism and that no absolute separation of religion and politics exists.[717] For

---

[713] See Tariq Modood, "Anti-Essentialism, Multiculturalism and the 'Recognition' of Religious Groups" 6 The Journal of Political Philosophy (1998) at 390. In his excellent article he claims and defends that the Western world should not act based on prejudices about Muslim groups who live in Europe. I claim vice versa for Turkey should not fear of providing for freedom religious minorities who are either Christians or Jews who live in Turkey.

[714] Id.

[715] Id, at 391.

[716] Id.

[717] Id, at 392.

example, most state holidays are based on Christian religious feasts. Furthermore, schools in these countries often offer Catholic-based education, though not Judaism or Islamic education. Finally he acknowledges that Muslims should not be excluded from recognition in multicultural states due to their belief in Islam; anything less does not fulfill the promise of Western secularism, since for there to be equality between religions, multicultural states should not favor one over another.[718] Modood, like the other liberal thinkers, believes that liberal states should support or encourage individualistic religions, maintaining a neutral stance rather than taking sides. He points out that "ethnic associations, businesses, trades unions, sport and film stars and so on should support or involve electoral candidates, but churches and religious groups are restricted. It makes weak of corporate representation and how much is it democratic?"[719] I think we should take his claim very seriously because each organization, religious or non-religious, has an ambition to influence politics. In the name of secularism, we provide this opportunity to non-religious groups, but not to religious groups. This is clearly undemocratic. Instead, I believe there has to be an ongoing dialogue, as well as tolerance among religious and non-religious groups in order to establish strong and peaceful societies in modern democracies.

Some authors believe that liberalism is a tool used to cover the secularist values held by authority figures such as legislators, executives, and judges.[720] Ze'ev Falk claims that secularist rhetoric about pluralism and personal liberty, in truth, comes from secular judgments which are "against the truth of metaphysics and religion."[721] The reality is that personal liberty and pluralism

---

[718] Id, at 392-3.

[719] Id, at 396. He calls that "there is a theretical incompatibility between multiculturalism and radical secularism." When there is no recognition of religious minorities, this incompatibility becomes a practical issue.

[720] See Ze'ev W. Falk, "Minority Religions in a Democratic Republic" 12 Journal of Law and Religion (1995-1996) at 450.

[721] Id.

has no guidelines for moral decisions, and there is no consensus or authority on most controversial issues. There is no common standard by which to judge what is good and evil.[722] Falk claims in his final remark that "the voices of religious individuals and institutions are therefore [as] legitimate in the political arena as those of their secular antagonists; and there is no "objective" solution to the problem of "Synagogue [Religion] and State."[723] Thus, in a broad sense, the question is how should political and social institutions in modern democracies treat people who would like to practice a different religion from that of the majority?[724] Here there is a misconception; the separation of Church [Religion] and State does not mean public institutions cannot " . . . accommodate [the] religious needs of people."[725] I think this is the balance point of our democratic philosophy. A multicultural state is responsible for accommodating religious groups, just as they do ethnic and linguistic groups. Thus we have to keep in our mind the question of "how far may government properly go in compelling individuals to perform obligations of citizenship which conflict with their beliefs or conscience?"[726]

Why do draconian secular systems [I am thinking here of France and Turkey] fail to protect religious pluralism and yet not lose their legitimacy in front of the public? Jonathan Fox quotes Mark Juergensmeyer who answers the question by suggesting that secular nationalism currently performs societal functions in modern world

---

[722] Id.

[723] Id, at 451. Falk gives little chance to the idea of "separation of Synagogue and State" may become the majority opinion in Israel. At 452.

[724] See Gloria T. Beckley & Paul Burstein, "Religious Pluralism, Equal Opportunity, and the State" 44 The Western Political Quarterly (1991) at 190.

[725] Id, at 191. At the above quoted sentence belongs to Judge William O. Douglas who spelled it out in Zorach v. Clausan, 343 U. S. 315, 1952.

[726] See Philip E. Jacob, "Religious Freedom-A Good Security Risk?" 300 Annals of the American Academy of Political and Social Science (1995) at 44.

democracies.[727] However, those systems are heading towards a "loss of faith" and this causes a legitimacy crisis. Juergensmeyer explains the reasons for loss of faith in secularism. Firstly, secular nationalists' governments do not keep their promises which were political freedom, economic prosperity, and social justice. Second, most of the time the non-Western world imported secular nationalism from outside thus the ideology does not have any domestic authority or legitimacy. Third, because of this importing from the outside, secular nationalism has been identified with cultural colonialism. Moreover, secular nationalism destroys or eliminates the traditional lifestyles of societies which are influenced by religious belief or practices. In addition, advocates of secular nationalists stand together with Western powers, which encourage people to believe in a global conspiracy against religion. These things break the legitimacy of secularism.[728] In short, our belief in religious liberty shapes the understanding of the "relations of morality and law, ethics and human government, moral purposes of government, and moral limitations that should restrain the state's use of coercive power."[729]

Mainly, this paper has highlighted the current debates of Will Kymlicka's multicultural citizenship theory with relevance to multicultural state or societies and then it touched upon the debates between secularism and religious freedom.

---

[727] See Jonathan Fox, "The Influence of Religious Legitimacy on Grievance Formation by Ethno-Religious Minorities" 36 Journal of Peace Research (1999) at 290. Fox rightly argues that Jurgensmeyer uses his theory for the Third World Countries, however those arguments are also applicable to more developed countries. At, 293.

[728] Id, at 291-2.

[729] See Daniel R. Heimbach, "Contrasting Views of Religious Liberty: Clarifying the Relationship between Responsible Government and the Freedom of Religion" 11 Journal of Law and Religion (1994-95) at 715.

The following essay was first published as: Introduction to Minority Issues in Turkey: The Constitution-Making Process and EU Integration, Volume 5-2 International Journal of Arts & Sciences, pg. 195-203 (2012)

7

INTRODUCTION TO MINORITY ISSUES IN TURKEY—THE CONSTITUTION—MAKING PROCESS AND EU INTEGRATION

Currently, Turkey stands between two worlds: Europe and the Middle East, or West and East. As Turkey prepares to join the European Union (EU), the country's problematic relationship with democracy needs to be re-examined. Under Turkey's current system, in operation for eight decades, the country has not been able to establish a stable democratic regime. Since the beginning of the republic, Turkey has created three constitutions. In addition, over the past 40 years, Turkey has faced four military coups or attempts thereof, the most recent in 1997. The EU is certainly not interested in the inclusion of a military state within its democratic structures. Yet, as it stands today, the formal democracy of Turkey is seriously weakened by its traditional reliance on a paternalistic military. Not only is the state of democracy in Turkey important in light of its EU application, it is also important internationally. If democratization can truly take hold and stabilize the country, Turkey could become a model state demonstrating the potential for congruency between democratic and Islamic values. Currently, the Turkish Parliament (TBMM) is trying to make up the Republic's first constitution, but the military will not take a stance on it. It is evident for Turkey that without the elimination of Turkish military power from civilian life there is no way to cure undemocratic problems within the country, for example, the recognition and protection of minorities.

Keywords: Minority issues, Turkey, Constitution.

Since its establishment in 1923 the Republic of Turkey has faced minority rights issues. In that year, the allies (France, the UK, Italy,

Greece, etc.) and the new republic signed the "Treaty of Peace" in Lausanne, which included minority subjects. However, until today the parties of the treaty have accused Turkey of violating the Lausanne Treaty. Turkey has never accepted these allegations. Turkey argues that all people residing in the country are citizens, and the republic recognizes only non-Muslims as the minority via the Lausanne treaty. However, the republic does not discriminate against anyone based on religion, ethnicity, and language differences. Furthermore, Turkey claims it is a unified state. In addition, the constructors of the republic and their followers believe that discussing this issue in public will mean enemies are going to attack the unification of Turkey and will try to divide Turkey's land. In truth, Turkey has adhered to dogmatic taboos that have precluded discussions of the *Turkish Armed Forces, Minority Rights*, and *Secularism*.

As a known phenomena, Turkish democracy runs under a military umbrella. Minority issues are considered a forbidden subject in Turkey. No Turkish legal books deal with this issue justly. Only a handful of sociologists and political scientists have written about it (see, for example, Etnik Kimlik ve Azinliklar [Ethnic Identity and Minorities], Birikim Magazine, Volume 71/72, March-April 1995, 3rd ed., Istanbul). Even as such, these materials do not clearly explain problems of minorities. They are written within a regime, requiring that certain truths not be explored. Thus, writing about this topic could define one as an enemy of the state. In December of 2004, the Commission of Human Rights of the Prime Minister's office prepared a report (only 16 pages!), entitled "Minorities of Turkey and Their Rights." However, before publishing the report, it was destroyed as a result of aggression from the military and Turkish Nationalists. Anyone who supported this study was declared a traitor of the country and aseparatist. Turkey began (in October 2005) the process to accession into the EU which will eventuallylead to full membership.

Minorities and their issues are hot topics around the world, however in Turkey it is more than that.When a person or people begin to discuss minorities or others in Turkey almost all nations believe that it is separatism and that it means only Armenians, Greeks and Jews of Turkey. This belief occurred because of historical events and religious faith. Even Turkish state tradition shares the same understanding as nations do. As a leading researcher in this area, Baskōn Oran rightly observes why the Turkish state and nations believe or believed in this way; because of the Millet system, a political and ideological reason.[730]

The Ottomans following Islamic law did not separate its citizens based on their race, nationality or citizenship. There are two kinds of citizens under Islamic law, (ra'iyye or teb'a) or Muslims and non-Muslims. In sum, current Turkish state follows Ottoman religious tradition on this topic even though it is against the secular system and its understanding.

Moreover, during the last two centuries of the Ottoman, Western states interfered with the internal problems of the Ottoman using the excuse of non-Muslim rights in the land, thus, still the nation of Turkey earned political belief when there were talks about non-Muslims. That is when separatism will come to the table (a political reason). Lastly, with the collapse of the Ottoman state only Anatolian land established a belief through the nation that religious minorities were separatist, but not Muslim minorities (an ideological reason).[731] Thus, the new republic's main frames are based on nationalism. The three main reasons being political, ideological and the millet system. Today, Turkey still believes that only non-Muslims are a minority of the country and Turkey also declared and made its beliefs accepted all over the world with

---

[730] Baskin, Oran, Türkiye'de **Azinliklar: Kavramlar, Teori, Lozan, İç Mevzuat, İçtihat ve Uygulama** [*Minorities in Turkey: Concepts, Theory, Lausanne, Domestic Law, Jurisprudence, and Practice*] (Istanbul, Iletisim, 2005) at 48-9.

[731] Oran, at 48.

the Lausanne treaty. With European Union accession Turkey has began to push and has tried to strike down this belief and practice, however, it seems Turkey does not wish to sacrifice this traditional path.

It is true that "every dispute has its own unique history and circumstances that need to be taken into account in devising a fair and workable solution."[732] In this paper, I will be aware and take into account the special conditions of Turkey without eliminating human rights standards. In previous and recent years, most of Turkish authorities argued that Turkey could not provide these standards (the UN and EU) to its own minorities because of its unique circumstances. However, the UN Human Rights Committee(General Comment No. 31; nature of the General Legal Obligation Imposed on States Parties to Covenant [ICCPR], dated on 26 May 2004) significantly remarked that: "— . . . the beneficiaries of the rights recognized by the covenant are I

"— . . . the beneficiaries of the rights recognized by the covenant are individuals . . . rights of members of minorities (article 27) may be enjoyed in community with others-States parties are required on ratification to make such changes to domestic laws and practices as are necessary to ensure their conformity with the covenant.-A failure to comply with this obligation (article 2, to take steps to give effect to the covenant rights is unqualified and of immediate effect) cannot be justified by reference to political, social, cultural or economic considerations within the state.-"

In this short paper, I will follow a classical enumeration in order to discover minorities of Turkey and their rights. First, I will explore the ethnic minorities who are Muslims; Kurds, Gypsies (Romas), Caucasians Groups, Arabs, and Balkan Immigrants. Second, I will look at other religious minorities; Alewis, including Zazas,

---

[732] See Will Kymlicka, Multicultural **Citizenship: A Liberal Theory of Minority Rights** (New York, Oxford, 1995) at 1.

Armenians, Greeks, Assyrians, and Jews including the Dönmes. Linguistic minorities of Turkey fall under the category of either ethnic or religious minorities such as Kurds, Laz, and Zaza . . . etc. Now, I would like to touch briefly on these groups and their problems. I will provide numbers related to the population of minorities.

Minorities of Turkey

Since the Ottoman era Turks and Kurds have lived together in Anatolia. Being Muslim, like Turks, Kurds were treated like Turks or other Muslim groups in those centuries. However, after the establishment of the republic in 1923, founders of the country had changed the ideology of the land from Ottomanism to Turkification[733] thus, it came out that any debate of minorities meant attacking the territorial integrity of Turkey and national unity. Like the others (referred to as minorities) Kurdish culture and identity came under attack then the founders of the country banned and denied all Kurdish language, identity and cultural rights. The current Kurdish population is 10 to 15 %. In other words, from 7 to 12 million Kurds live in Turkey. There is no trusted or secure statistic about these people. Until 1965, with the general census counting, it was possible to find out the numbers of ethnic minorities in Turkey.[734] I think Turkey needs a new general census system which would provide a clear number of minorities in order to realize and solve their problems. Most of these Kurds are Sunni, a small amount are Alewi. Kurds of Turkey are still fighting against the limited use of their native tongue and cultural identity suppression. A few Kurdish separatists claim self-determination for the Kurdish population; however this issue should be explored

---

[733] See more Fatih Öztürk, **Constitutional Law Readings for Turkey**, (Istanbul, Filiz Kitapevi, 2008).

[734] See more about general census and minorities in Turkey, Fuat Dündar, **Türkiye Nüfus Sayimlarinda Azinliklar** [*Minorities in Turkey's General Censuses*], (Istanbul, DOZ Yayōnlarō, 1999).

in another study. In sum, the Kurdish issue is the main minority problem in Turkey.

Around 300 thousand to an half million Romas live in Turkey. Some are Christian, the majority is Muslim. Unfortunately, most of the Romas' living area has a higher crime rate than their neighbors. Turkish society owns a lot of prejudice about their life style and culture. The main problem of Romas in Turkey is that they likely live outside of mainstream society.[735] Around the world Gypsies seem to have the same problem: how can they incorporate themselves without being assimilated into mainstream society?

Caucasian Groups include Circassians (around 800,000), Georgians (100,000) and Lazs (150,000).[736] Circassians are originally from Russia, today around 1 million live in Turkey. Around the 1860s they immigrated to Turkey because of Russian persecution. Today, elder's of these people may be able to speak their mother languages. Almost all of them are Muslim, like the Turks, who follow the Hanefi school of Islam. Around 10,000 Georgians are Christian. Caucasian groups are assimilated into society because of their religious beliefs. There exist no claims made against authorities in terms of right to language or education.

Almost all of the Arab population is Alewis, who call themselves Nusayri.[737] However, their Alewi beliefs are different from the

[735] See more Mustafa Aksu, **Türkiye'de Çingene Olmak** [*Being Gypsy in Turkey*] (Ankara, Anekdot Yayinevi, 2009). Ali Arayici, **Avrupa'nin Vatansizlari: Çingeneler** [*Europe's Stateless: Gypsies*], (Istanbul, Kalkedon Yayinlari, 2008). Elena Marushiakova, Vesselin Popov, **Osmanli Imparatorlugu'nda Çingeneler** [*Gypsies in the Ottoman Empire*], (Istanbul, Homer Yayinlari, 2006).

[736] See Aleksandre Grigoriantz, **Kafkasya Halklari, Tarihi ve Etnografik Bir Sentez** [*Cacuasian People: A Synthesis of History and Ethnography*], (Istanbul, Sabah Gazetesi Yayini, 1999).

[737] See Hüseyin Türk, **Nusayrilik: Anadolu'nun Gizli Inancı & Inanç Sistemleri ve Kültürel Özellikleri** [*Nusayris: Secret Belief of Anatolia & Belief Systems and Cultural Characteristics*], (Istanbul, Kaknüs Yayinlari, 2010).

Turkish version of Alewism. Their population stands at around 1 million. However, some nationalist authors believe that their ancestors were from Middle Asia who in essence was Turks. Because of their Alewi beliefs they are assimilated by Arab Alewis. Today, Nusayri have claims against assimilation or Turkicization and may able to use the Arabic language solely in private spheres. Around 10,000 Arabs are Christian and they face problems from Kurdish Sunnis or Nusayri because they live in the same neighborhoods. After the 1880s Balkan states

After the 1880s Balkan states began to have independence from the Ottoman states which gave rise to many Balkan immigrants.[738] Many Muslims like Bosnians, Pomaks, and Albanians from this region escaped from persecution and immigrated to Anatolia. Their current situation is like the Caucasian group, they are almost assimilated into Turkish society. The estimated number for Balkan immigrants is around 2 to 3 million.

Alewis are the biggest religious minority group in Turkey.[739] Historically, their claims have been on the table since almost the establishment of the Ottoman state. During the Ottoman era, many hot fights occurred between state forces and Alewis. Most of the Alewis are ethnically Turks. Around 8 to 12 million Alewis live in Turkey. One third of Alewis are Kurds. Current Alewis of Turkey sometime claim societal prejudices which are produced from their religious belief. In addition, the state does not provide any support to establish or develop Alewi religious places of worship, whereas Sunni Turks receive all benefits from the state.

---

[738] See Ahmet Halaçoglu, **Balkan Harbi Sonrasında Rumeli'den Türk Göçleri** [*Turkish Immigrations from the Balkan Region During the Balkan War*], (Ankara, TTK, 1995).

[739] See Orhan Türkdogan, Alevi-Bektasi Kimligi [*Identity of Alevi and Bektasi*], (Istanbul, Timas, 2004).

Catharina Raudvere, Elisabeth Ozdalga, Tord Olsson, **Alevi Identity: Cultural, Religious, and Social Perspectives** (Istanbul, Swedish Research Institute, 1998). Elise Massicard, **The Alevis in Turkey and Europe: Identity and Managing Territorial Diversity**, (London, Routledge, 2012).

Some researchers believe Zazas are Kurds, while others believe that they are Turks.[740] However, modern Zazas have the same attitude as their ancestors did. A good guess is that from half million to 1 million Zaza speakers live in Turkey. Most Zaza speakers are Alewi but a minority is Sunni. Thus, Zazas will be examined under Alewis. Zazas actually fall under the category of linguistic minorities. However, in Turkey, with the exception of Kurds, there is no wide out crying about the use of mother language from other Muslim minorities.

Currently, around 100,000 Armenians reside in Turkey.[741] Mainly they are Orthodox Christians. Their main claims are that they are not able to open enough educational institutions-legal status of Patriarchateand that they may not be able to have their own charitable properties. However, very hot debates began between the Armenian Diaspora and Turkey in the 1915-18 events, thus, Armenians of the Western world made it be believed and declared that the Ottoman state committed an ethnic cleansing or genocide against Armenians and therefore Turkey should compensate victims' families. However, the Turkish nation or state never seemed to accept these claims.

Yusuf Sarinay, **24 Nisan 1915'te Ne Oldu? & Ermeni Sevk ve Isyaninin Perde Arkasö** [*What Happened on April 24, 1915 & The Background of Armenian Expedition and Rebellion*], (Istanbul, Ideal Kültür Yayöncölök, 2012) See Guenter Lewy, **The Armenian Massacres in Ottoman Turkey: A Disputed Genocide**, (The University of Utah Press, 2005).

---

[740] See David McDowall, **A Modern History of the Kurds**, Third Ed., (London, I. B. Tauris Co. Ltd., 2004).

[741] See Mehmet Perinçek, **100 Belgede Ermeni Meselesi** [*Armenian Issue on Hundred Documents*], (Istanbul, Dogan Kitap, 2007).

There are no more than 5,000 Greeks left in Turkey.[742] Their main issues are that they may not be able to have religious training institutions and that they may not be able to operate or own charitable properties—legal statues of Patriarchate. However, the Turkish state argues that if Greece provides full rights to Turkish minorities in Greece, that it will do the same for Greeks in Turkey.

Around 25,000 to 50,000 Assyrians live in Turkey.[743] They are a forgotten nation. They are Christian, but not recognized as minority under the Lausanne Treaty. They have no legal status. The Turkish state denies them rights to have their own social and charitable institutions. Most of them immigrated to Western European countries in previous years. I have to note that during the Ottoman era (for six centuries) many different cultures and religious groups survived, however, interestingly, in the new republic regime within half a century almost all of these groups have been assimilated or have disappeared.

Around 30,000 Jews live in Turkey.[744] Historically, Turks have protected Jews from persecution. Some nationalist or a few religious radicals in Turkey, like other world countries including Western democracies, have anti-Semitic ideas about Jews in Turkey. Turkish

---

[742] See Jesse Russell & Ronald Cohn, **Greeks in Turkey**, (Bookvika Publishing, 2012).

Reene Hirschon, ed., **Crossing the Aegean: An Appraisal of the 1923 Compulsory Population Exchange between Greece and Turkey**, (NY, Oxford, Berghahn Books, 2006)

[743] See Eyyüp Tanriverdi, Ahmet Tasgin, Canan Seyfeli, **Süryaniler ve Süryanilik I, III, III, IV** (Ankara, Orient Yayinlari, 2005).

[744] See Erol Haker, **Bir Zamanlar Kirklareli'de Yahudiler Yasardi** [*Once Upon A Time There Jews Lived in Kirklareli*], (Istanbul, Iletisim Yayinlari, 2002).

Stanford J. Shaw, **The Jews of the Ottoman Empire and the Turkish Republic**, (London, McMillan, NY University Press, 1991)

Avner Levi, **Türkiye Cumhuriyetinde Yahudiler** [*Jews in the Republic of Turkey*], (Istanbul, Iletisim Yayinlari, 2010).

Jews declare every year that they do not have any problems living in Turkey as a minority group.

Dönmes are known as converts and there is no acceptable or trusted number about them.[745] Dönme are the Jewish followers of Sabatay Sevi who declared himself a Messiah. Around 1660s religious Jewish leaders made accusations and complaints against him to the Sultan thus, he was sentenced to capital punishment. To save his own life he converted to Islam before the Sultan. After that he told his followers to go under ground and Sevi developed a belief system which had elements from Islam and Judaism.

Neither Jews nor Muslims accept them into their society. They hide their identity to avoid discrimination among people. Thus, it is almost impossible to count their numbers. A rough guess would be about 100,000. However, they are known to be very successful in bureaucracy, politics, business and other professions.

The Constitution-Making Process and EU Integration[746]

After winning the 2011 general election the current Prime Minister (PM) Erdogan's Justice and Development Party promised to all of Turkey that his party would prepare and enact a new

---

[745] See Cengiz Sisman, *The History of Naming the Ottoman/Turkish Sabbatians* in **Studies on Istanbul and Beyond**, Robert G. Ousterhout, (Penn, The Joukowsky Family Foundation & American Research Institute, 2007).

   Abdurrahman Küçük, **Dönmeler (Sabayitisler) Tarihi** [History of Converters (Sabbatians], (Ankara, Berikan Yayinevi, 2010).

   Marc David Baer, **The Dönme: Jewish Converts, Muslim Revolutionaries, and Secular Turks**, (Stanford, California, Stanford University Press, 2009).

[746] See more about EU Integration, Yves Meny & Andrew Knapp, **Government and Politics in Western Europe:**

   Britain, France, Italy, Germany, Third Ed., (NY, Oxford University Press, 1998) at 354-85.

constitution that would not be intervened by military powers. PM Erdogan: "With a civilian, participatory, liberating and democratic constitution, we will be making the democratization process permanent. In drafting the new constitution, the AK Party group will not leave the table. If we see that it isn't working, then we will see which party we can do it with and will welcome them to join us. We have always been reconciliatory and we will continue to be so, because, we continue to do what we do."[747] Constitution-making processes require public participation, or at least demands a minority groups' involvement.[748] However, "the aim of Turkish policy is to stay within the boundaries of the Treaty of Lausanne and prioritize national security considerations over minority issues."[749] Still, Turkey claims it does not have any minorities other than Armenians, Greeks and Jews.[750] The EU has no common requirement for protection of minorities, even if there is a certain expectation from member states.[751] When we look at EU member states Germany, France, Italy, Slovakia, and Luxembourg deny having minorities or discriminating against them.[752] Lately, EU reports on Turkey argue that Turkey needs to provide efficient and sustainable regimes for minorities and should comply with Copenhagen criteria. The EU put Turkey under pressure to sign the Framework Convention for the Protection of National Minorities; however Turkey, has still not signed it. I think Germany, France, Greece, and other member states have given Turkey some bad examples. It is evident that the EU has no control on minority

---

[747] See "PM Erdogan 'We will Draft the New Constitution'," dated July 1, 2012, available at: http://english.sabah.com.tr/National/2012/04/23/pm-erdogan-we-will-draft-the-new-constitution (accessed on July 1, 2012).

[748] See Jeffry Thomas, *Anayasa Yapmak ve Anayasayi Degistirmek: Türkiye'nin Anayasal Reformu Üzerine Karsilastirmalar ve Hukukun Ustunlugu Perspektifleri* in **Yeni Anayasa İçin Yol Haritasi**, ed. Fatih Öztürk, (Istanbul, Bion Matbaacilik, 2012) at 43.

[749] See Sule Toktas & Bülent Aras, *The EU and Minority Rights in Turkey*, 124-4 Political Science Quarterly (2009-10) at 697.

[750] Ibid, at 699.

[751] Ibid, at 706.

[752] Ibid.

issues of member states.[753] At minimal, the EU expects Turkey to improve freedom standards for minority. To sum up, since 2000, the EU has demanded the following articles and Turkey has responded . . . [754]

Solve the problems of internally-displaced persons (Kurds): Return to Village and Rehabilitation Project further implemented, A circular for facilitating the voluntary return of internally displaced persons, A strategy document, the Internally Displaced Persons Problem and Measures on Village Return and Rehabilitation Project, on August 17, 2005, The Law on Compensation of Losses Resulting from Terrorist Acts with 173,208 applications, With respect to Internally Displaced Persons, progress continued on the process of compensation, The process of compensation of losses due to terrorism continued to make progress.

Provide rights to non-Sunni Muslims (Alevis): Some improvements on the legal status of non-Sunni associations in 2003, The opening of the first Alevi Institute, A municipal council recognized a Cem House as a place of worship and applied mosque tariffs to its water charges, Three municipal councils recognized Cem Houses as places of worship and granted them the same financial advantages as mosques, Administrative courts in Antalya, Ankara, Izmir and Istanbul ruled that Alevi students should be exempted from attending the mandatory religion and ethics course

Eliminate the problems of religious foundations, Provide and implement property rights to/of religious foundations: Applications for the registration of foundations started to be received in 2003, Establishment of equal treatment for Mosques and Christian

---

[753] Ibid, at 709.
[754] This section was drawn from "*Is There A Puzzle? Compliance With Minority Rights in Turkey*", by Gözde Yilmaz, No. 23, January 2011, KFG, The Tronsfarmative Power of Europe, Working Paper. Available at: http://userpage.fu-berlin.de/kfgeu/kfgwp/wpseries/WorkingPaperKFG_23.pdf (missing web address)

churches regarding free access to water, A Protestant church was established as an association in Ankara, The Protestant church in Diyarbakôr was finally able to register as a place of worship in 2005, Further implementation in the registration of religious associations in 2006, The Bahai community's request to renovate its garden was approved, Official registration of the Association for Supporting Jehovah's Witnesses, 2,285 applications for registration of property, New foundations Law was adopted, Implementation of the Law on Foundations adopted in February 2008 proceeded smoothly.

Eliminate restrictions on broadcasting in other languages and implement them: Limited implementation in state television, Broadcasting in languages other than Turkish/limited, A radio station broadcasting programs on Christianity, Further implementation of broadcasting in languages other than Turkish, A new radio channel in Diyarbakôr, Çarô FM, received authorization to broadcast in Kôrmanchi and Zaza Kurdish, Broadcast nationally, all day long, in languages other than Turkish on state television, TRT, In January 2009 TRT started operating channel TRT-6, broadcasting in Kurdish 24-hours a day, Four local TV and radio channels started broadcasting in languages and dialects traditionally used by Turkish citizens, Broadcast in Armenian began on TRT (TV) for half an hour twice a day, Applications for three dialects in Kurdish and Arabic radio stations were approved, The public radio network started to broadcast in Armenian in March 2009.

Eliminate restrictions on education in other languages and implement them: Private schools have started to teach languages other than Turkish—but limited implementation, Teaching in languages other than Turkish/limited, The Higher Education Board (YÖK) endorsed the application from a Turkish University (Artuklu University in Mardin) to establish a "Living Languages Institute" which would provide postgraduate education in Kurdish and other languages spoken in the country, Kurdish as a language course offered in Bilgi University, Istanbul.

Eliminate restrictions on the use of languages in the public sphere: Registration of names in languages other than Turkish /limited and varied, Governorships in several cities in the Southeast have started offering public services in Kurdish.

Revise the curricula in schools and remove discriminatory language from textbooks: Finalization of the redrafting the descriptions of Christian denominations in religious education textbooks.

Eliminate the problems in construction permits for places of worship: Istanbul's main synagogue was reopened, A complex comprising of a mosque, church and synagogue was opened, "the garden of religions" was opened in Belek.

Improve the situation of the Roma: The new Law on Settlement, which eliminates any discriminatory provisions against the Roma was approved by the Parliament.

Ensure the implementation of minority rights (non-Muslim minorities), Solve the problems of minorityschools: The new Law on Private Education Institutions eased the limitations in schools where the language of education is not Turkish and in schools established by foreigners, including minority schools, Minority Circular published in 2010.

Improve the situation in the Southeast in terms of socio-economic development and cultural rights: Ensure the exercise of cultural rights of minorities: A plan for development of the Southeast was adopted, Contrary to previous years, the *Newroz* celebrations in March 2009 passed by peacefully overall. Governorates in the region gave permission for celebrations.

Eliminate the ban on training clergy (comprising the issue): The Ecumenical Patriarchate's applications for work permits were answered positively.

Solve the Kurdish Problem: A debate was launched by the prime minister and 34 PKK members as a peace activation group, who were not related to violent acts, were welcomed from base from a PKK base (Kandil Mountain) and not punished (2009), A wide-range public debate was initiated by Prime Minister Erdogan to solve the Kurdish issue.

Turkey should, at minimum, provide legal status to religious foundations, remove the village guard system, amend the law of movement and residence of Aliens discriminating against Romas, provide opportunity to non-Muslim minorities to attain bureaucratic and military careers, provide opportunity to children to learn their mother tongues in public schools, and finally to recognize all minorities of the country.

During the constitution-making process regarding EU integration and what Turkey should do there is one realistic goal: Inserting an article to the new constitution declaring that Turkey recognizes and respects all of minorities and accepts minority rights as a group right. Another serious issue is after drafting the new constitution Turkey should definitely receive advice from minority groups' representatives in order to realize a healthy balanced constitution-making process. Turkey should not forget that public participation of constitution-making processes is widely accepted as an international right.27

In sum, once more, without the elimination of military power from Turkish politics or civilian life, Turkey will not be able to cure minority problems in Turkey as is the same for other problems in the Turkish democracy. I am also aware that law alone cannot heal social problems. For centuries people have been inventing, changing, and discarding laws and legal systems in the hope that particular social problems could be resolved. Ignorance can only be defeated through education; however, like every problem in human life everything ultimately depends on human beings themselves and their actions. Education is the most effective vehicle regardless of whether or not we have a paralyzed social and political system or whether we have one operating with clockwork precision.

In 2012, at the foot of the EU door, Turkish democracy runs under status quo, and the elite is above the Turkish system, like Damocles' sword. I hope one day Turkey will be full of freedom of expression, respect for others' ideas and beliefs, acceptance of criticism from any one or group. People of Turkey are beginning to believe again, as they once did during Ottoman times, that diversity is not a crime; it is one of the greatest facets of life given to us to hold and cherish.

References

1. Alexandris, Alexis. The Greek Minority of Istanbul and Greek-Turkish Relations, 1918-1974 (Athens: Center for Asia Minor Studies, 1983).

2. Aydin, Mehmet Akif. Islam ve Osmanli Hukuku Arastirmalari [Researches of the Law of Islam and Ottoman] (Istanbul: Iz, 1996).

3. Baderin, Mashood A. International Human Rights and Islamic Law (Clarendon: Oxford, 2005).

4. Bass, Gary Jonathan. Stay the Hand of Vengeance (Princeton, Oxford: Princeton University Press, 2000).

5. Berch Berberoglu (ed.). The National Question: Nationalism, Ethnic Conflict & Self-Determination in the 20th Century, (Philadelphia: Temple University Press, 1995). 27 See more Christina Murray, *"Anayasa Yapimina Halkin Katilimi ve Gelecek"*, at 17-30 in **Yeni Anayasa İçin Yol Haritasi**, ed. Fatih Öztürk, (Istanbul, Bion Matbaacilik, 2012). *Introduction to Minority Issues in Turkey* 203

6. Boyle, K. and Sheen, J. (eds.) Freedom of Religion and Belief (London and New York: Routledge, 1997).

7. Chaszar, Edward. The International Problem of National Minorities (Pennsylvania: Indiana University of Pennsylvania, 1988).

8. Cumper, P. and Wheatley, S. (eds.) Minority Rights in the New Europe (The Hague: Martinus Nijhoff, 1999).

9. Dorsen, Norman and Rosenfeld, Michel & Sajo, Andras and Susanne Baer (eds.). Comparative Constitutionalism: Cases and Materials (St. Paul: West Group, 2003).

10. Gotlieb, Yosef. Self-Determination in the Middle East (New York, Praeger, 1982).

11. Guler, Ali. Osmanli Devletinde Azinliklar [Minorities in the Ottoman] (Istanbul: Turan, 1997).

12. Hamidullah, Muhammed. Islam Anayasa Hukuku [Constitutional Law of Islam] (Istanbul: Beyan, 1995).

13. Kaboglu, Ibrahim (ed.). Ulusal, Ulusalustu ve Uluslararasi Hukukukta Azinlik Haklari: Birlesmis Milletler, Avrupa Birligi, Avrupa Konseyi, Lozan Antlasmasi [Minority Rights in National and International Law: The United Nations, the Council of Europe, the Treaty of Lausanne] (Istanbul: Istanbul Barosu Insan Haklari Merkezi, 2002).

14. Kelly, Paul (ed.). Multiculturalism Reconsidered: Culture and Equality and Its Critics (Malden, MA: Polity, 2002).

15. Kurt, Ismail and Tuz, Ali. Turkiye'de Aleviler, Bektasiler, Nusayriler [Alewis, Bektasis, and Nusayris in Turkey] (Istanbul: Ensar, 1999).

16. Kymlicka, Will. Multicultural Citizenship: A Liberal Theory of Minority Rights (New York: Oxford, 1995).

17. —————(ed.). The Rights of Minority Cultures (New York: Oxford, 1995).

18. —————and Norman, Wayne (eds.). Citizenship in Diverse Societies (Oxford: Oxford University Press, 2000).

19. Mehta, R. Sampat. Minority Rights and Obligations (Ottawa: Canada Research Bureau, 1973).

20. Onder, Ali Tayyar. Turkiye'nin Etnik Yapisi: Halkimizin Kokenleri ve Gercekler [The Ethnic Structure of Turkey: The Ancestors of Our Nation and Truth] (Istanbul: Pozitif, 2005).

21. Oran, Baskin. Turkiye'de Azinliklar: Kavramlar, Teori, Lozan, Ic Mevzuat, Ictihat, Uygulama [Minorities in Turkey: Concepts, Theory, Lausanne, Domestic Law, Jurisprudence, and Practice] (Istanbul: Iletisim, 2005).

22. Rehman, Javaid. International Human Rights Law: A Practical Approach (Harlow: Pearson Education, 2003).

23. ————The Weaknesses in the International Protection of Minority (The Hague: Kluwer, 2000).

24. Reyna, Yuda and Zonana, Moreno. Son Yasal Duzenlemelere Gore Cemaat Vakiflari [According to Current Legal System; Non Charities of Groups] (Istanbul: Gozlem, 2003). 2003.

25. Sekerci, Osman. Islam Ulkelerinde Gayri Muslimlerin Temel Haklari [Basic Rights of Non-Muslim in Islamic Countries] (Istanbul: Nun, 1996).

26. Sener, Cemal. Turkiye'de Yasayan Etnik ve Dinsel Gruplar [Ethnic and Religious Groups in Turkey] (??2004).

27. Sofuoglu, Adnan. Fener Rum Patrikhanesi ve Siyasi Faaliyetleri [Fener Greek Patriarchate and Its Political Activities] (Istanbul: Turan, 1996).

28. Soykan, T. Tankut. Osmanli Imparatorlugunda Gayrimuslimler [Non-Muslims in the Ottaman Empire] (Istanbul: Utopya, 2000).

29. Thornberry, Patrick. International Law and Rights of Minorities (Oxford: Clarendon, 1992).

30. —————Minorities and Human Rights Law (London: MRG, 1991).

31. —————and Estebanez, Maria Amor Martin. Minority Rights in Europe: A Review of the Work and Standards of the Council of Europe (Brussels: Council of Europe, 2004).

32. Tierney, Stephen (ed.). Constitutional Law and National Pluralism (Oxford: Oxford University, 2004).

33. Turkdogan, Orhan. Alewi Bektasi Kimligi [The Identity of Alewi and Bektasi] (Istanbul: Timas, 1995).